AJANTA MAHĀPIṬAKA 6-1.

Antarpiṭaka 6.

Concise Buddhist Legends.

Pratyantara Piṭaka 1.

Ajanta Paintings: A Compilation of 84 Abridged Narratives.

Cover illustration: *Ajanta Cave 17, narrative no. 58, Siṃhala Avadāna, scene 27. Siṃhala leaves with an army through the city gate to avenge an attack by the* rākṣasis *(demonesses) of an island.*

Singh, Rajesh Kumar, 2019-

Ajanta Paintings: A Compilation of 84 Abridged Narratives, = Ajanta Mahāpiṭaka 6-1 / By Rajesh Kumar Singh. 2nd ed.

ISBN 978-81-925107-6-7. Hard cover.

First edition: *Ajantā Paintings: 86 Panels of Jātakas and Other Themes* (Baroda: Hari Sena Press, 2013). Paperback ISBN 978-81-925107-3-6, mobi ISBN 978-81-925107-4-3, epub ISBN 978-81-925107-5-0.

1. Buddhist art—India—Deccan. 2. Buddhist studies—India—Deccan. 3. Buddhist art—India—Ajanta caves. 4. Art history—India—Ajanta caves. 5. Ajanta caves (India) 6. Ajanta paintings (India).

ISBN 978-81-925107-6-7.

Second edition of Rajesh K. Singh, *Ajantā Paintings: 86 Panels of Jātakas and Other Themes* (Baroda: Hari Sena Press Private Limited, 2013). Paperback ISBN 978-81-925107-3-6, mobi ISBN 978-81-925107-4-3, epub ISBN 978-81-925107-5-0.

Published by Hari Sena Press Private Limited, Baroda, India. Email: harisenapress@gmail.com.

Production and distribution by Abhikalp, Baroda, India. Email: info@abhikalp.net.

The re-telling of the Buddhist legends are adapted from the following publications, courtesy of Prof. Dr. Dieter Schlingloff and Prof. Dr. Monika Zin:

Schlingloff, D. *Ajanta: Handbook of the Paintings 1,* I-III (New Delhi: IGNCA, 2013), vol. I.

Zin, M. *A Guide to the Ajanta Paintings 2: Devotional and Ornamental Paintings* (Delhi: Munshiram Manoharlal, 2003).

Frontispiece: a panorama of the Ajanta caves.

AJANTA PAINTINGS

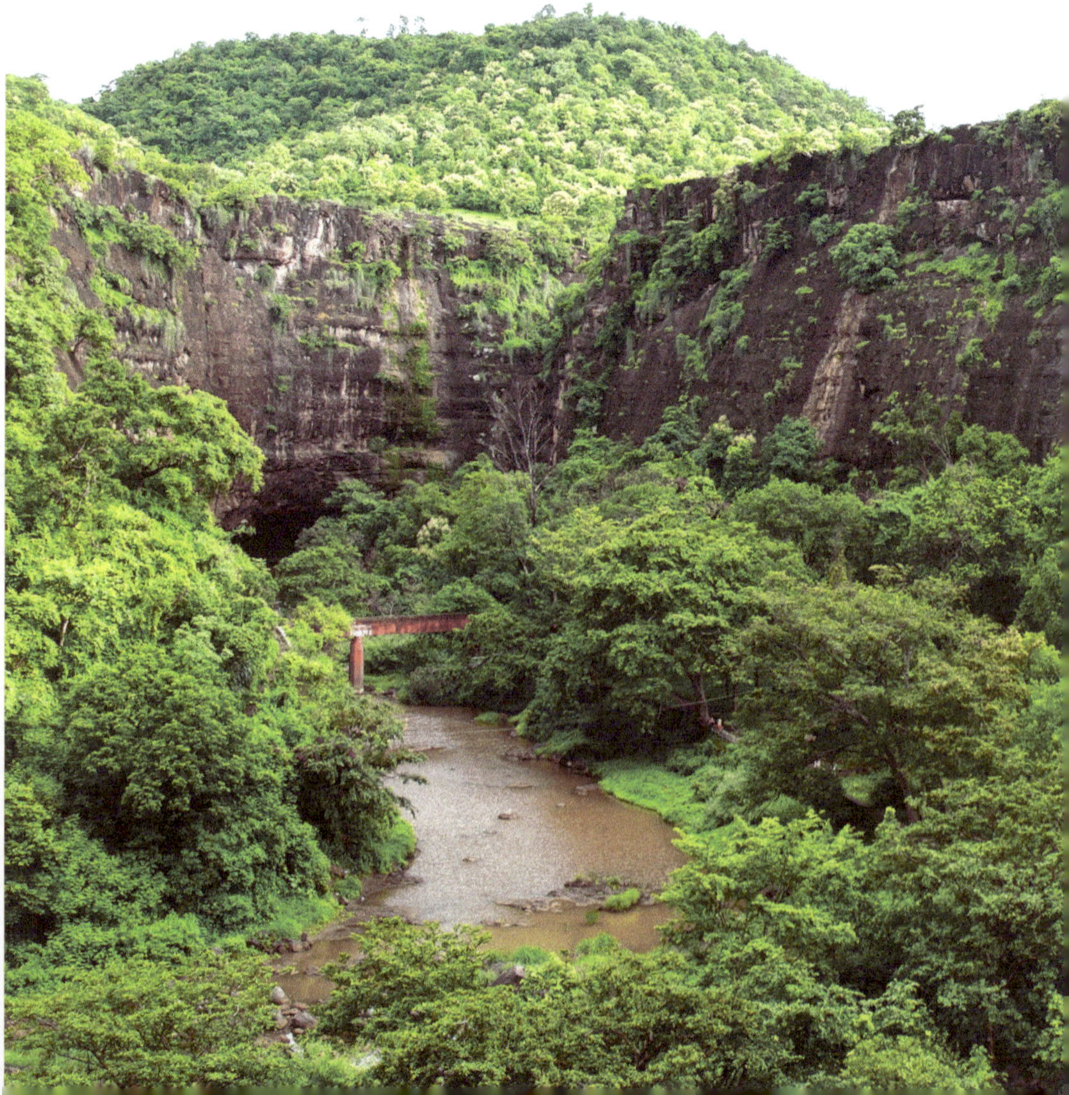

AJANTA PAINTINGS

A compilation of 84 abridged narratives

RAJESH KUMAR SINGH

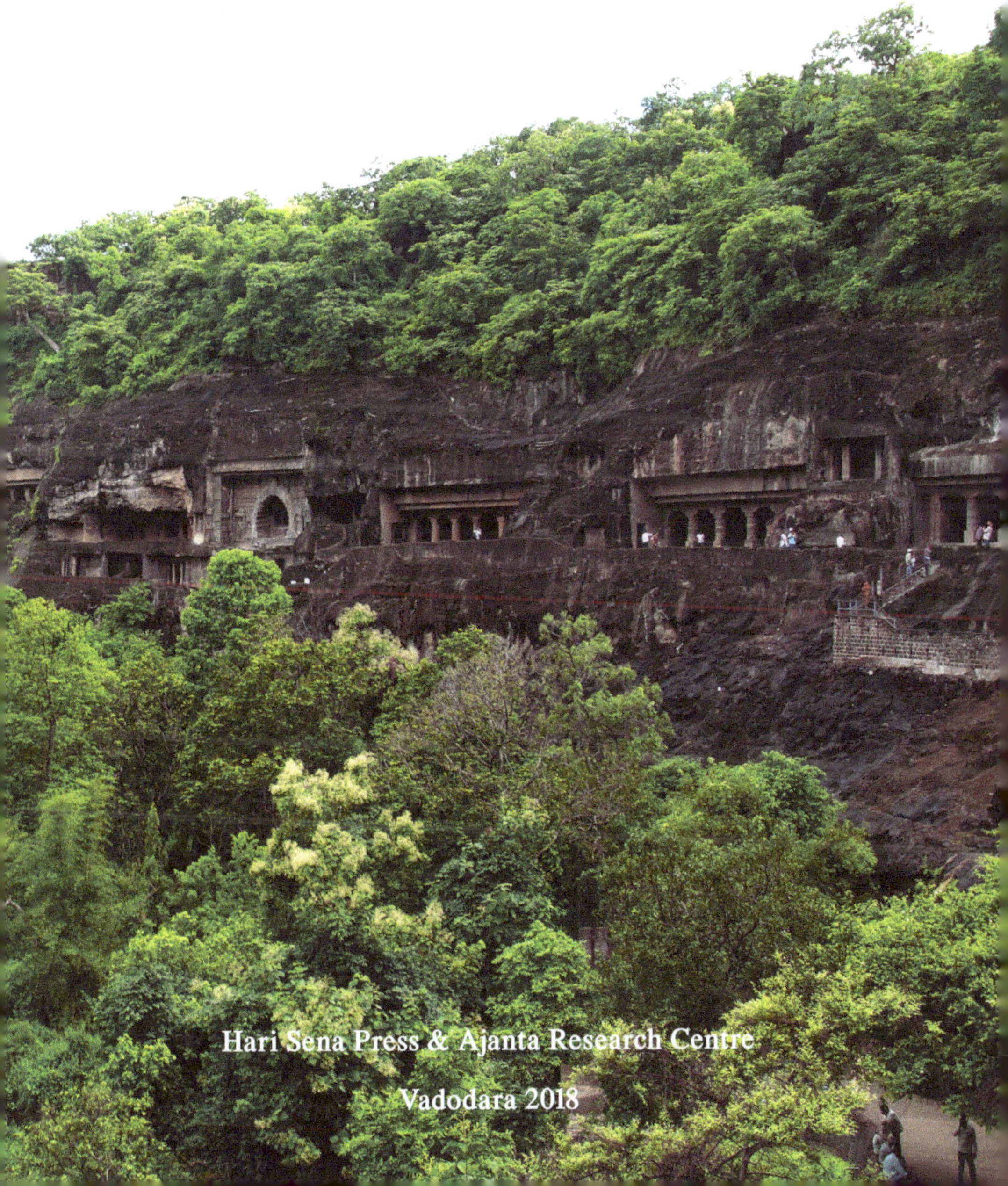

Hari Sena Press & Ajanta Research Centre

Vadodara 2018

For

Late Shri Ranjitsingh Gaekwad, Deepak bhai, Shailendra bhai, Jayaram, Rekha, and Surendran

the patrons of a student in the early 1990s.

Preface to the second edition

I should like to clarify at the outset that this book does not include my individual research. Being an art historian I have not yet studied the Buddhist scriptures. This is of course my shortcoming.

The logic of why this book was compiled remains in the fact that it is going for the new, slightly revised, edition. The book has been liked by the Indian students and general readers. It is for them that the book was conceived. This book is like a primer, an elementary text book, on the subject of the Ajanta paintings, which were executed in two periods: 2nd–1st century BCE and late 5th century CE.

Scholars know well that the subjects of the Ajanta paintings have not been easy to identify. Different identifications were proposed in the last two centuries of the Ajanta scholarship. There is an older school of thought that linked the Ajanta narratives either to the *jātakas* as found in the Pali canon or to the *avadānas* as found in the Mahāyāna texts. Although the links with the scriptures of the Mūlasarvāstivāda school—which was not a sect and whose character, philosophy, vinaya, and religious practices have still not been fully defined—were certainly traced, it took a long time for such attempts to be recognised fully within the frontier research, and it is only scarsely recognised in other reference works of the art history of South Asia. Educators teaching the subject in the classrooms go back to some of the older and popular works stacked in the Indian libraries, which suffer with the condition of not being able to acquire as many recent works as needed.

In the recent decades, Dieter Schlingloff (2013, 1999, 1987) and Monika Zin (2003a, 2003b) published their most comprehensive works. They published line drawings and offered new identifications and analyses subjoined with copious critical apparatuses. We learn that almost 52% of the (nearly 45 of about 86) Ajanta narratives have the nearest textual versions in the Mūlasarvāstivāda scriptures. The rest are from other sources, some even from the non-canonical Sanskrit literature of the times. On one hand, the Mūlasarvāstivāda scriptures were written in Sanskrit, on the other hand, the late 5th-century epigraphs of Ajanta are also in Sanskrit without exception. In view of some of these basic facts—and a volume of other complicated details—our understanding of the Buddhism of Ajanta is set for a major overhaul. It is no longer possible to apply binary labels to anything that is there in Ajanta, be it the Hīnayāna/Mahāyāna model, the *caityagṛha/vihāra* model, the Sātavāhana/Vākāṭaka model, or the completed/incomplete caves model.

The confusion must linger, for there are various problems to reconcile. The scholars of Buddhist studies must negotiate with art historians, epigraphists, scholars of numismatics, and vice versa. But the gravest problem is that the majority of the original texts of the Mūlasarvāstivādins, which were in Sanskrit, have not come down to us. The Indian researcher is indebted to the larger Buddhist world, for these texts of the Mūlasarvāstivādins have been substantially preserved in the ancient translations in the Chinese, Khotanese, Mongolian, Tocharian B, and Tibetan. However, the tragedy for the modern Indian scholar is that most of these ancient translations are not found in the modern Indian languages. There are some critical editions and translations in English, German, and French.

Amid the above situations, Schilingloff's *Ajanta: Handbook of the Paintings 1* (2013), which was originally in German, offers much help to the Indian reader.

Inspired by the same work, it was always my wish to aggregate all the Ajanta narratives at one place, and illustrate them with at least one colour photograph from my collection. The challenge was that it should be a small booklet for the beginner. The plan required that the narratives must be retold in a highly abridged format to accommodate all the narratives and a photograph for each extant painting.

The idea was discussed with Prof. Schlingloff and Prof. Zin in 2011 and 2012. They agreed to help, and granted me permission to use their research for the abridgement of the stories. I prepared the drafts assisted by two of my former students: Sandeep Joshi and Snehal Tambulwadikar. The same was seen by Prof. Schlingloff (in 2012). He commented that there was a scope for improvements. However, neither he nor I had the time to devote for the perfection.

Actually, the act of abridging or retelling any story involves modifications. Quite frankly, it has been beyond me to ensure absolute accuracy and faithfulness to the source material. Therefore, I stake no claim to accuracy and authenticity here. I only offer a broad contour of what the stories contain. The curious reader may consult the readings provided at the end of this booklet for further insight; and forgive the present author for any inadvertent distortion.

Ajanta has 94 painted depictions of 84 narratives (or versions thereof). This booklet presents the short summaries of the 84 narratives. I have been able to produce photographs of only 70 narratives. The reason why the rest could not be included is because either the painting is so badly damaged, or it survives in an extremely fragmentary state, or it has not been possible or feasible for me to do the photography work.

The short summaries of the legends were first included in my work, *An Introduction to the Ajantā Caves* (2012) that also included my study of the sequence of the excavations of four select caves of Ajanta. That is a larger work and has some technical details on the chronology of the caves. The price was also higher. It was not affordable to many students. Therefore, I compiled a separate booklet *Ajantā Paintings: 86 Panels of Jātakas and Other Themes* (2013) meant exclusively for the students. The present is the second edition of the same booklet with a slightly modified subtitle.

I have excluded the introduction to the Sātavāhanas and Vākāṭakas from this edition and focused on the paintings alone. The syntax, flow, and lucidity have been slightly improved. The layout, typefaces, and photographs have also been improved. I have added the keywords and identification numbers assigned to the themes by Schlingloff and Zin. The sequence of the stories in this booklet is based on how today's visitor enters the caves and views the paintings in the clockwise fashion beginning from Cave 1 to Cave 17. Indices to the narratives have been provided both numerically and alphabetically. These are placed at the end of the booklet. Owing to certain inadequacies the following narrative paintings could not be included:

No. 6.	Cave 10. Śyāma.
No. 7.	Cave 10. Ṣaḍdanta.
No. 8.	Cave 10. Bhagavān.
No. 9.	Cave 10. Udayana.
No. 66.	Cave 7. Bhagavān.
No. 81.	Cave 6. Māravijaya.
No. 87.	Cave 21. Devāvatāra.
No. 90.	Cave 6. Mahāprātihārya.

Besides, the majority of the non-narrative paintings have not been included.

—RKS, Dharma Day/Āṣāḍha Pūrṇimā, 2019.

Acknowledgements

Primary research. During my research since 2006 many permissions were availed from the Archaeological Survey of India for the in-situ research and photo documentation. I would like to thank the Director General's office in New Delhi and the Office of the Superintending Archaeologist, Aurangabad Circle; in particular Dr V. N. Prabhakar, Dr Shivanand V., Dr D. Dayalan, Mr M. Mahadevaiah, and Mr Vilas Jadhav.

Secondary research. In the first edition of this book much help was received from Prof. Dr. Dieter Schlingloff (Hon. Professor, Leipzig University, Germany) and Prof. Dr. Monika Zin (Kucha Project, Saxon Academy of Sciences, Leipzig). The concise texts of the narratives are adapted from the following publications: (*1*) Dieter Schlingloff, *Studies in the Ajanta Paintings, Identifications and Interpretations* (Delhi: Ajanta Publications, 1988); (*2*) *A Guide to the Ajanta Paintings*, vol. 1, *Narrative Wall Paintings* (Delhi: Munshiram Manoharlal, 1999); (*3*) *Ajanta: Handbook of the Paintings*, vol. 1 (New Delhi: IGNCA, 2013); and (*4*) Monika Zin, *A Guide to the Ajanta Paintings*, vol. 2, *Devotional and Ornamental Paintings* (Delhi: Munshiram Manoharlal, 2003).

Individuals. Md. Sayyed Abid, Sayyed Asak, Sayyed Rajek, and Sayyed Azhar of Hotel New K. P. Park, Fardapur always help me during my field tours by providing free or subsidized lodging and boarding. I am fortunate that I have four brothers in Ajanta, and an *abba* and *ammi.*

While abridging the stories, I was helped by my art historian friends Sandeep Joshi and Snehal Tambulwadikar while Tanveer Ajsi suggested useful improvements.

My friends in the history departments of M. J. College, Jalgaon and BAMU, Aurangabad provided encouragement.

Funding. My larger research work (not included in this book) has recieved the support from 'Dharohar,' SML, Udaipur under the Corporate Social Responsibility policy. I am very thankful to Dharohar for the generous support.

If the work is found useful in any measure it is due to the above persons and institutions, whereas the defects, if any, are entirely mine.

Contents

III. CAVE NO. 9

IV. CAVE NO. 16

V. CAVE NO. 17

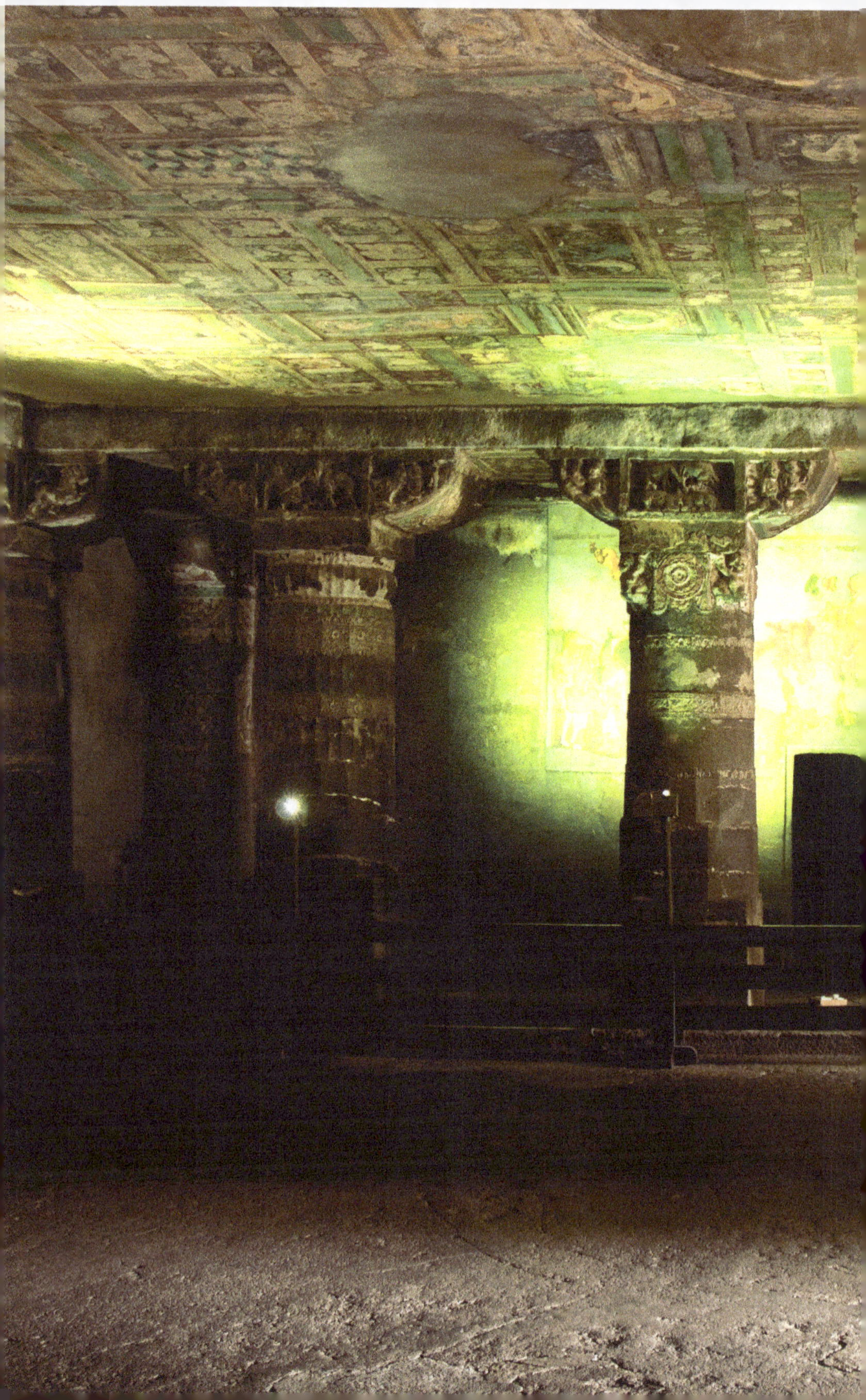

I. Cave No. 1

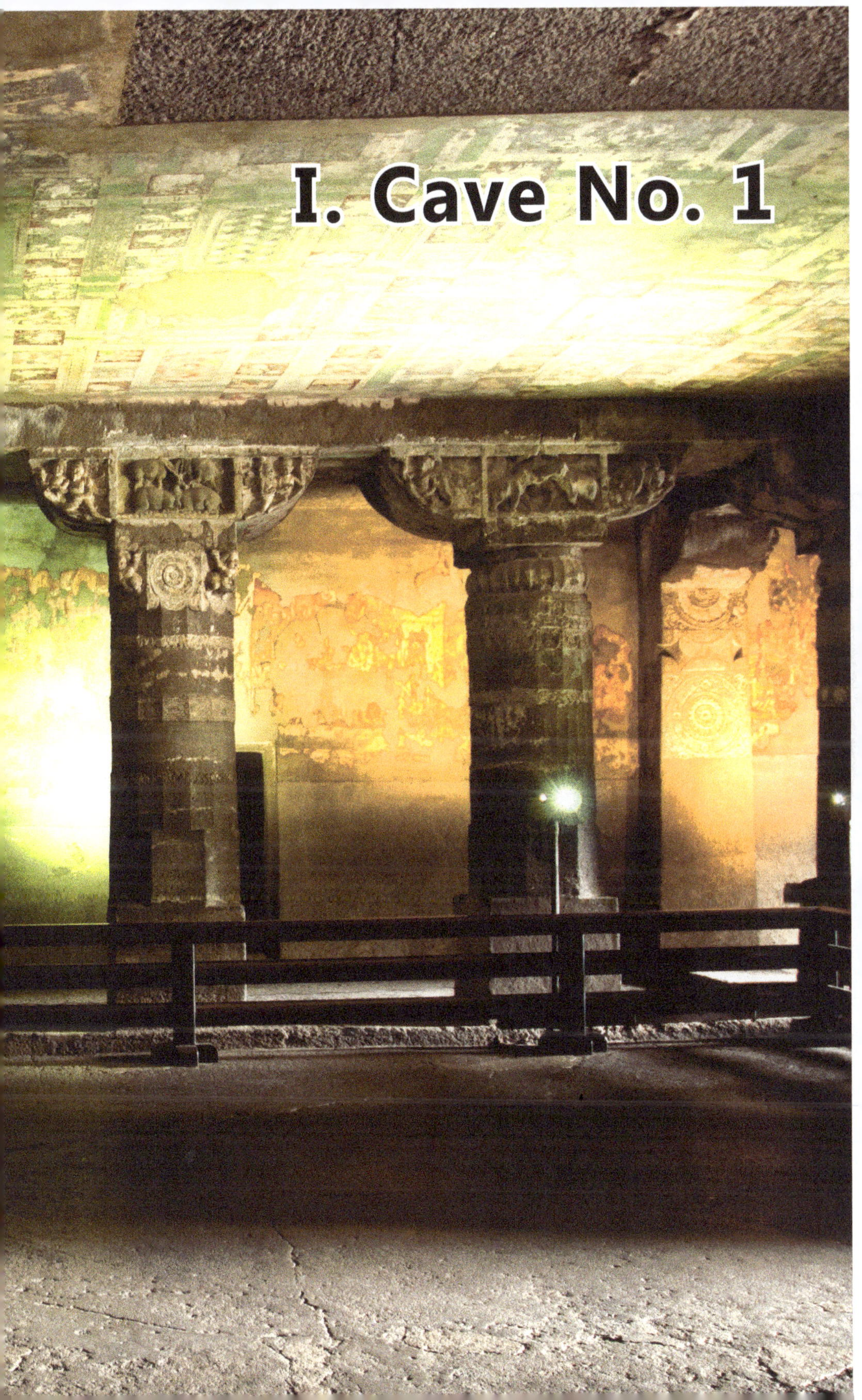

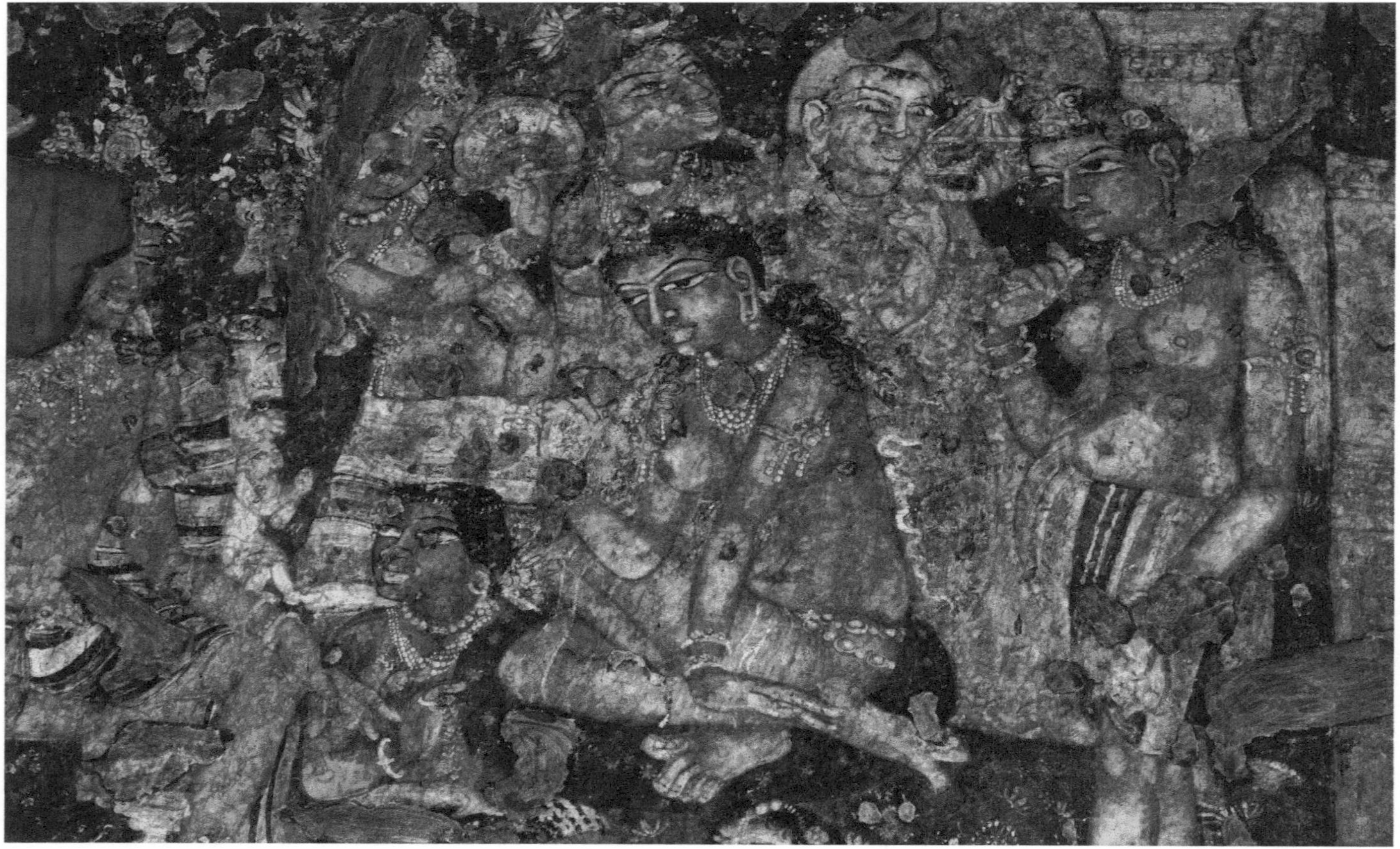

No. 50. *Scene 1. King Maitrībala is seated in his palace with the queen. They are surrounded by the royal household. The king discusses with his wife the virtues of benevolence.* Hall, front aisle, right wall.

NARRATIVE THEMES.

No. 50.[1] Maitrībala.

Identification: Schlingloff (1977b, p. 913).—There lived a king by the name of Maitrībala ('The Power of Benevolence'). He was extremely benevolent towards his subjects. Five demons, disguised as brahmans, entered his kingdom. They saw a lonely cowherd and asked him why he was not afraid of living on his own. The cowherd told them that in the kingdom of Maitrībala no one had any fear. Agitated, the demons went to the king's court and begged for food. The king ordered for food to be served, which was vegetarian. The demons morphed into their original forms and said that they are demons and they only eat flesh, blood, and bone. The king's nature was neither to harm anyone nor to refuse anyone who asks for something. So he ordered his sergeants to cut a chunk of flesh from his own body (despite all-round protests) and offered it to his guest. Overwhelmed, the demons asked the king to kindly stop. The king extracted a promise from them that henceforth they would not harm anyone. Upon this, Indra descended from the heaven, and there was accompanied a divine flower shower. Indra healed Maitrībala's wounds with herbs.—King Maitrībala was none other than the Buddha in a former existence.

No. 44. Mahāsudarśana.

Identification: Schlingloff (1987, p. 59f.).—A great king, Mahāsudarśana, ruled over the ancient and prosperous city of Kuśāvatī (Kuśinagara). The king was known for his sense of justice and was loved by the people. Once, some citizens went to him and offered him gold, jewels, and other precious objects. The king hesitated to accept the gifts, still the people left behind the riches. Later, the king consulted his vassals and built a magnificent temple open to all religions. This temple became a daily banquet hall for migrant Brahmins and ascetics. The king went there for meditation and spread his goodness, compassion, rejoice, and calmness among the people and animals of his kingdom.—King Mahāsudarśana was none other than the Buddha in a former existence.

1 The numbers under the *narrative* themes refer to those assigned by Dieter Schlingloff to the *narrative* paintings of Ajanta, vide Schlingloff 2013.

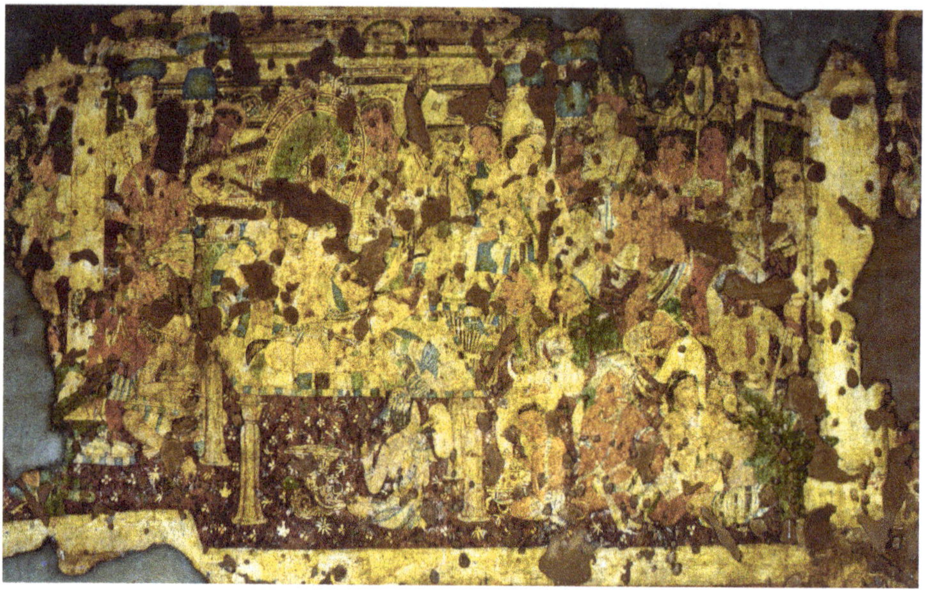

No. 44. *The legend of King Mahāsudarśana. The citizens offer precious gifts to the king who is reluctant to accept the items.* Hall, front wall.

No. 46. Śibi-Kapota.

Identification: Foucher (1921, narrative no. 15).—When Lord Indra complained about the imperfections of human beings, his architect Viśvakarmān drew his attention to King Śibi who was an archetype of justice and compassion. To test Śibi, Indra asked Viśvakarmān to assume a pigeon's (*kapota*) appearance, while he became a falcon chasing the pigeon. When the king granted a word of protection to the pigeon, the falcon argued for his right to the prey, complaining that he would, otherwise, die of hunger. The king, known for his justice announced that he could sacrifice his own body to save the life of the pigeon. Then, the king chopped off a portion of his own flesh as much as the weight of the pigeon. On the balance, however, Indra as pigeon kept on increasing his weight. The king too continued cutting more and more flesh from his body to match the weight. When this was not enough, King Śibi attempted to offer his whole body on one side of the balance. Thereupon, Indra and Viśvakarmān assumed their original forms and explained the scenario. The king was given back his original body.—King Śibi was none other than the Buddha in a former existence.

No. 75. Udrāyaṇa.

Identification: Schlingloff (1987, p. 60). The legend is from the life

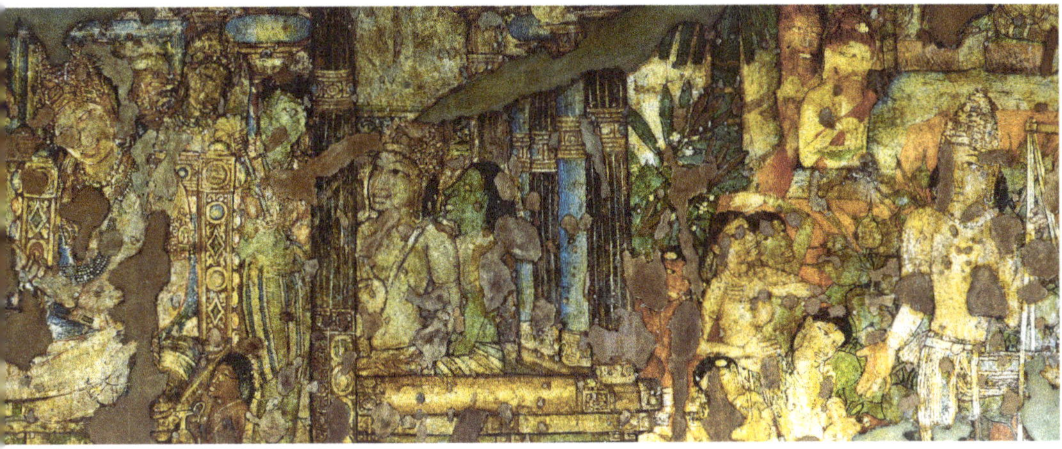

of the Buddha.—King Udrāyaṇa of Roruka received a painting, representing the Buddha, as a gift from his friend, Bimbisāra, the king of Rājagṛha. Udrāyaṇa was so impressed by this painting that he summoned a monk to preach the Buddhist doctrine to him and his advisors. One day, Udrāyaṇa observed the signs of death on his queen's face, even as she danced. Seven days later, when the queen passed away, Udrāyaṇa was so distressed that he moved out of the city, bidden farewell by the beggars. He reached Rājagṛha, where Bimbisāra greeted him with great honour and took him to the Buddha who accepted him into the monastic order. Then, Udrāyaṇa's evil son murdered him for the kingdom, which soon was ruined in a sandstorm.

No. 46. *The legend of King Śibi and a pigeon.* Hall, front wall.

No. 75. *The legend of King Udrāyaṇa. Beggars on the left side bid farewell to King Udrāyaṇa while brahmans seen on the right are listening to the sermon of the Buddha.* Hall, front wall.

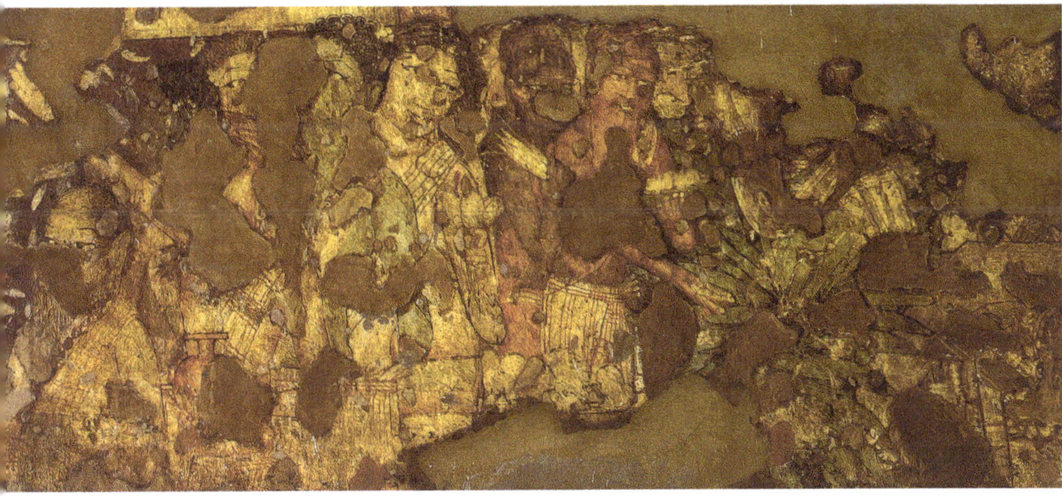

No. 40. Sudhana.

Identification: Schlingloff (1973a, p. 155–167).—There was a *nāga* (one of a race of semi-human serpents) prince who ruled over a kingdom abutting his father, the nāga king's, kingdom. Once a snake charmer sent by a human king to capture the nāga prince was killed by a hunter. On hearing how the prince was saved by the hunter, the nāga king invited the hunter to his palace and honoured him with precious objects. However, on the advice of a hermit, the hunter requested for an additional present, an unfailing noose. Initially, the nāga king refused to give the noose in order to protect the nāgas from *garuḍas* (eagles), but then gave in at his son's request.

The hunter came to know from a hermit about a *kinnarī*, a princess of a fairy-land high up in the mountains, who bathed in a forest lake every full moon night. He caught the *kinnarī* in the subsequent full moon night with the help of the unfailing noose even as her attendants flew away. The *kinnarī* requested the hunter not to touch her and handed over her crest-jewel (which gave her the power to fly) as security. When the hunter learned that Sudhana, the son of a human king had a soft spot for the pretty *kinnarī* he handed her over to Sudhana.

Sudhana spent some happy days frolicking with the *kinnarī*,

No. 40. *The legend of Prince Sudhana, scene 5. With a hand sign the fairy princess reveals to a friend her love for Sudhana, who is standing with the same gesture and a walking-staff in the gateway of the princess' palace, where the fairy princess is hiding him from the king.* Hall, front wall.

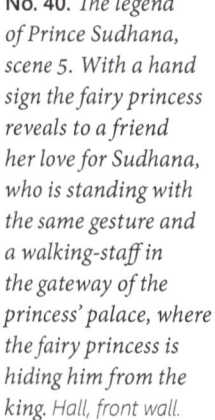

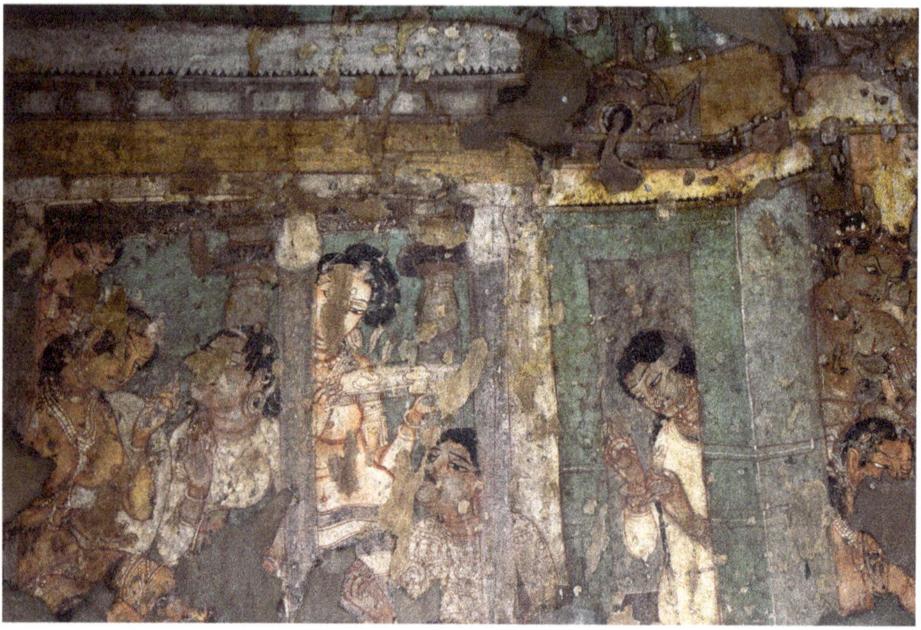

far from his father's kingdom. But a jealous and scheming court brahmin, who intended to himself possess the *kinnarī*, sent Sudhana on a military operation against a hill tribe and performed some atrocious rituals involving animal sacrifice. The brahmin thought that if the prince returned alive from the operation, he would die grieving over his beloved, which would allow him to gain dominance at the court. When the *kinnarī* got a hang of this plot, she asked the queen for her crest-jewel, which the prince had entrusted to her, and flew away.

She related all this to the hermit in the forest. She also disclosed to him the road map to her father's palace. When the prince returned from the campaign unharmed, he straightaway went in search of his beloved. The hermit faithfully described to him the way to the *kinnarī*'s father's palace. The prince overcame many obstacles to reach the destination. He flung a signet ring into one of the jugs of water prepared for *kinnarī*'s bath. The *kinnarī* saw the ring fall into her lap when water was being poured over her body by the attendants. By this she became aware of the prince's arrival. To add to her joy, her father was ever so delighted with Sudhana, who, however, had to pass a few more tests before he could marry the daughter. The prince passed all exams with flying colours and wedded the beauteous *kinnarī*. They lived happily in the fairy-castle and then took off for the prince's hometown. The king welcomed them back and made his son an administrator of his kingdom.—Prince Sudhana was none other than the Buddha in a former existence.

No. 59. Śaṅkhapāla.

Identification: Foucher (1921, narrative no. 13).—A *nāga* (serpent) king named Śaṅkhapāla visited a hermit to find out the reason behind his rejection of the worldly life. The hermit instructs the nāga king that he must practice asceticism to be reborn as a human. Thereafter when Śaṅkhapāla was practising asceticism a group of young people started dragging him with a noose in his nose. A cattle dealer offered sixteen heads of cattle to secure the release of the nāga. The nāga invited the cattle dealer to his splendid palace in the waters. He accepted the invitation and experienced the heavenly life meant for kings for a year. Thereafter, he returned to the world. The nāga decided to become a hermit and expressed his wish to be reborn as a human and suffer all the pains

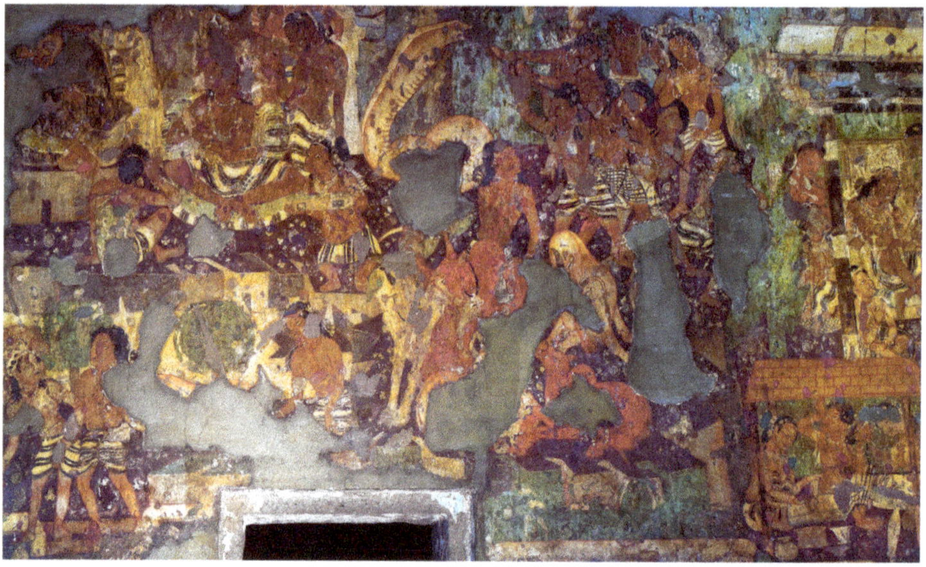

No. 59. *Legend of the serpent king Śaṅkhapāla.* *Hall, left wall.*

as only humans could, to gain salvation.—Nāgarāja Śaṅkhapāla was none other than the Buddha in a former existence.

No. 45. Janaka.

Below. Left: **No. 45.1.** *Janaka.* Right: **No. 41.1.** *Kalyāṇakārin.* *Hall, left wall.*

Identification: Goloubew (1927, p. 16).—King Janaka of Videha believed that a person's willpower was responsible for his successes. Once he was rescued from a shipwreck by a deity after

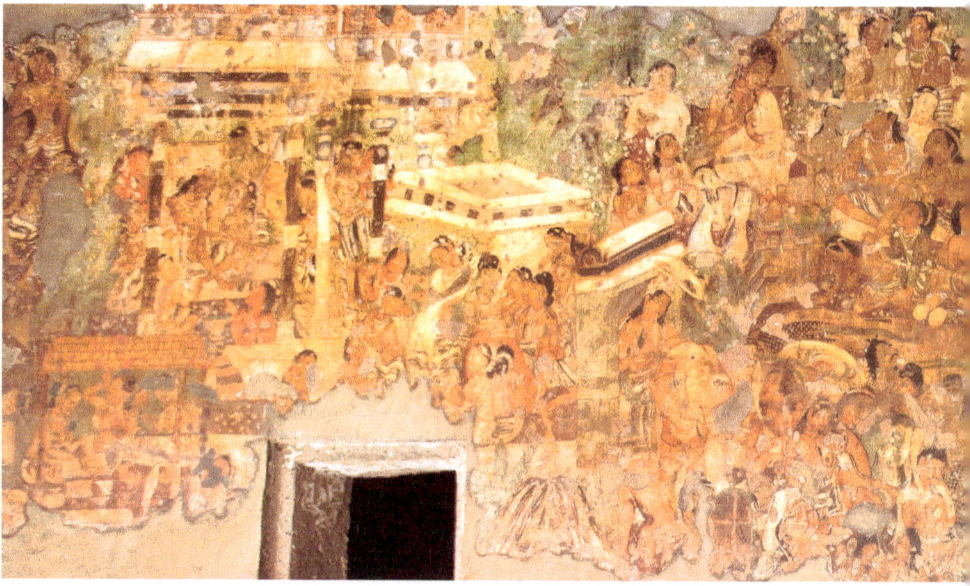

he managed to keep afloat for a while on the sheer strength of his will. His will power also helped him secure the kingship of Mithilā as also Princess Sīvalī's hand. But Janaka was aiming even higher, he wished to be free of all human desires and live as a hermit. He refused to hold dance performances in his court and was not at all amused at the sight of animals that roamed in his park. He had decided to leave the palace and renounce the worldly life. Even the seven hundred ladies of his court could not make him change his mind. Nor was he moved by the double blow of a fire in his palace and the capture of his kingdom by forest tribes.

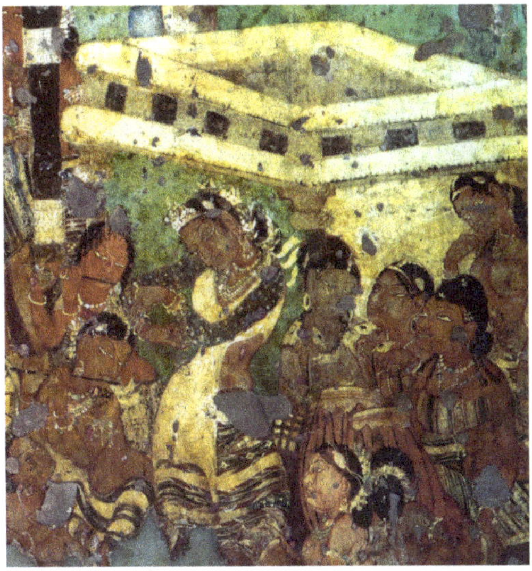

No. 45.2. *Janaka, scene 2. A dance performance is organised to lure King Janaka who has decided to follow the path of renunciation.*

When he left his palace with his advisors, a forest hermit, Nārada, asked him why he had taken this tough decision. He replied that a person could lead a free and happy life without belongings and possessions. He anointed his son the king on Sīvalī's request and asked her to follow him on the path to renunciation. The queen was infuriated when Janaka ate food discarded by a dog. So Janaka

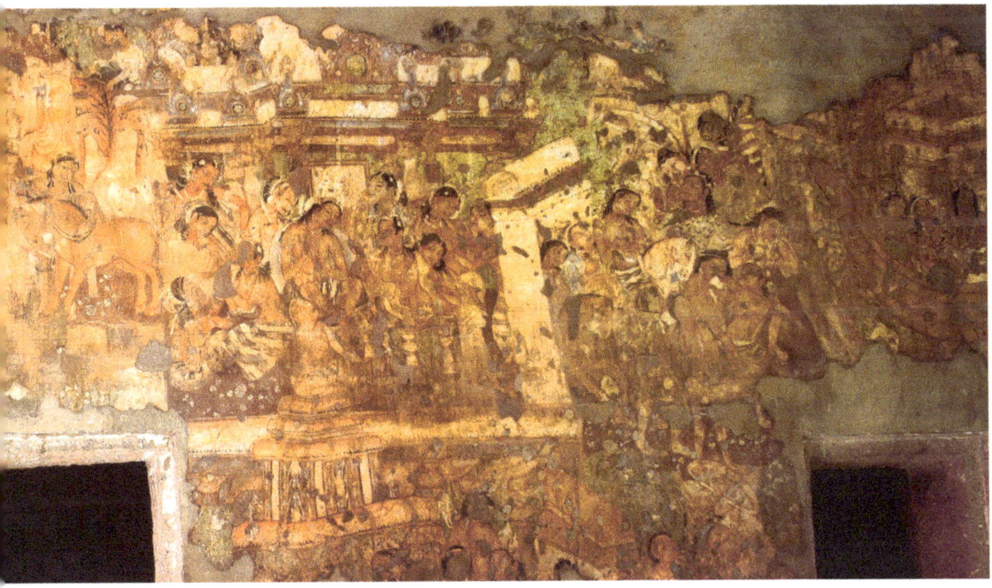

decided to leave his wife and go alone. He observed that if one bangle was worn it would not make a noise and a bow maker was able to check the curvature of the bow with closed eyes. On the basis of these two observations, he asked his wife to leave him and decided to remain alone for the rest of his life.—King Janaka was none other than the Buddha in a former existence.

No. 41. Kalyāṇakārin.

No. 41.2. *The legend of Princes Kalyāṇakārin and Pāpakārin, scene 1. They sail to a jewel island to get the riches because due to excessive charity of Kalyāṇakārin the royal treasury had become empty.* Below right: *they are attacked by sea monsters.* Hall, left wall.

Identification: Schlingloff (1976, p. 5–16).—Two princes, Kalyāṇakārin ('Doing Good') and Pāpakārin ('Doing Evil'), bore the characteristics of their names. Once, Kalyāṇakārin, accompanied by Pāpakārin, embarked on a sea voyage in search of wealth as endless charity had emptied out the royal coffers. During their voyage, Kalyāṇakārin found a blue wishing-stone in a jewel island. On the return leg, the ship, overloaded with precious stones, drowned along with its passengers who were then also attacked by sea monsters. Kalyāṇakārin managed to save himself and his brother with the help of the wishing-stone, and gave half of rescued jewels to Pāpakārin. However, to acquire the

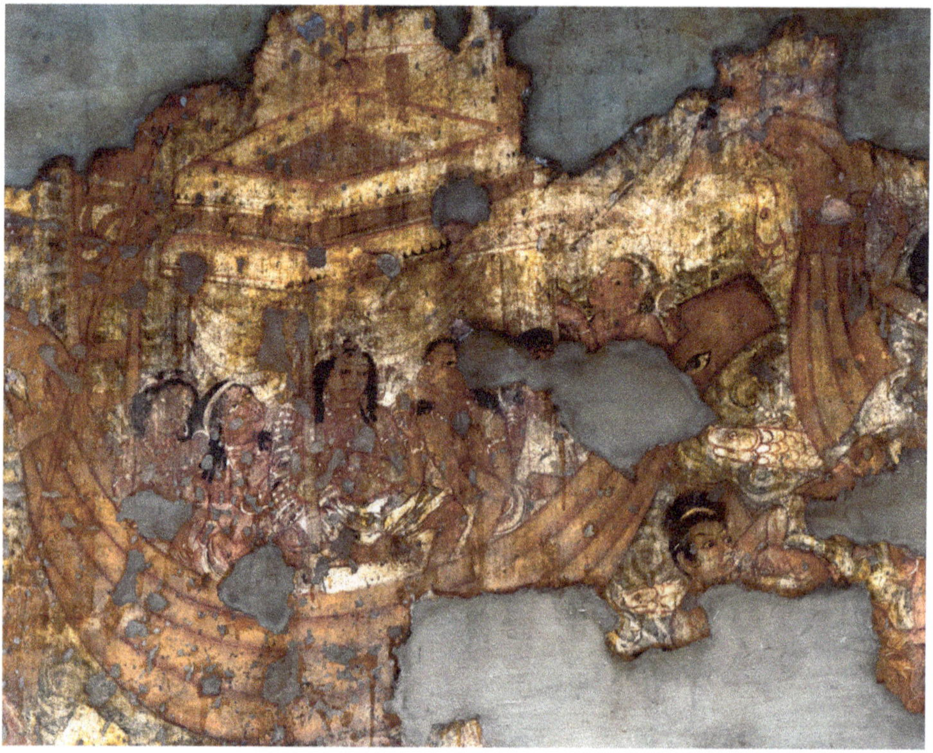

kingdom and his brother's power and resources, Pāpakārin gauged Kalyāṇakārin's eyes out as he slept, and ran away with the jewels.

Some cowherds found the blind and abandoned Kalyāṇakārin and looked after him. They gave him a flute to earn alms as a musician. The head gardener of a royal residence, impressed by his flute playing, hired him as a garden hand. One day the princess saw him and instantly fell in love with him. She asked her father for permission to marry this blind musician, something which her father granted her, albeit unwillingly. They lived in the princess' palace together. By and by Kalyāṇakārin suspected his wife's fidelity and asked her to heal one of his eyes by a spell of truth and thus prove her sanctity, which she did. When Kalyāṇakārin gained sight in one eye, he told his wife his back story, including the misdeeds of his evil brother. After that, he gained vision in his other eye as well. The princess invited her father to behold the miracle. The king recognised his son-in-law as Prince Kalyāṇakārin because he had heard about him, and he accepted him happily. Later, Kalyāṇakārin returned to his father's kingdom with his wife.—Prince Kalyāṇakārin was none other than the Buddha in a former existence.

No. 74. Unidentified.

Schlingloff (1999; 2013) had identified the painting as a depiction of the legend of Sumāgadhā. He now maintains that his identification is incorrect (personal communication). Still, however, we are giving the story of Sumāgadhā and two photographs of the painting in the hope that a reader might attempt proper identification.—

Anāthapiṇḍada, the merchant of the city of Śrāvastī, was a disciple of the Buddha. His daughter, Sumāgadhā, was married to the son of a merchant of the city of Puṇḍravardhana who was a follower of some naked beggar ascetics. She was disappointed with the ascetics who came to her palace for alms and hoped to draw her father-in-law to Buddhism. One day, with the permission of her father-in-law, she invited the Buddha for food with disciples. Her invitation was in the form of offering flowers. Her flowers flew and landed right on the Buddha's feet. The Buddha and his disciples miraculously travelled through the air and reached the merchant's house at Puṇḍravardhana. Sumāgadhā welcomed them with food and drink.

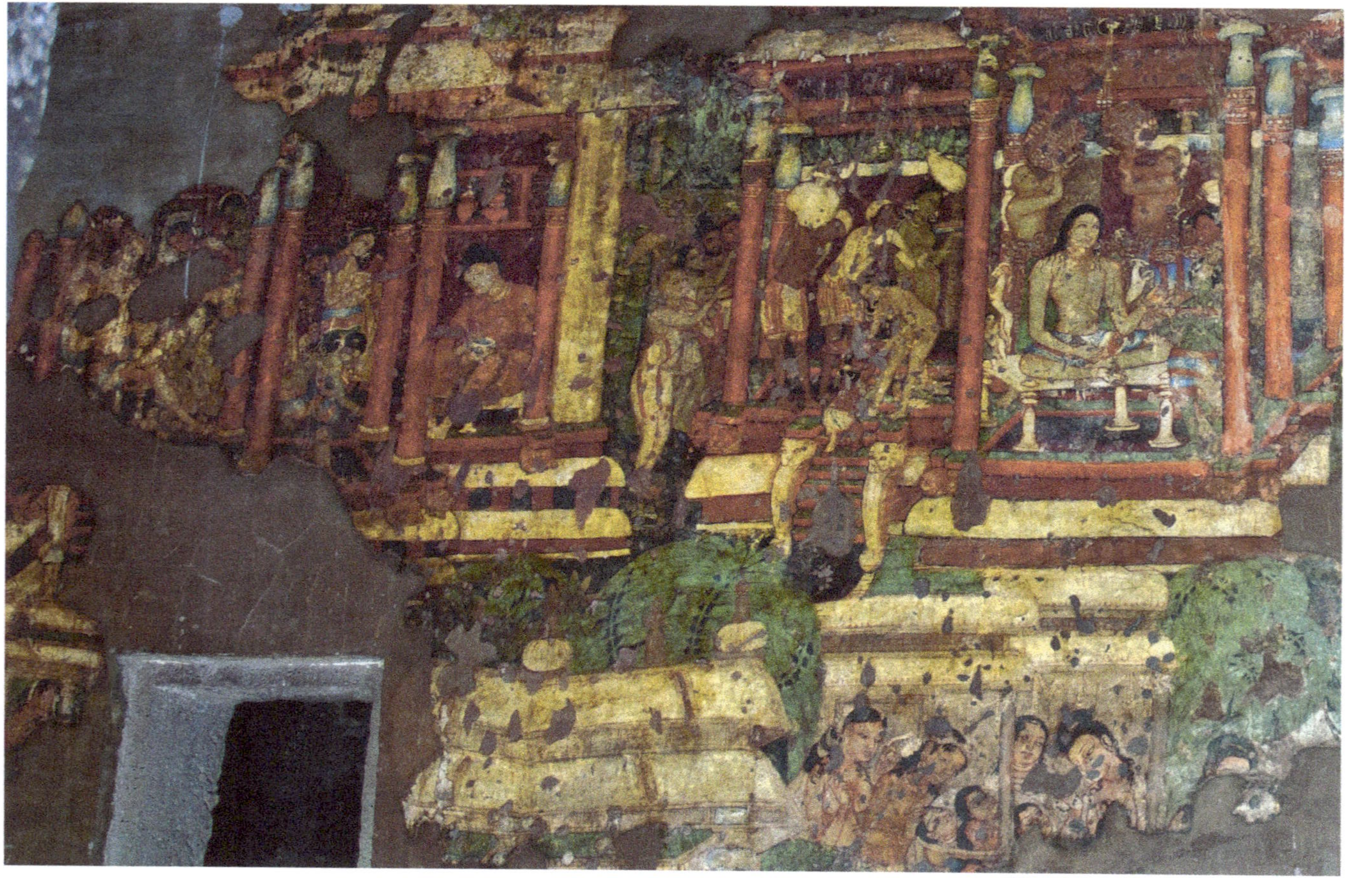

No. 74. Left: *an unidentified narrative*. Right: *the legend of a brahman named Mahoṣadha coronated as king of Videha*. Hall, left rear wall.

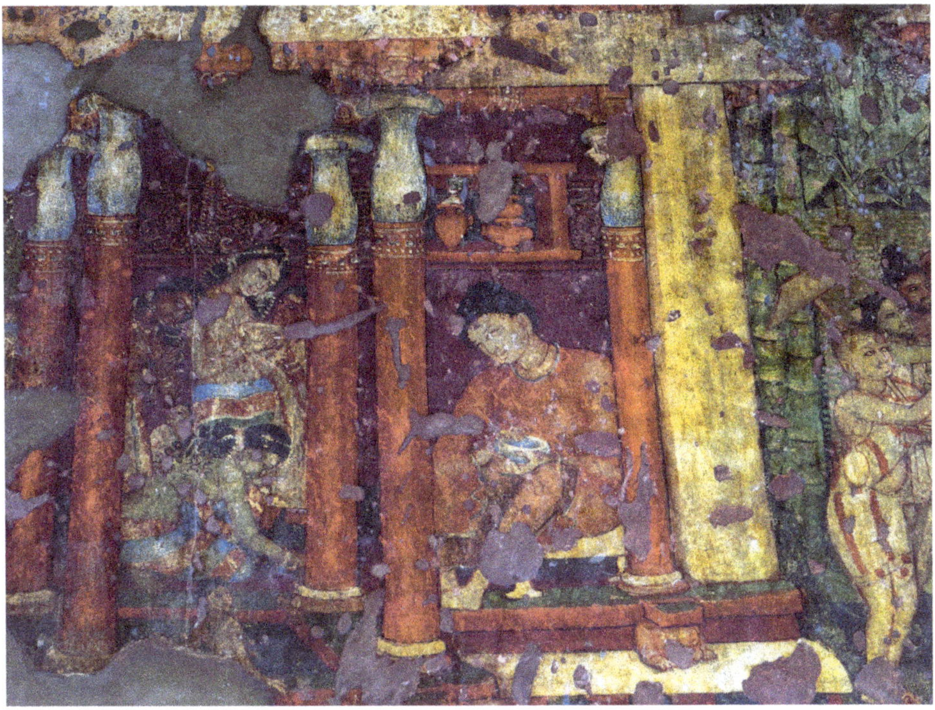

No. 74. *An unidentified story.* Hall, left rear wall.

No. 38. Mahoṣadha.

Identification: Goloubew (1927, p. 16).—A prince was banished from his kingdom due to a court intrigue. He managed to reach Videha, his uncle's kingdom. Shortly, the uncle died. So, the prince was crowned as the king of Videha. He found that there were six very corrupt ministers. So, he curtailed their powers after appointing a prime minister who was the mayor's son named Mahoṣadha.

Mahoṣadha was renowned for his intellect and acumen in law. His wife was Viśākhā, the daughter of a carpenter. She was a mix of beauty and brains.

The six lecherous ministers used to make unwelcome advances to her in order to corrupt her too. Wise Viśākhā made a plan to expose them. She pretended to be attracted to them. One day, she invited each of them to her chamber at different times in the night. They arrived at their respective hours. One by one, she shoved them into different baskets. Next day, she dragged them all to the royal court and exposed them before the king in her husband's presence.

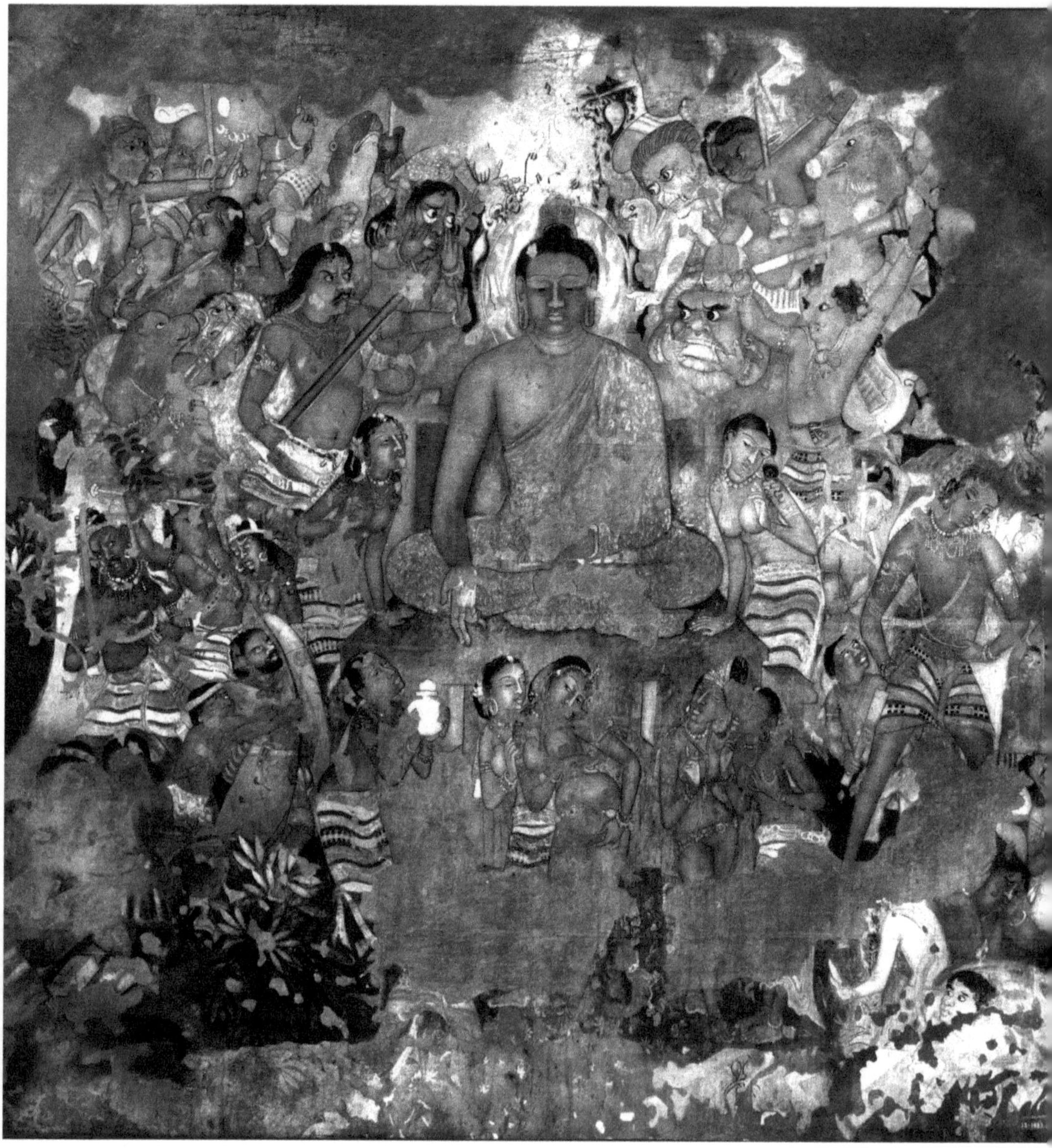

No. 80. *The legend of Māravijaya (Buddha's victory over Māra). Left wall of the vestibule to the sanctum sanctorum. Hand painted copy by John Griffiths. Photo courtesy of D. Schlingloff, M. Zin, and V&A Museum, London.*

The king was very impressed by her intelligence. He desired to have a wife like her. So, he sent Mahoṣadha to win over the daughter of a neighbouring king. Mahoṣadha did the job.

Thereafter, the six ministers were removed from their positions and exiled from the kingdom.—The Prime Minister Mahoṣadha was none other than the Buddha in a former existence.

No. 80. Māravijaya.

Identification: Griffiths in Burgess (1879, p. 14). The legend is from the life of the Buddha.—Indra, disguised as a grass-cutter, offered a bundle of straw to the Bodhisattva who had reached the stage just before the enlightenment. The Buddha first sat in the *vajrāsana* posture (*vajrāsanam abhiruhya* or Diamond Seat), then *paryaṅkam baddhvā* (crossed legged). He decided to remain in the position until he achieved the enlightenment. Meanwhile, Māra, the ruler of the world of sensuality, was hell-bent on making the Bodhisattva and other human beings permanent prisoners of sensuality. He went to the Bodhisattva in the guise of a postman and gave him the false news about a terror attack at his hometown Kapilavastu.

Though initially taken aback, the Bodhisattva recognised the messenger as Māra. So, he was unmoved. Māra then declared that Gautama was not virtuous enough to achieve the enlightenment. The Bodhisattva replied that he had sacrificed three world-ages and had given up all his belongings, even his body, to achieve the enlightenment. Māra alleged that his own great position is the proof of his past great deeds of many sacrifices. He accused that the present position of the Bodhisattva is the proof that he did not have any such sacrifice in the previous births.

Thereupon, the Buddha called the Earth Goddess as a witness. The goddess appeared and confirmed that what the Bodhisattva had said was true. Discouraged but still not defeated, Māra fled away, and sent his three daughters, namely, thirst, lust, and desire, to entrap the Bodhisattva. They tried to seduce him in various ways. However, the Bodhisattva transformed them into old women. When they returned to Māra, their unholy forms made Māra extremely worried and depressed.

Then Māra fought back by assuming himself as a warrior. His soldiers turned into animals and demons with many kinds of terrible weapons. But, when they flung the weapons at the Bodhisattva, they fell on the ground. To see an incapacitated army, the indefatigable Māra created a poisonous storm and a millstone shower to annihilate the Bodhisattva. Upon this, the deities of Sukhāvati (the Pure Land) protected the Bodhisattva by creating a secured leaf-hut for him.

Eventually, to distract the Bodhisattva, Māra turned the leaves of the Tree of Enlightenment into crystals, which started to make

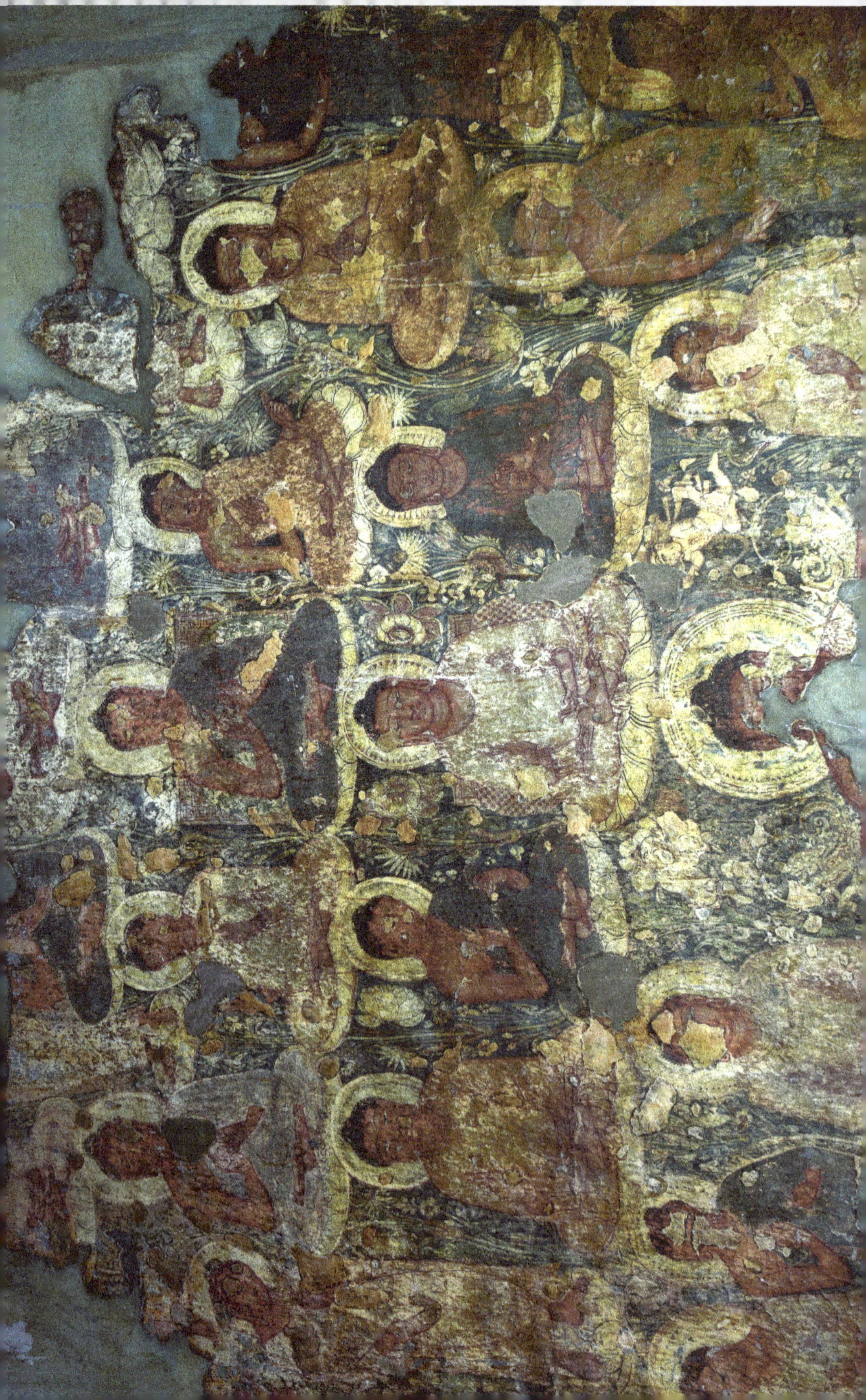

a great noise in the thunderstorm. But the deities of the Pure Land removed all such attacks. Then, they relegated Māra's warriors into the underworld. It was the same night when the Bodhisattva achieved enlightenment and became the Buddha.

No. 88. Opposite page. *Detail from the legend of Mahāprātihārya or the Buddha's Great Miracle at Śrāvastī.* *Shrine antechamber, right wall.*

No. 88. Mahāprātihārya.

Identification: Foucher (1921, narrative no. 57). The legend is from the life of the Buddha.—There were six ascetics, who misled the followers of the Buddha when he preached about the path to salvation. They wanted to challenge the Buddha's spiritual power in a contest. They sought King Bimbisāra's endorsement, which was not given. But King Prasenajit thought otherwise and requested the Buddha to participate in this event. Initially, the Buddha stated that he had not taught superhuman feats to his disciples, but simply instructed them to fight against evil. But finally, he agreed to participate. He performed the Great Miracle of Śrāvastī, since performance of a miracle was a precondition to achieving the state of nirvāṇa (beatitude attained by extinction of individuality and desires, with release from effects of karma). King Prasenajit arranged the event in a place between the city of Śrāvastī and the Jetavana monastery. The king, his advisers, the ascetics, their disciples, and many spectators assembled at the site.

The king ordered Uttara to request the Buddha to come. Uttara returned, in flight mode (thanks to the Buddha's magical powers), and announced the Buddha's arrival. The Buddha conjured rays of light that burst into the hall, illuminating it; he produced golden light which brightened up the whole world. The monastery's gardener, Gaṇḍaka, placed a Karṇikāra tree in front of the hall. A second gardener, Ratnaka, placed an Aśoka tree behind the hall. On the Buddha's arrival, the earth started shaking, the sun and the moon became brighter, instruments spontaneously sounded holy music, and gods showered flowers upon the Buddha.

After the Buddha took his seat the monk Maudgalyāyaṇa asked for the Buddha's permission to demonstrate a few superhuman skills that he had picked up from his master. But the ascetics had challenged the Buddha, not his disciples. Therefore, on the king's request, the Buddha had to demonstrate his superhuman powers by going into a deep meditative state, disappearing from his seat, reappearing in air above the seat, moving eastwards, and assuming four postures, namely, perambulation, standing, sitting and lying. When he entered into a fire, his body glowed in six colours. He performed various miracles in all four directions and then returned back from the spiritual state.

However, all these acts could be learnt and performed by any of the Buddha's disciples, so was felt by the erudite gathered in the hall. So, the king requested the Buddha to perform Mahāprātihārya (Great Miracle). Then, on the Buddha's call, Gods Brahmā and Indra appeared from heaven and sat on the Buddha's right and left, respectively. The *nāga* (serpent) kings, Nanda and Upananda, offered him a lotus decorated with pure gold. The Buddha sat cross-legged in the lotus, set his body, focused his mind and made another Buddha appear above the lotus and all four sides. This multiplicity of images rose to the visible heavens. These Buddha forms appeared in different positions and some even entered fires and produced miraculous manifestations with sentences of the doctrine. He made all the appearances required by the monks, and only then, took his seat. Finally, it was the turn of the ascetics, but no one had the courage to rise to the occasion. The ascetics' pavilions were hit by a thunderstorm fashioned by the commander of the army of *yakṣas* (a class of semi-divine beings whose master is Kubera, the God of Wealth). The most important ascetic, Purāṇa, drowned himself in a pond. The episode ended with the Buddha preaching a sermon, directing his people towards salvation.

No. 60. Campaka.

Identification: Foucher (1921, narrative no. 2).—The miffed wife of a *nāga* (serpent) king went to a royal court to complain that a hunter had caught her husband just so that he could put up his catch for display and earn some cheap brownie points. So far, the nāga king had been leading a perfectly blameless existence and had recently observed a fortnight's fast. So, weakened, he had allowed himself to be captured. But, all knew that he was powerful enough to destroy the entire city, if the nāga so desired.

The king asked the hunter to compensate for the nāga's capture. The hunter stubbornly held his ground but later he released the nāga. Thereafter, the nāga king invited the human king over to his palace. The king initially refused because he was rather scared of the nāgas. He then agreed when the nāga king assured him that he would not be harmed. When the king entered the glittering living quarters of the royal serpent and saw all precious objects casually scattered around, he wondered aloud about the virtuous life of the nāga king and how it would be to be reborn in the world

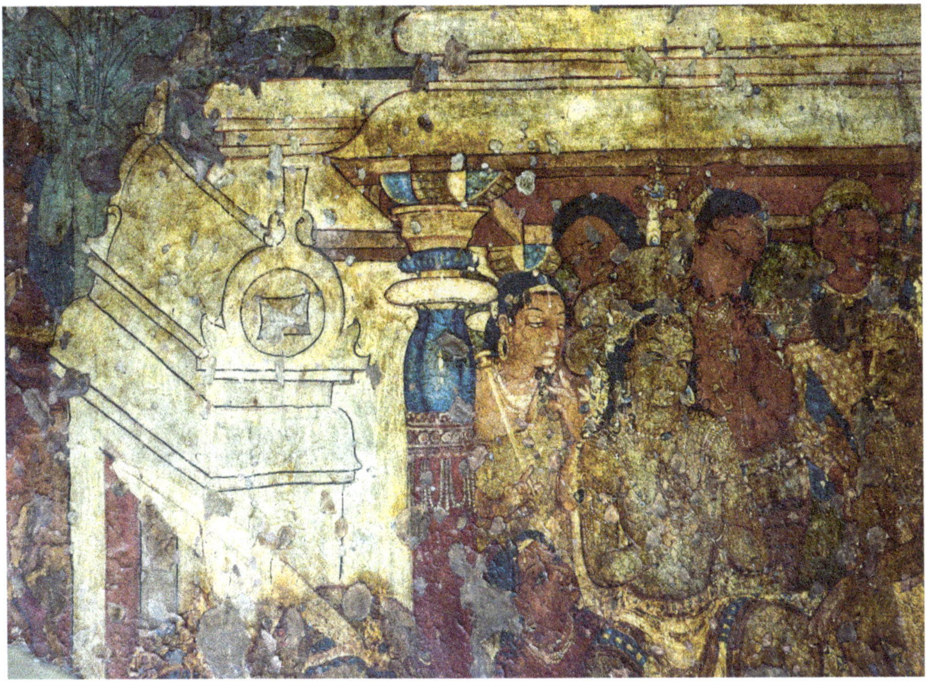

No. 60. *The legend of a nāga king called Campaka, scene 6. Campaka is seated in his palace with royal companions and is instructing his guest (partly visible on right) on the unique value of reincarnation as a human being, for only a human can become a Buddha.* Hall, rear wall, right side.

of humans. The nāga king explained that only human beings, as against mere nāgas, could escape the cycle of rebirths.—Nāgarāja Campaka was none other than the Buddha in a former existence.

No. 76. Nāgakumāra.

Identification: Schlingloff (1977b, p. 913–917).—In a previous age when a Buddha named Kāśyapa was living, a *nāga* (serpent) prince died in the claws of a *garuḍa* (eagle). Before his death, he saw some monks meditating in the hills and wished to become a monk in his next life. He was reborn as a human and achieved sainthood. As he meditated, he had a vision of his previous life's parents, who were still grieving over his demise. He flew to them with superhuman powers and revealed his identity. His parents offered him a delightful meal and he promised to visit them daily for meals. His attendant observed his absence during the meal time, so one day he followed him. The parents offered a scrumptious feast to their former son but only an ordinary meal to the novice. The novice flew into a rage at such abject discrimination and uttered a vow to be reborn as a nāga and even to dislodge the present nāga king. As soon as he uttered this evil vow, water, the vital element

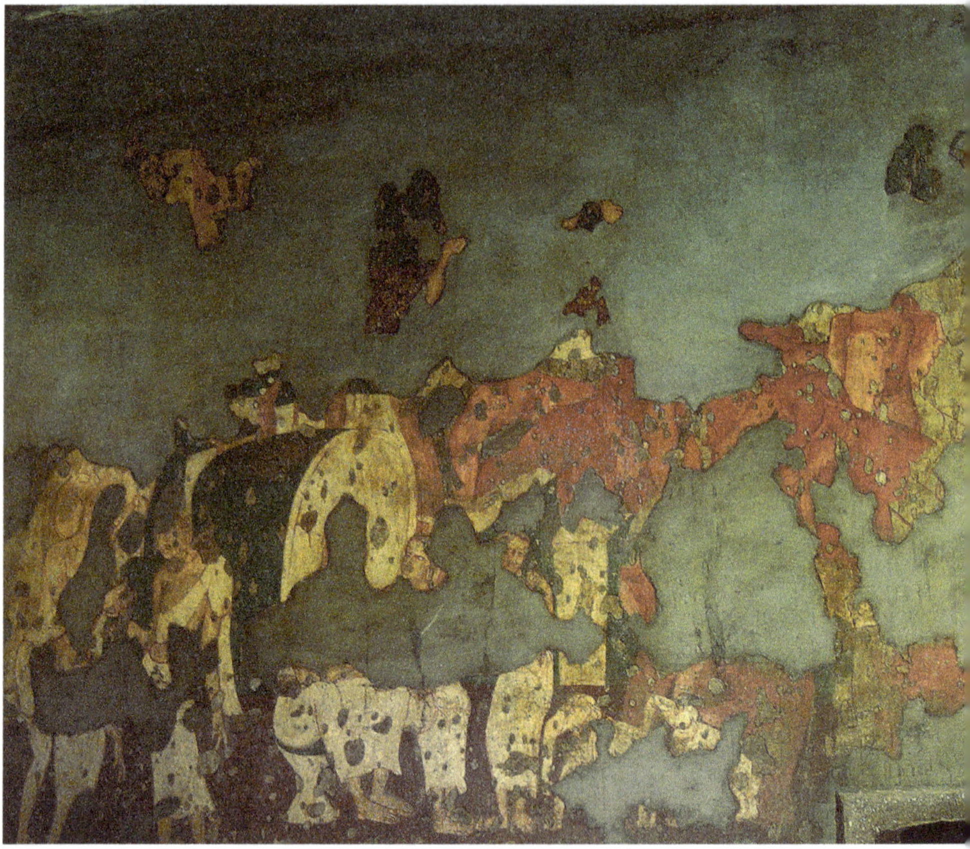

No. 76. *nāgakumāra (on the left)*

No. 53. *Prabhāsa (centre and right).*

Hall, right wall.

of the nāgas started dripping from his finger.—The Nāgakumāra was none other than the Buddha in a former existence.

No. 53. Prabhāsa.

Identification: Schlingloff (1977c, p. 152).—King Prabhāsa caught an elephant. He trained the animal and decided to take him out for a walk one fine day. The elephant sniffed out the odour of a female elephant, it being the mating season, and was immediately aroused. In the flurry of jumbo activity that followed, the king and his mahout saved themselves with the help of a stout branch of a tree. The elephant spent several days with his mate. Afterwards, the mahout took him back to the royal court. The king blamed the mahout for his improper training methodology but the mahout convincingly argued that he was not at fault and that no amount of coaching could tame animal instincts. To prove his point, the mahout ordered the elephant to eat a heated iron ball. The elephant prepared to eat the hot iron ball. The king was mighty impressed by the elephant's subservience as well as his virility. Later, the king

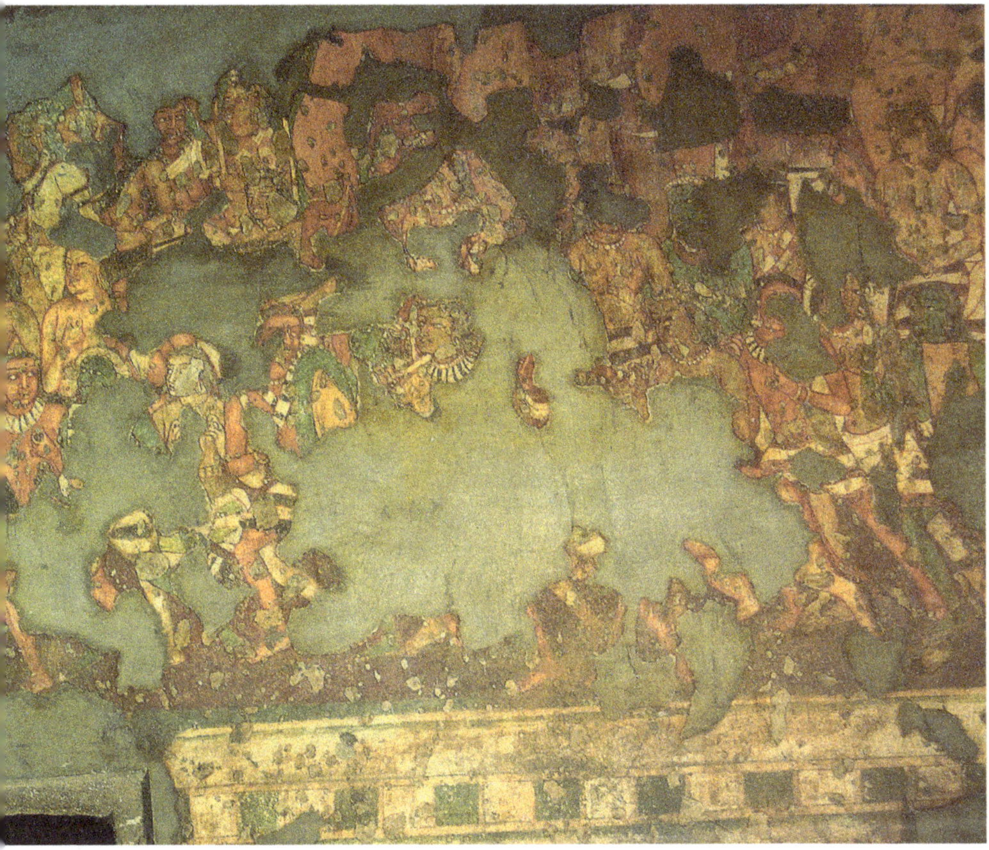

heard that only the Buddha could conquer carnal desires. Then, he made up his mind to take the path of a Bodhisatva.—King Prabhāsa was none other than the Buddha in a former existence.

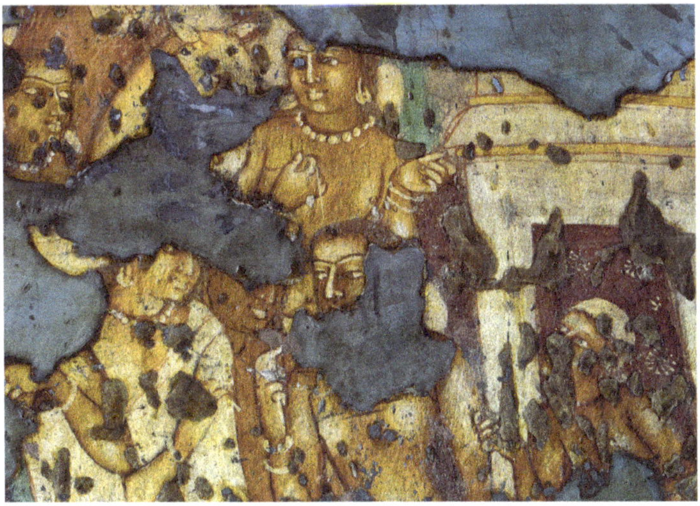

No. 53. *Prabhāsa, scene 4. Escorts discuss the dangerous beguilement of the elephant of King Prabhāsa.*

A NON-NARRATIVE THEME.

No. 42.[1] Bodhisattva kings in mountains (hall).

1 The numbers under the *non-narrative* themes including the captions refer to those assigned by Monika Zin to the *non-narrative* themes of the Ajanta paintings, vide Zin 2003a.

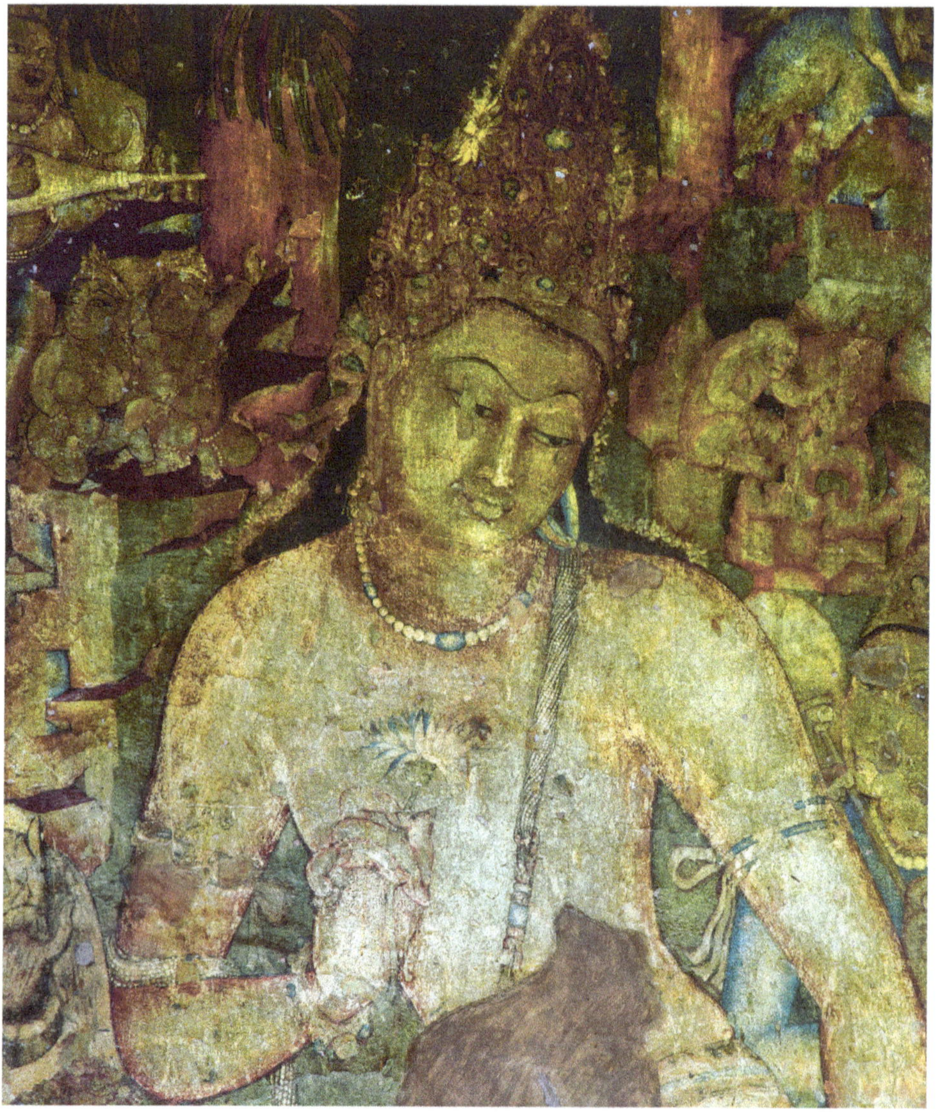

No. 42.1. *Bodhisattva King in a mountainous landscape. Hall, rear left wall.*

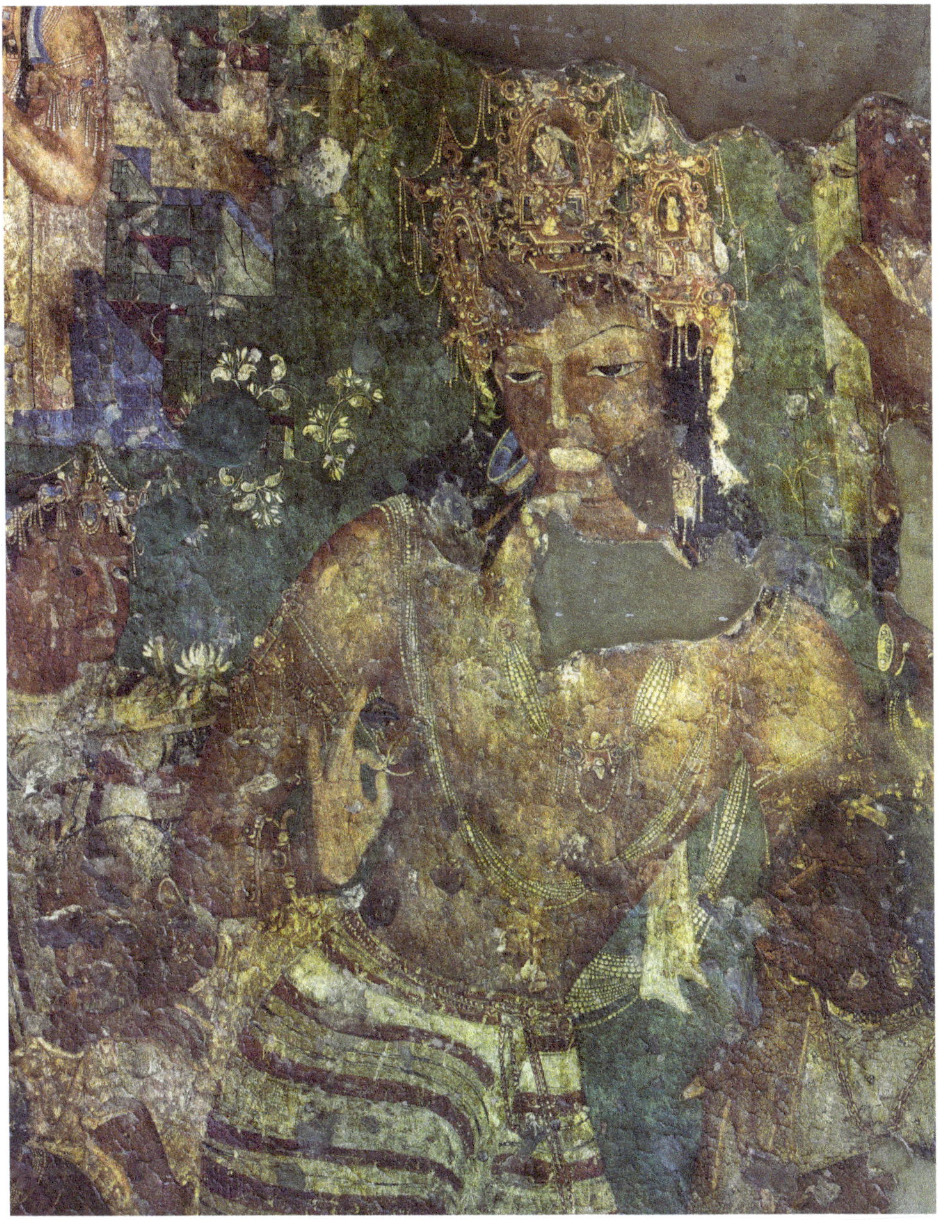

No. 42.2. *Bodhisattva King in a mountainous landscape.* *Hall, rear right wall.*

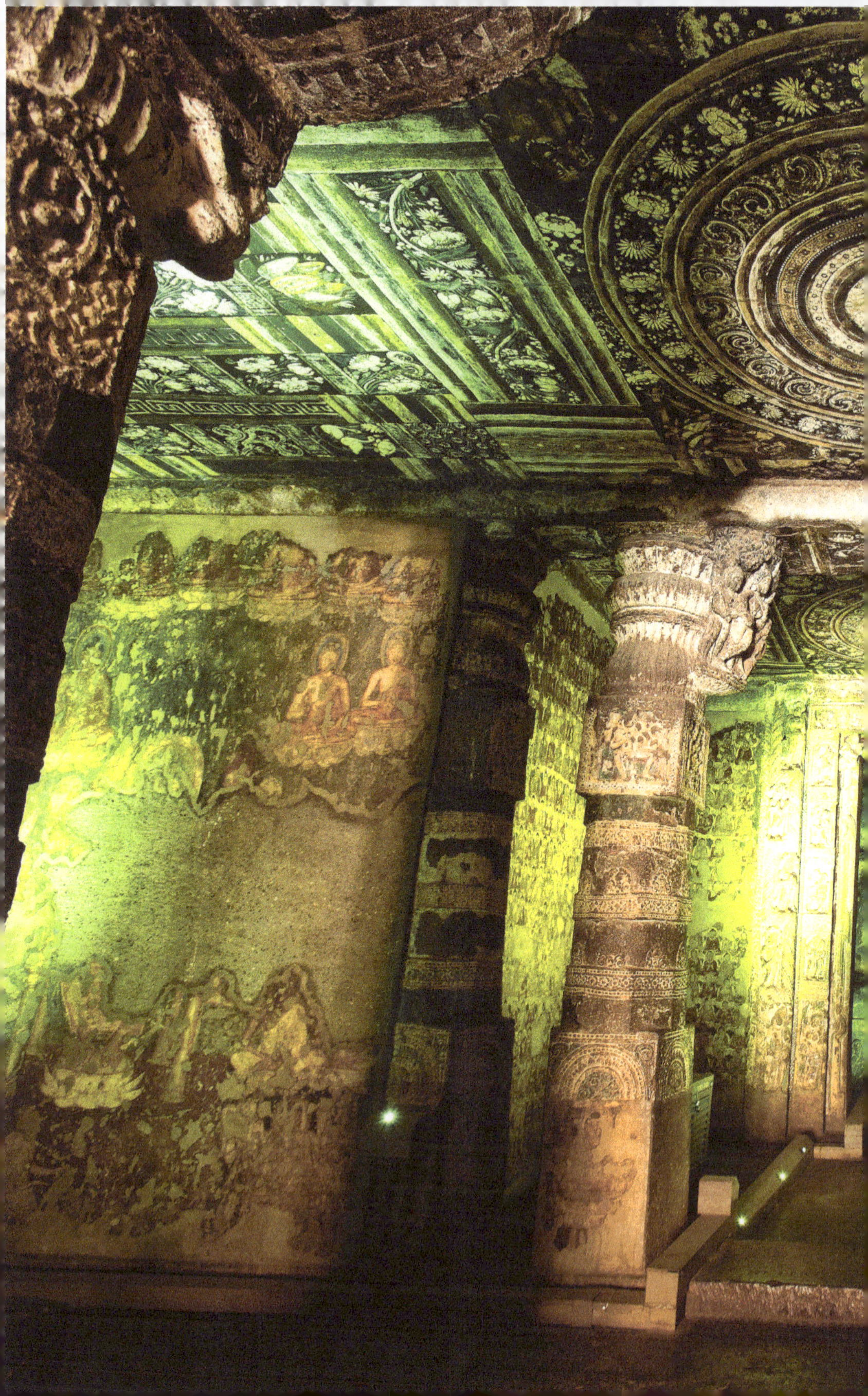

II. Cave No. 2

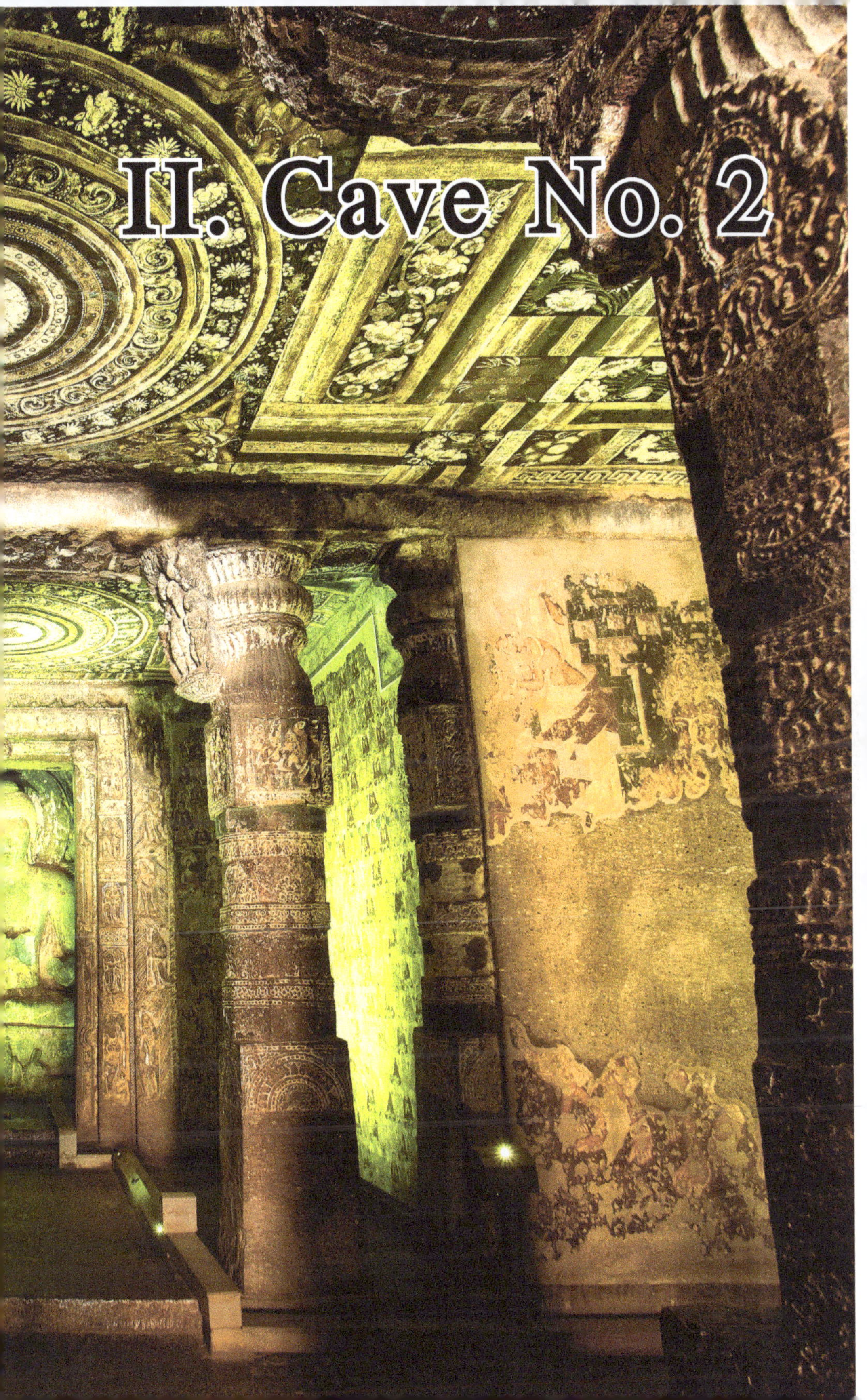

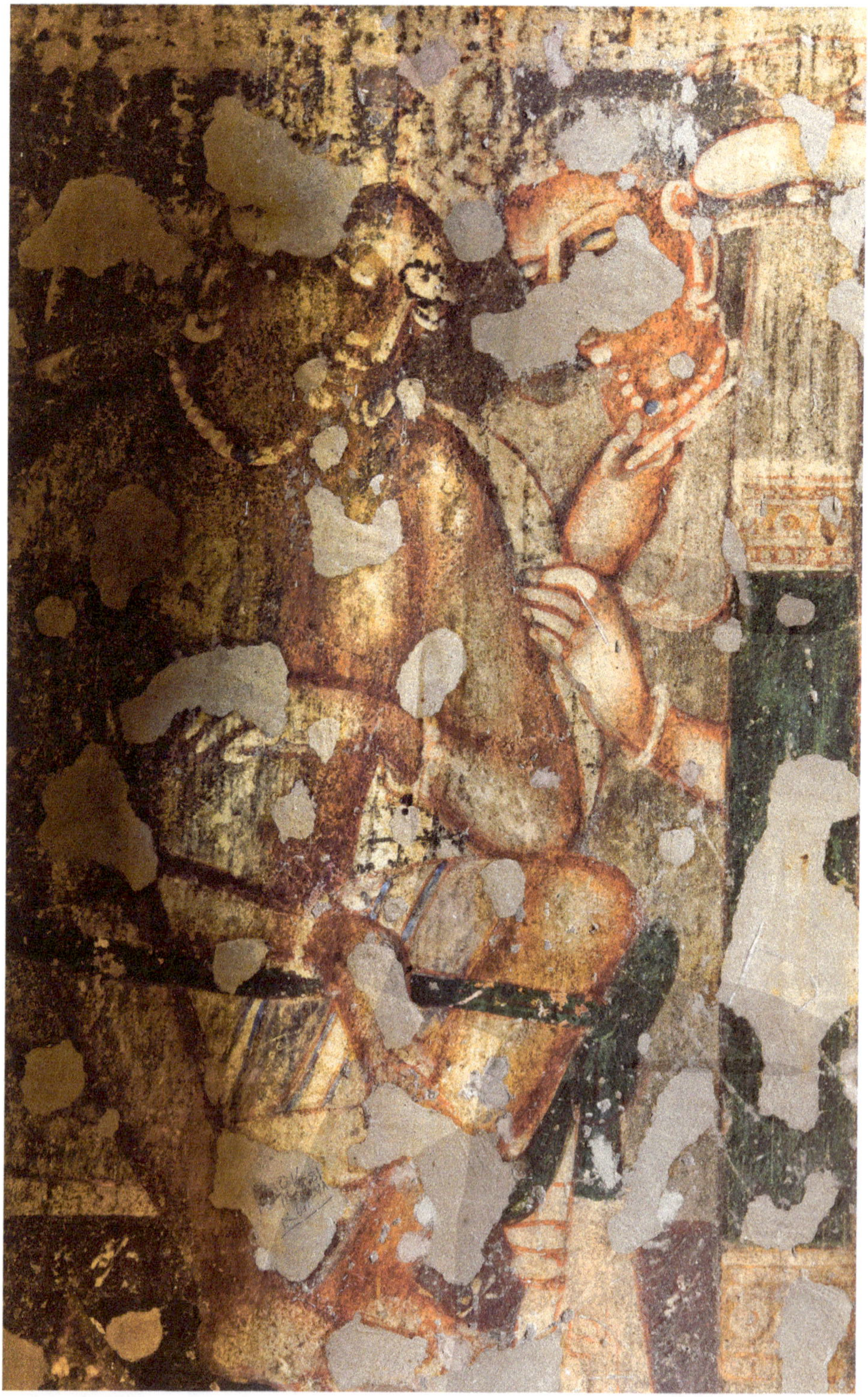

NARRATIVE THEMES.

No. 61.[1] Bhūridatta.

Identification: Schlingloff 2013.—A *nāga* (serpent) king sent his representatives to propose to the daughter of the king of Banaras. But the king was not agreeable to the concept of a human-nāga union. Later, he agreed on the condition that the nāgas would not harm anybody. After marriage, the princess gave birth to four sons. Her second son, Bhūridatta, was not satisfied in his magnificent palace and departed with the avowed aim of practising asceticism so that he could be reborn in Indra's heaven. He suffered many hardships because of evil brahmans. Finally, he was brought back to his palace by his relatives, where he exposed the futility of sacrifices and rituals performed by brahmans and shed light on their caste-related hubris.—The cobra Bhūridatta was none other than the Buddha in a former existence.

No. 61. Opposite. *The king of Benaras seated in despair after receiving the proposal from a nāga king to marry his daughter.* *Porch, right pillared pavilion.*

No. 54. Prabhāsa.

Identification: Schlingloff 2013. For the story, vide Cave 1, No. 53.

No. 34. Kṣāntivādin.

Identification: Oldenburg (1895, narrative no. 12); Lüders (1902, p. 758 f. = trans. 1903, p. 326 f.).—There was an ascetic, Kṣāntivādin (Preacher of Meekness and Forgiveness), who lived and preached in a forest. On a hot summer's day, a king came to the forest with his female companions. They took a communal dip in pond. After the lively bath session, the king fell fast asleep, while his companions explored the forest, ultimately reaching the ascetic's hermitage. They sat around him and listened to his preaching. When the king awoke, he noticed the ladies' absence and went in search of them. When he found them listening to the ascetic in rapt attention, he rushed towards him with his sword, accusing him of stealing the ladies. The ascetic spoke to the king softly but the king cut off his hands and other limbs. At this, the king was swallowed by the earth. The ascetic promised to his ministers that

1 The numbers under the *narrative* themes refer to those assigned by Dieter Schlingloff to the *narrative* paintings of Ajanta, vide Schlingloff 2013.

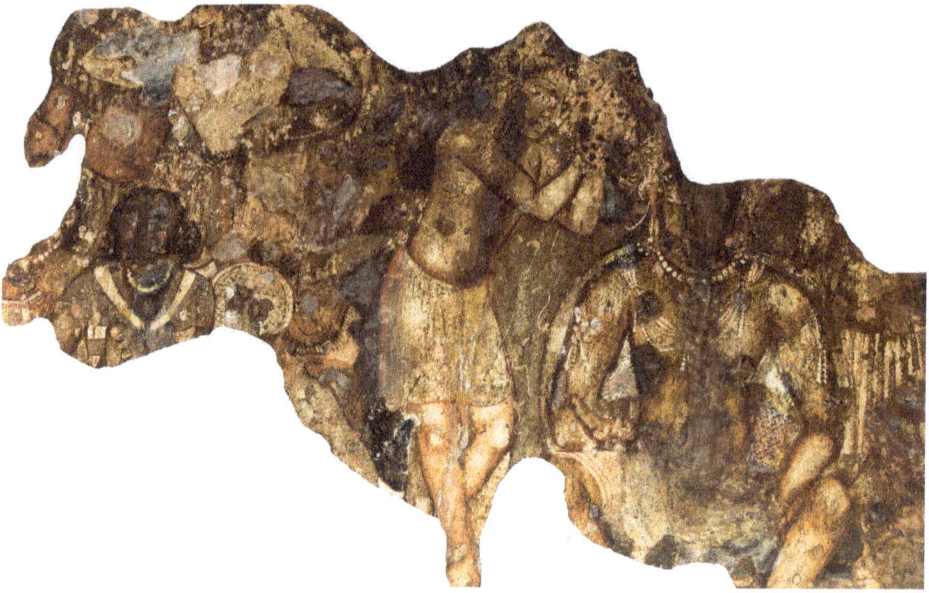

No. 54. *The extant fragment of the legend of King Prabhāsa who is seated majestically on the right while deciding to take a ride on the newly tamed elephant.* Porch, right pillared pavilion.

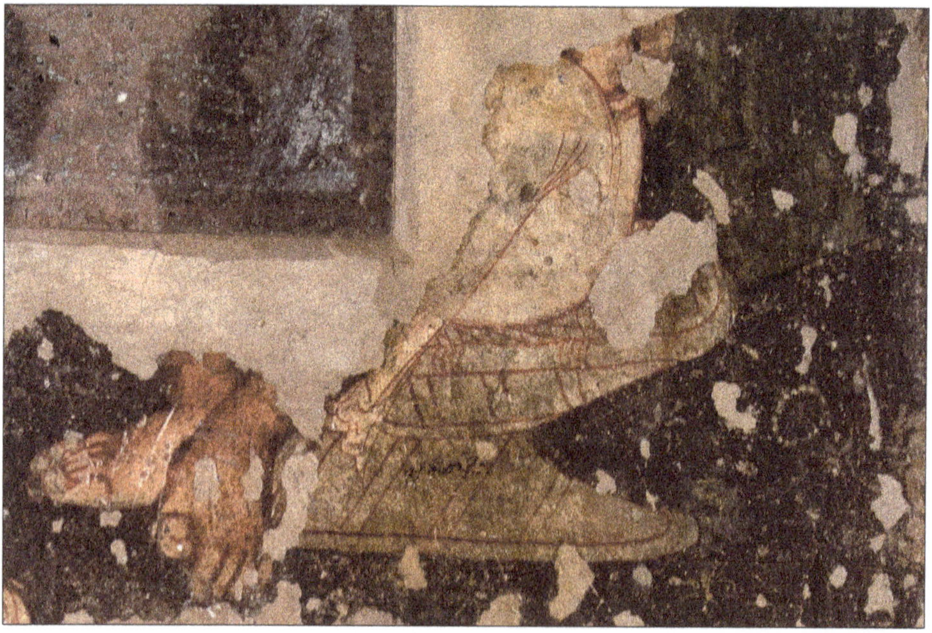

No. 34. *The extant fragment of the figure of the ascetic Kṣāntivādin. He is seated in a cane-stool that bears an inscription informing us his name.* Porch, left pillared pavilion.

their country would not suffer due to the king's sin as he ascended to the heavens.—The brahman ascetic Kṣāntivādin was none other than the Buddha in a former existence.

No. 51. Maitrībala.

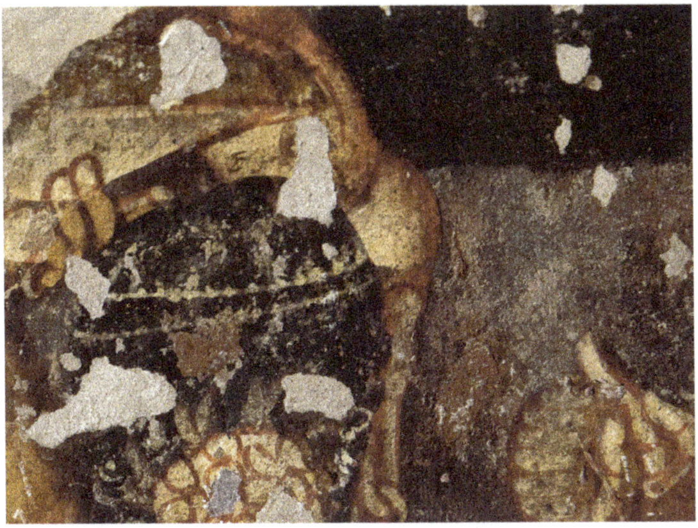

No. 51. *The extant fragment of a figure from the Maitrībala narrative who is standing next to the King who serves the vegetarian food to the five demons disguised as brahmans.* Porch, left pillared pavilion.

Identification: Lüders (1902, p. 761 f. = trans. 1903, p. 328). For the story, vide Cave 1, No. 50.

No. 47. Śibi-Kapota.

Identification: Schlingloff (1977, p. 57–68). For the story, vide Cave 1, narrative no. 46.

No. 13. Haṃsa.

Identification: Oldenburg (1895, narrative no. 1).—A king of the geese (*haṃsas*) lived on the shores of a lake in the Himalayas with his general and a huge flock of geese. Sages and commoners alike admired their beauty and wisdom, which even became a topic in the assemblies of kings. On hearing this, the king of Banaras made a beautiful lotus pond to lure them. In a moonlit night, some geese flew to the pond. They returned home in the rainy season and told the others about the fabulous pond. Soon enough, the entire flock set off for Banaras despite warnings from the general. The palace

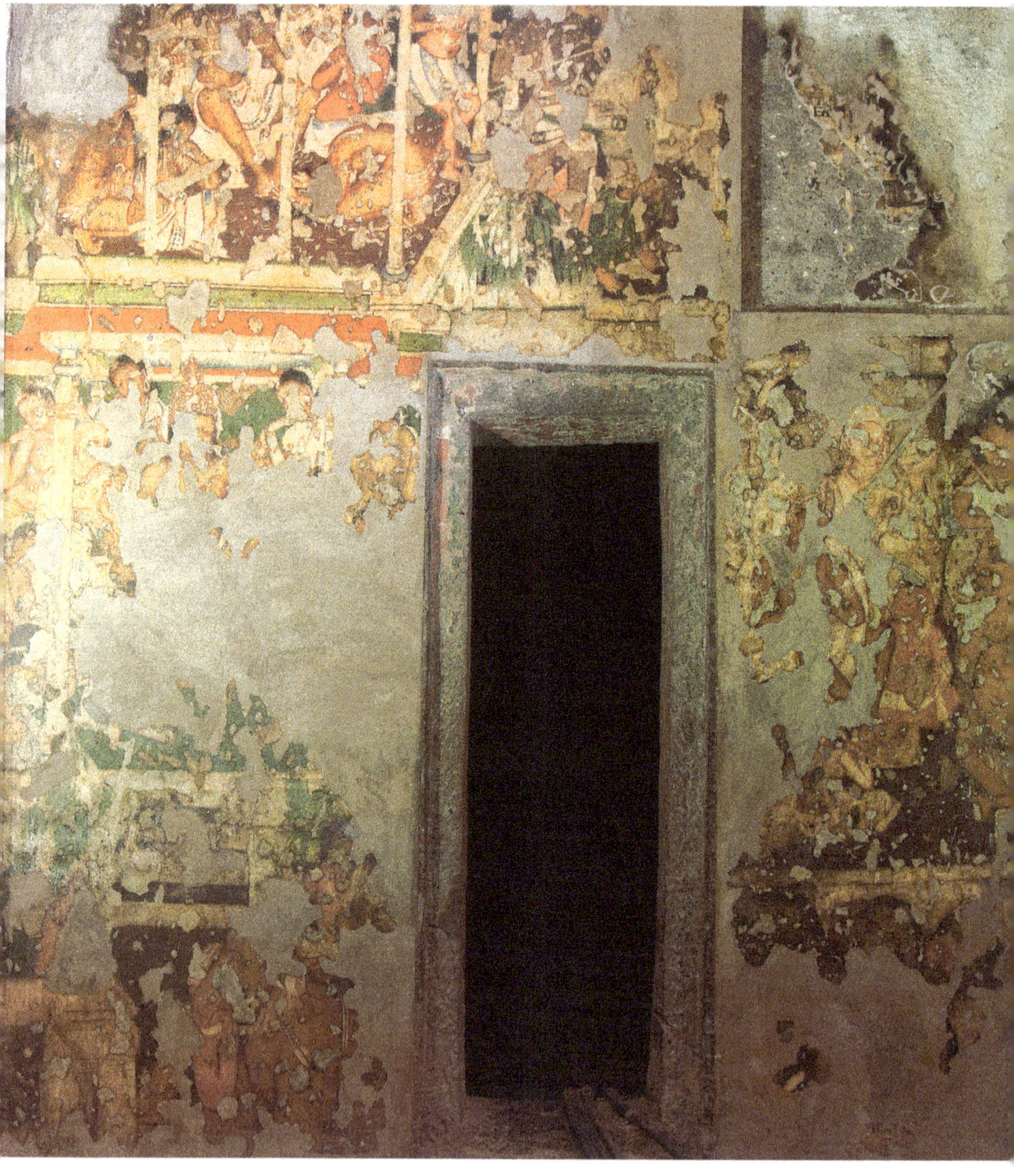

No. 47. *The wall with the Śibi-Kapota narrative. Hall, front aisle, right wall.*

guards informed the king about the two beautiful leading geese. The king gave orders to trap them and the goose king was caught in a snare. The goose king warned his flock to fly away. All flew away except the general, who remained with his king even as he saw the fowler approaching. This moved the fowler, who freed the goose king and related the story to the king. The general told him to take them to the king, who treated them with awed respect and

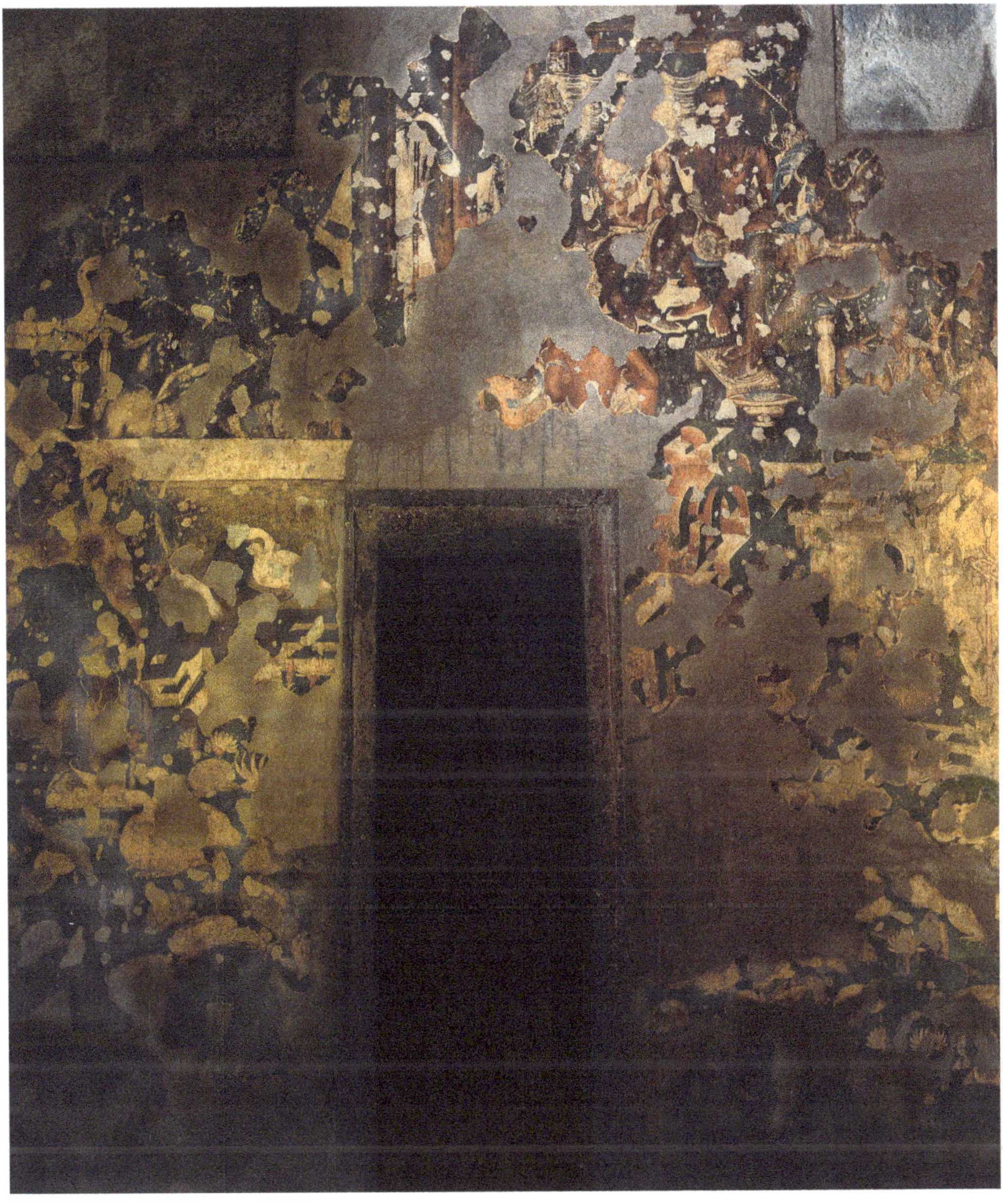

offered a seat near him. The king asked the goose king to instruct him about the virtues of a just ruler and loyalty. Subsequently, he freed both of them.—The goose king was none other than the Buddha in a former existence.

No. 13. *The wall with the Haṃsa narrative.*
Hall, front aisle, left wall.

No. 65. Bhagavatprasūti.

Identification: some episodes by Foucher (1921), others by Schlingloff (1983; 1987), cf. Schlingloff (2013, vol. I, p. 378). The legend is from the life of the Buddha.—

When the time had come for the Bodhisattva to have his last rebirth, celestial hymns were chanted. After that, he went to the assembly of the gods and informed them about when, where, and how he would take his last birth on earth. Then, on a full moon night, he took the form of a young, white, six-tusked elephant. The queen, Māyā, wife of King Śuddhodana of Kapilavastu, saw this sequence in her dreams and related it to her husband in the morning. On the king's request, the brahmans interpreted the queen's dream, saying she would give birth to a son who would become either a universal monarch or an enlightened Buddha. The king, pleased by this prediction, offered presents to the needy people in his city. A palace was built by the deities so that the queen could stay there during her pregnancy. She neither suffered physical or mental anxieties associated with women in her state, nor did she feel lust for a man. The queen could feel the Bodhisattva in her womb. As the time for delivery neared, Māyā requested her husband to send her to Lumbinī Park, where she could enjoy nature in full bloom.

No. 65.1. *The legend of Bhagavatprasūti (the Birth of the Enlightened One), scene 1. The Bodhisattva, in conversation with the gods of the Tusita Heaven, is planning his last birth in the saṃsāra.* Hall, left wall.

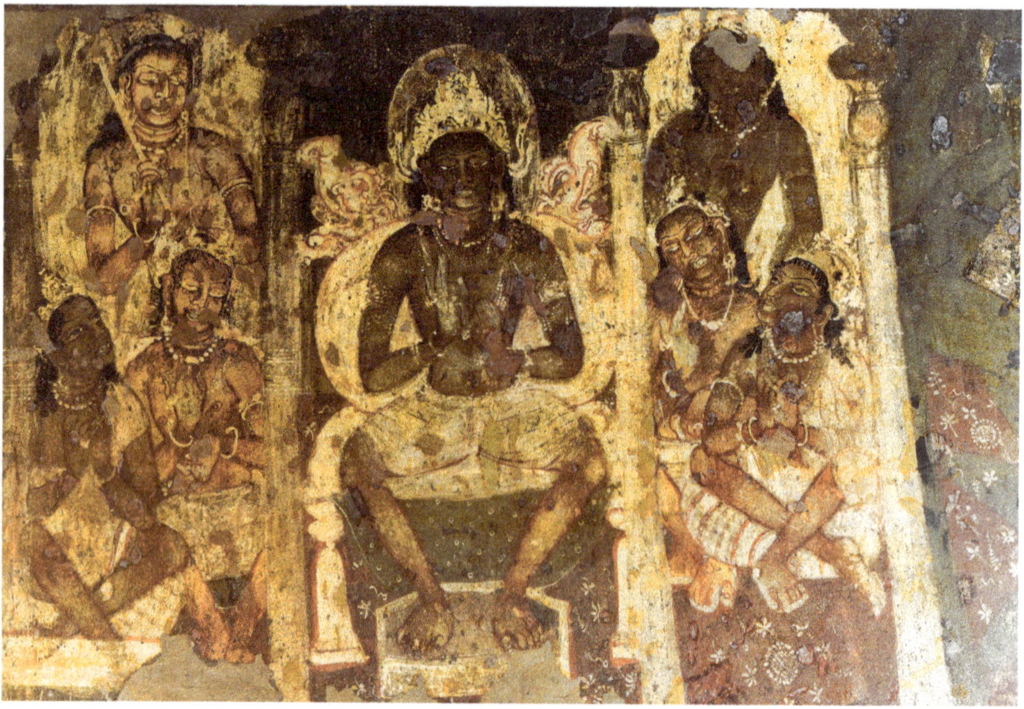

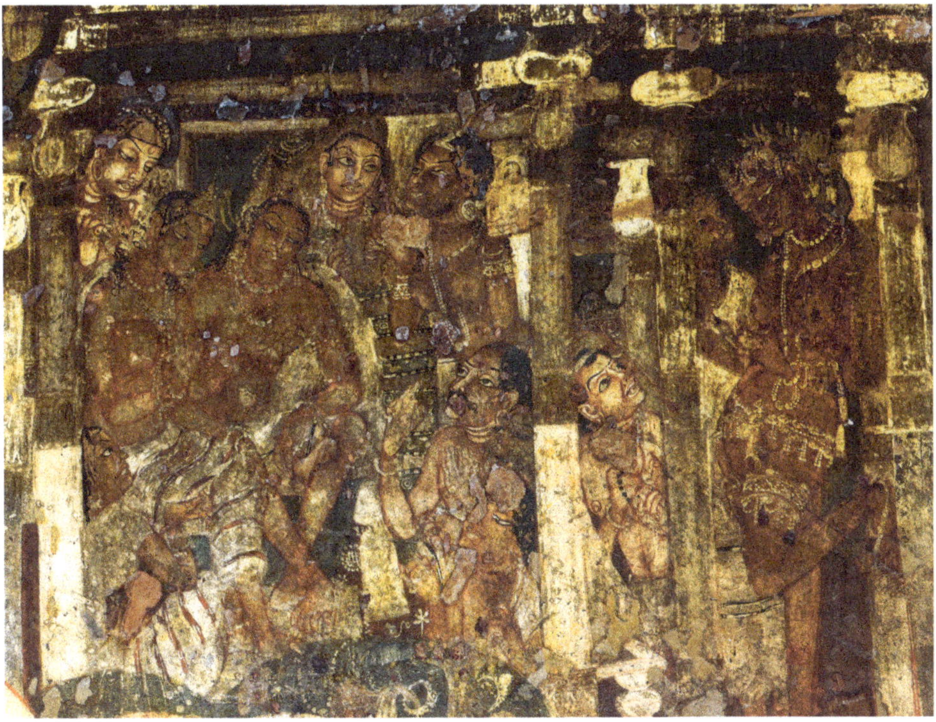

No. 65.2. Left: *scene 4. Three brahmans interpret the dream of queen Māyā to the royal couple.* Right: *scene 6. Māyā experiences the Bodhisattva inside her womb.*

The king arranged her trip and she left in a chariot with a number of attendants. In the grove, she found a fig tree decorated with cloths and pearls. As soon as she held a branch of that tree with her right arm, the Bodhisattva appeared from the right side of her body. Then, Indra and Brahmā appeared, received the infant and covered him with a divine silk cloth. When the Bodhisattva stood on the ground, two Nāga kings, Nanda and Upananda, emerged from the earth with a flow of warm and cold water to cleanse the Bodhisattva. Then, the Bodhisattva opened his divine eyes, looked over the world, took seven steps in all directions and announced his mission. Though the queen's body was clean and intact, ponds of water and fragrant oil materialised before her, with heavenly girls to serve her. One week after the Bodhisattva's birth, the queen died and the infant was taken to Kapilavastu and handed over to his aunt. The Bodhisattva was to be offered to the gods, according to custom. As soon as Śuddhodana entered the temple with the Bodhisattva, all the gods moved from their respective positions and fell at the Bodhisattva's feet to worship him.

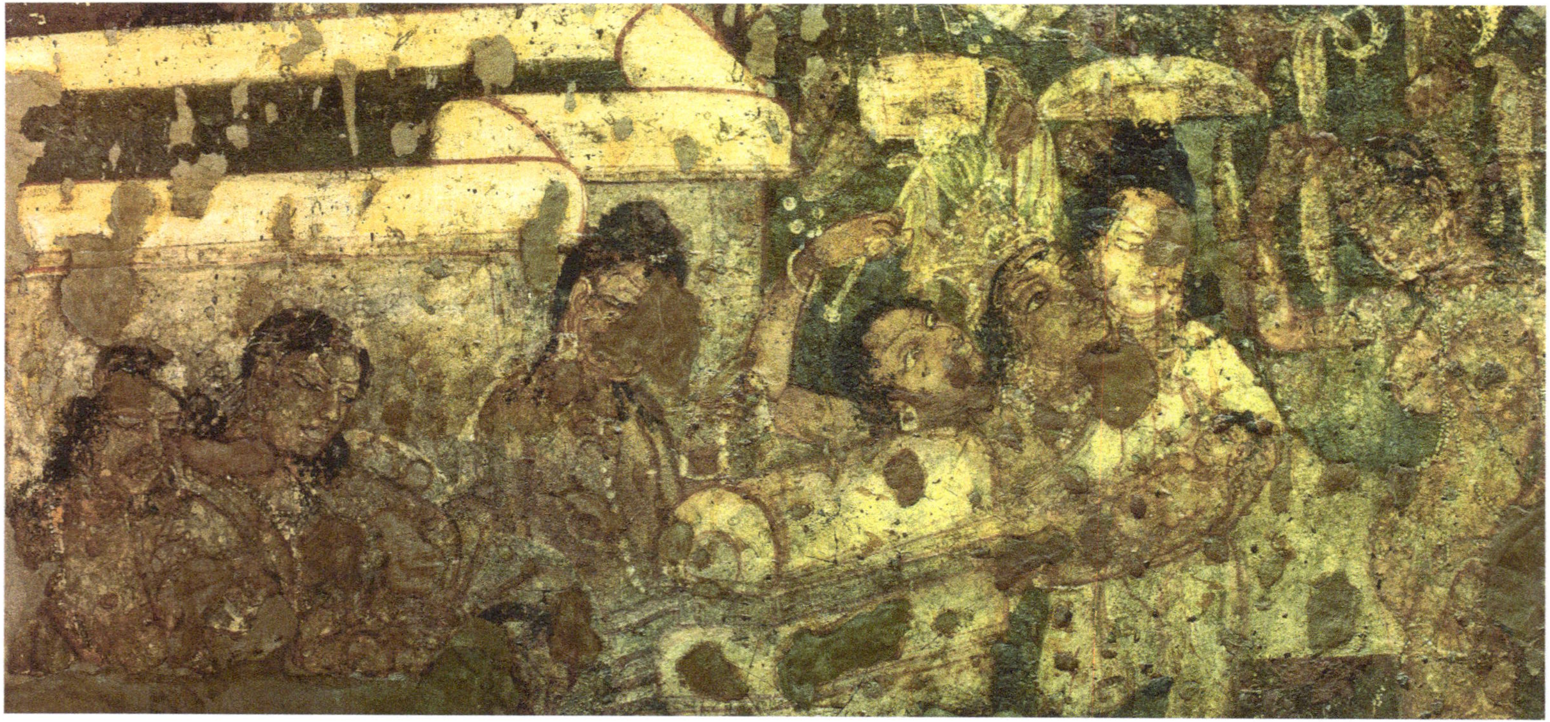

No. 65.3. *Bhagavatprasūti, scene 9. In Lumbinīvan, outside the city gates, the Gods Indra and Brahmā have taken the newborn in their hands as the Bodhisattva emerged from the queen's right side who has clasped the branch of a tree.*

No. 89. Mahāprātihārya.

Identification: Foucher (1921, narrative no. 57). The legend is from the life of the Buddha.—For the abstract of the story, vide Cave 1, No. 88.

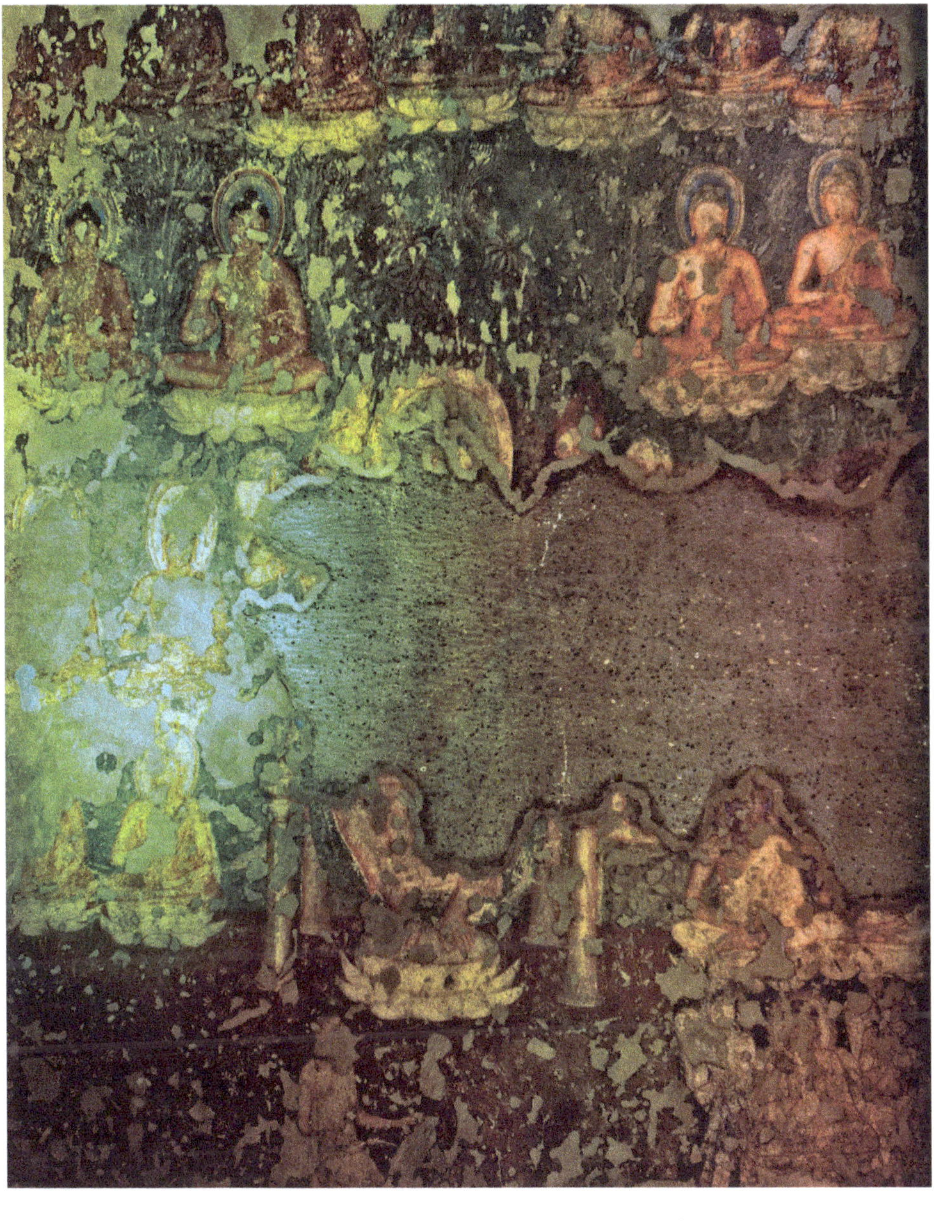

No. 89. *Flanked by Indra and Brahmā, the Buddha performs Mahāprātihārya (the Great Miracle of Śrāvastī) where a thousand Buddhas emanate from him.* Hall, rear wall, left side.

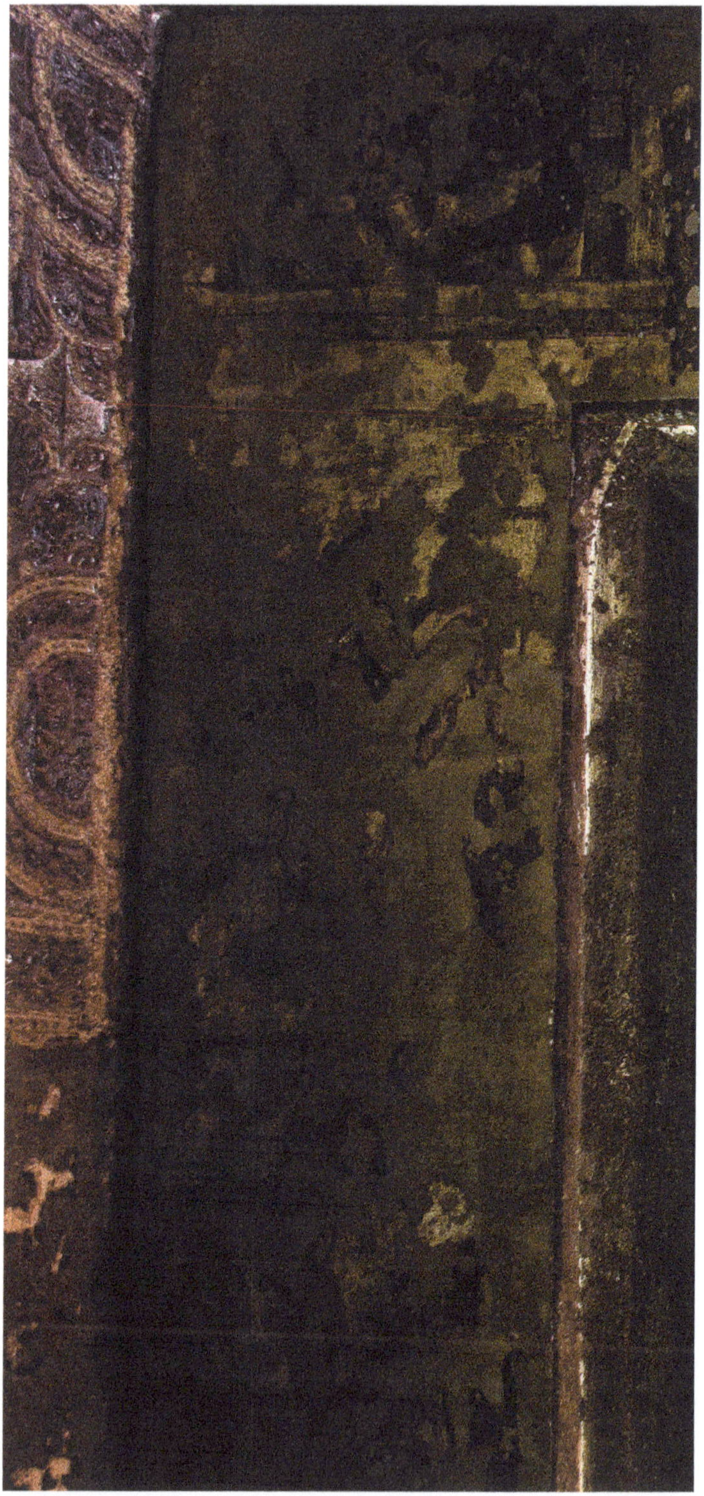

No. 16. ***The extant fragments of the Rúru narrative.*** *Hall, right wall.*

No. 16. Rúru.

Identification: Foucher (1919/1921, p. 60).—There was a golden-fleeced *rúru* or *svarṇa-mṛga* (stag) who lived near a torrent. Once, he rescued a drowning man, and thereafter requested the man not to tell anyone about his whereabouts so that the humans would not come after him to get his golden fleece.

Around this time, the queen of the land saw a vision of a golden-fleeced stag on a throne, delivering a sermon to the royal family. To fulfil her dream, the king declared a grand compensation for the person who could help him find such a stag. When the rescued man heard the king's declaration, he revealed the stag's location in the royal court. He led the king and his staff, armed with bows and arrows, to hunt down the stag. The crew managed to locate the stag but failed to catch him. The king also saw the stag and tried to wound him with an arrow, but the stag started to narrate the incidence of betrayal to the king. The king heard out the stag's story and was ready to punish the betrayer. The stag asked the king to forgive the culprit and even give him his reward. The king followed his instructions and led the stag to his palace; there the golden-fleeced animal delivered the sermon from a throne to the residents, advising them to practise kindness, an episode the queen had dreamt.—The stag was none other than the Buddha in a former existence.

No. 37. Vidhura.

Identification: Foucher (1921, narrative no. 11).—Vidhura, the loyal Prime Minister of the Kuru king, was famous for his wisdom even in the kingdom of the *nāgas* (serpents). One day, the nāga queen requested for the heart of Vidhura. Thereupon, the nāga king asked for the help of the nāga princess to fulfil the queen's desire.

The princess decided to search for a husband who could help her in the mission. As she let everybody know her wish to marry, the Yakṣa Puṇṇaka came riding a flying horse and presented himself as a candidate for marriage. The princess took the *yakṣa* (genius, a class of semi-divine beings) to her father. The king agreed to the marriage on the condition that Puṇṇaka must bring the heart of Vidhura.

Puṇṇaka went to Kubera, the Lord of the *yakṣas*, and obtained his permission to go on the mission. Subsequently, he flew away to obtain a magical jewel, which mirrored the whole world. Finally, he flew to the Kuru land and challenged the Kuru king in a game of dice. He placed the magic jewel against Vidhura. The Kuru king lost the game, and took the *yakṣa* to Vidhura.

Vidhura taught the lessons of wisdom to them and followed the *yakṣa*. Vidhura came to know about the nāga queen's desire for his heart, and came to the conclusion that she actually desired

No. 37.1. *The wall with the Vidhura narrative.* *Hall, right wall.*

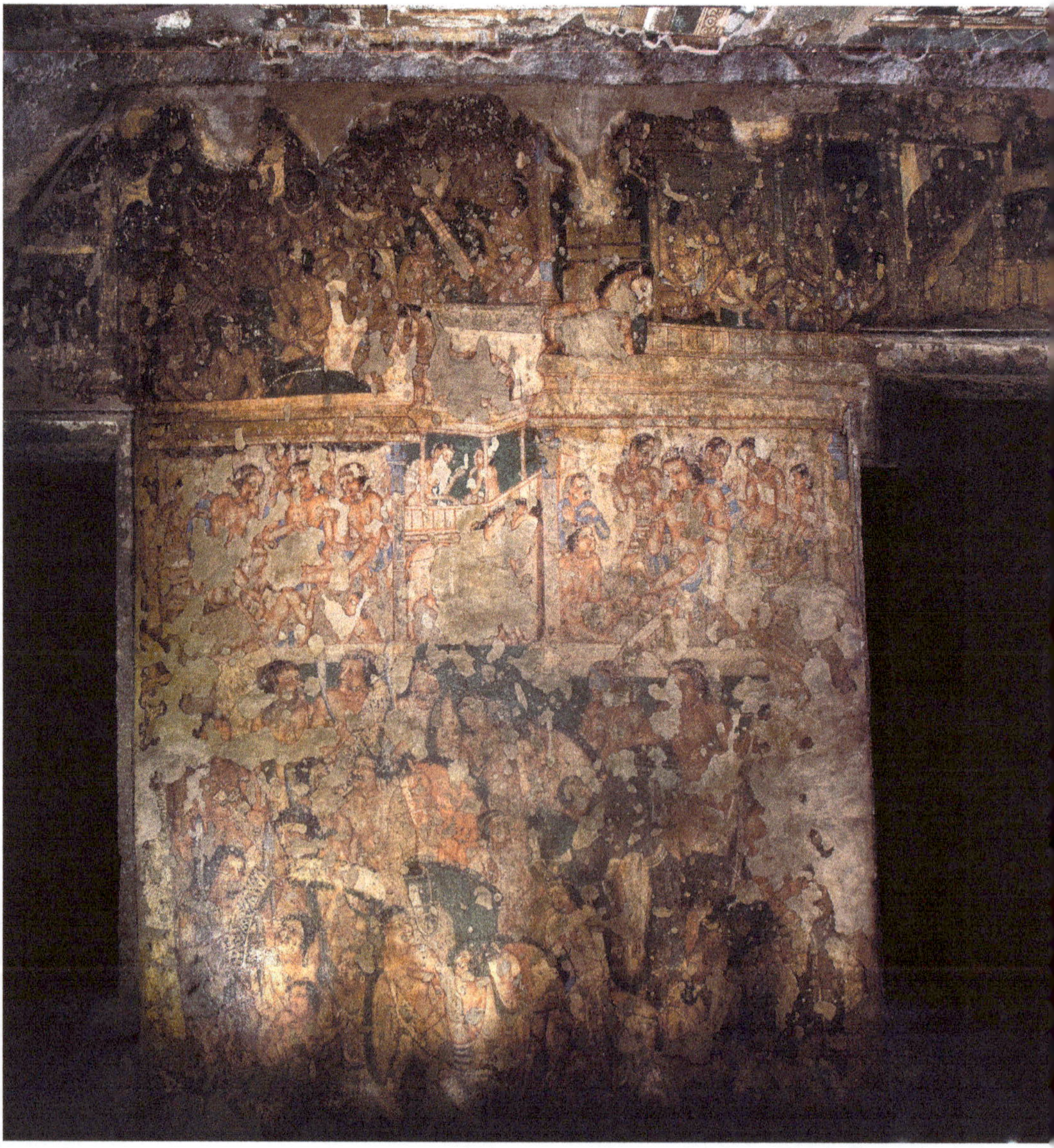

his words of wisdom. He flew with the *yakṣa* on the horse to the palace of the nāgas and gave the lessons of wisdom to the nāga king and queen. When Vidhura returned to his hometown, the king arranged a grand parade and feast in his honour.—**Prime Minister Vidhura** was none other than the Buddha in a former existence.

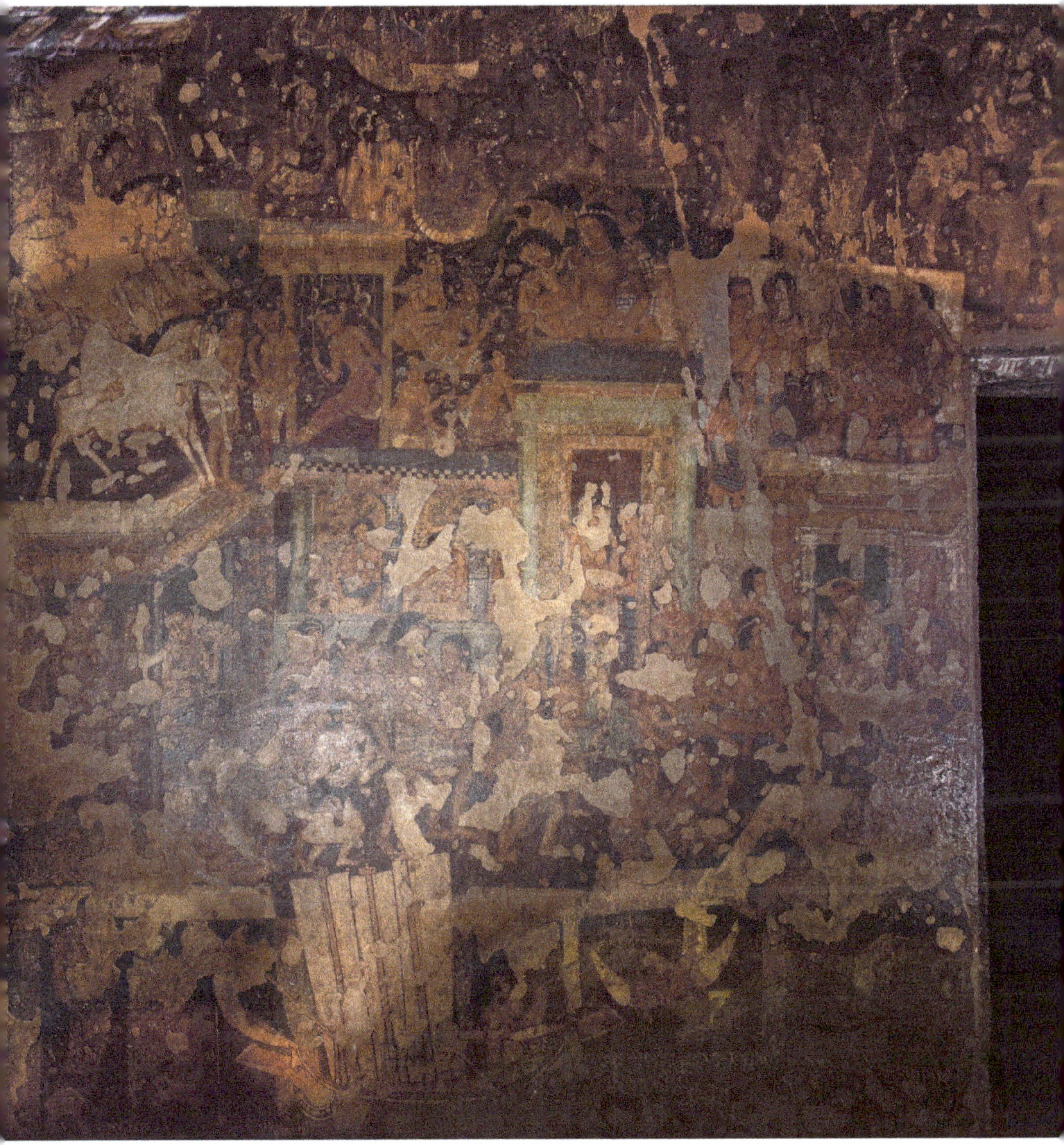

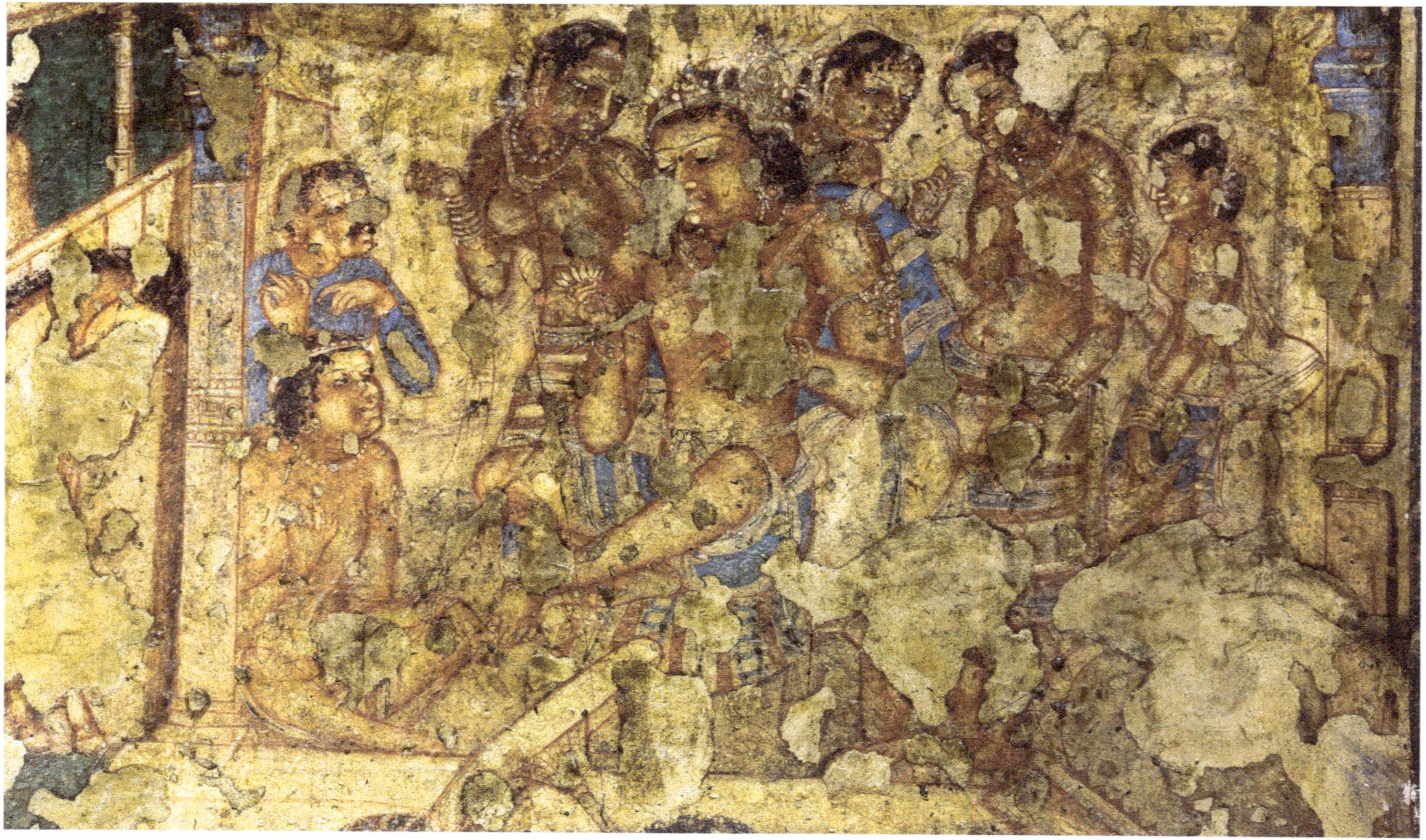

No. 37.2. *The legend of Vidhura, scene 7. Puṇṇaka, the yakṣa (genius) has come to his master Kubera for the permission to marry the nāga princess.*

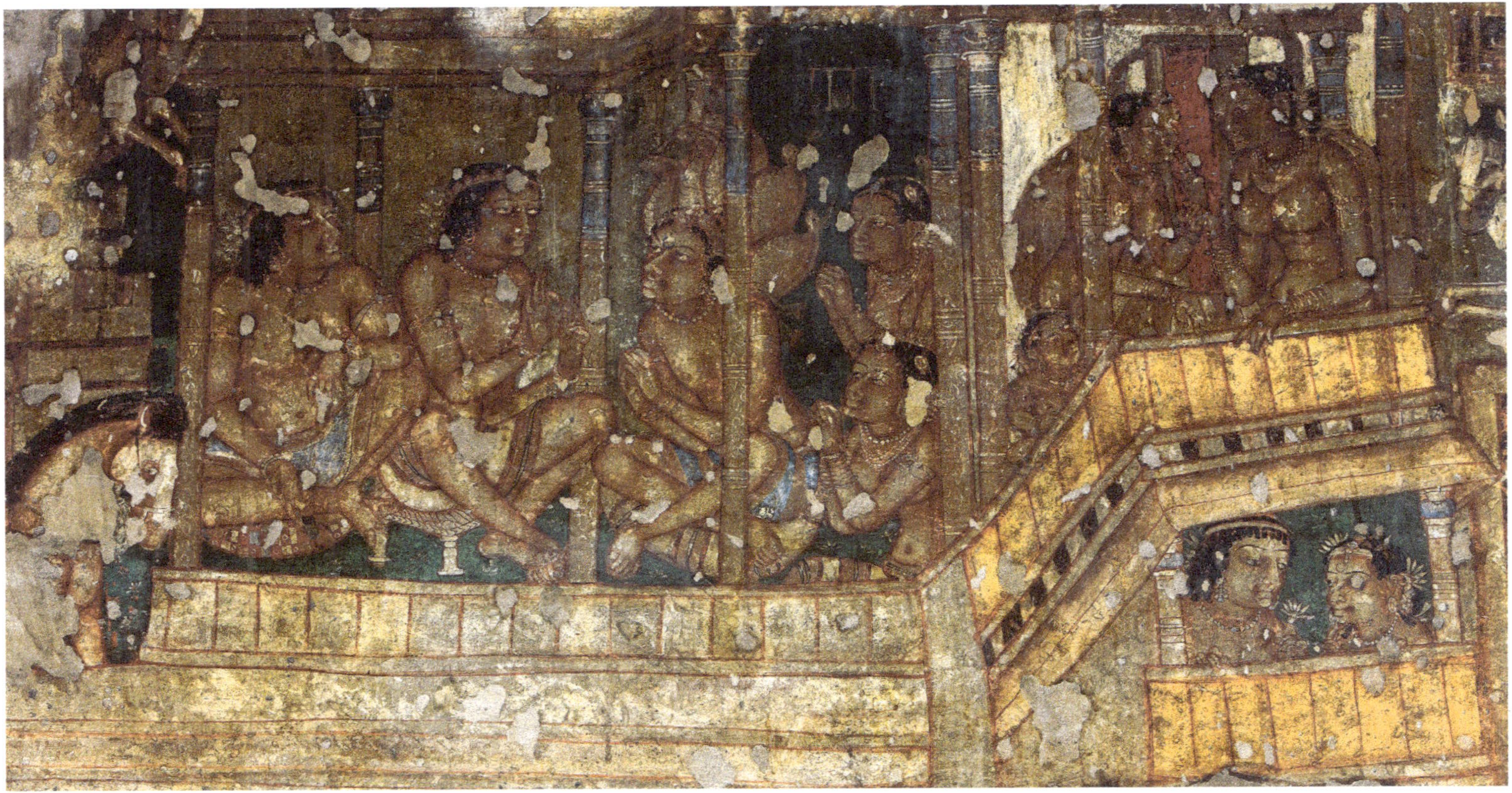

No. 37.3. *The Vidhura narrative, scene 13. Yakṣa Puṇṇaka has brought Vidhura to the nāga palace. Vidhura fulfils the nāga queen's craving for the revelation of his wisdom.*

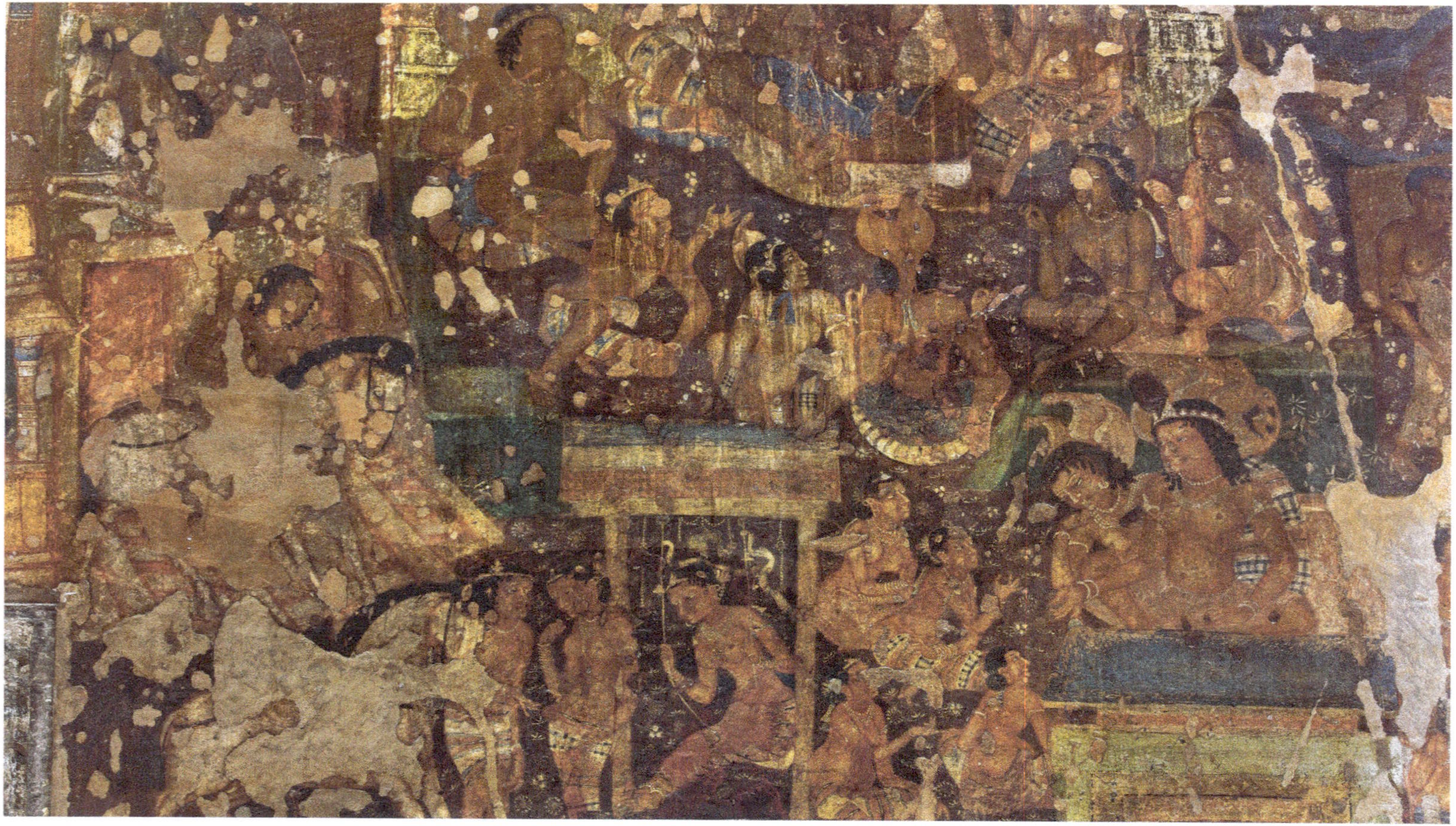

No. 37.4. *Various other scenes from the Vidhura narrative.*

No. 79. Pūrṇa.

Identification: Foucher (1921, narrative no. 3). The legend is from the life of the Buddha.—Bhava was a merchant from the ancient city of Śūrpāraka or Śroṇāparāntaka, today's Nala Sopārā in the Mumbai region. When he fell ill, his wife and sons refused to take care of him. Instead, a maid nursed him back to health. So, he offered a reward to the maid. Instead she requested him to accept her as a partner by law. Bhava accepted the proposal.

In due course, she gave birth to a son from Bhava, his fourth son through whom all wishes were supposed to be fulfilled. So, the son was named Pūrṇa (fulfilment) who grew up to become a successful businessman. Once, when his three elder brothers returned from a sea voyage, Bhava lay in his deathbed. He summoned all of them and advised them to stay together, and to defy their wives if they tried to separate them. He especially asked his eldest son to look after Pūrṇa.

After Bhava's death, the brothers embarked on yet another sea voyage, assigning Pūrṇa the job of looking after the business and family. Pūrṇa was always honest and just. However, once, by chance, the wives of his two brothers received their shares of profit somewhat late while the elder brother's son received his portion in time. When the three brothers returned, the two younger wives complained about this, putting the blame squarely on Pūrṇa. They persuaded them to abandon the joint family system and go

No. 79. *The legend of Pūrṇa, scene 9. The Buddha (seen in the centre) has come flying through the air with his monks to the home town of Pūrṇa. He is being welcomed with gifts by the inhabitants of the town of Śūrpāraka (Nala Sopārā). Hall, right wall.*

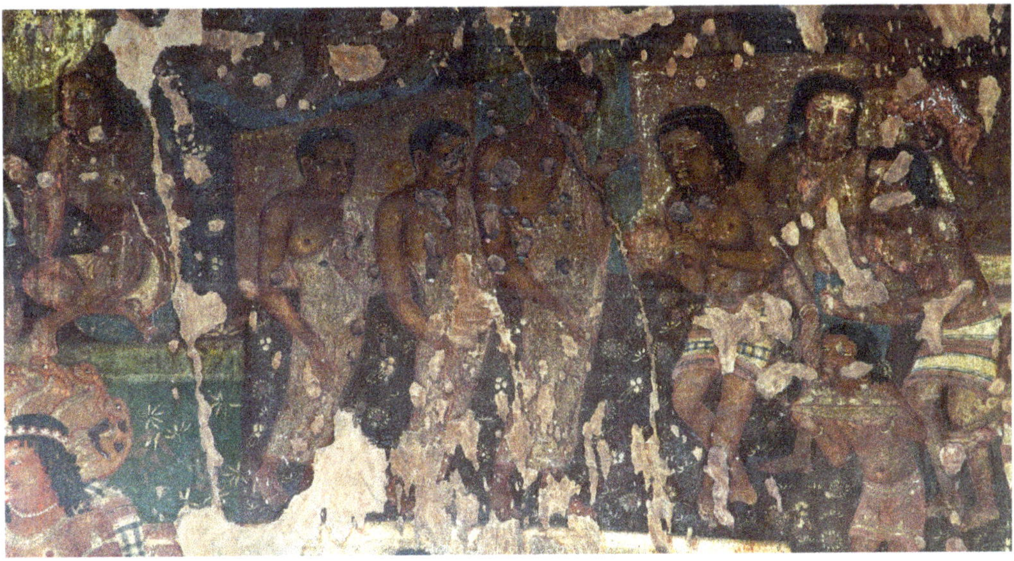

their separate ways. At the time of settlement, Pūrṇa was denied his share of the property as he was the maid's child. The eldest brother, who was committed to the promise made to his father, inherited Pūrṇa by renouncing his own share.

Once, the children were crying because they were very hungry. Pūrṇa's eldest sister-in-law gave him a coin to buy some food. In the market, Pūrṇa traded in sandalwood with a single coin and ended up multiplying it due his business acumen. He not only brought the food home but also some left over sandalwood.

Gradually, Pūrṇa became a noted sandalwood trader with a licence for overseas trade. His fame as a successful tradesman spread as far as the city of Śrāvastī. The other merchants also went to Śūrpāraka to commence a sea voyage under Pūrṇa's direction. Pūrṇa heard the teachings of the Buddha when he lodged at the Jetavana monastery in Śrāvastī. He was deeply impressed. He wanted to become a monk and obtained his brother's permission to visit Śrāvastī. After he enrolled in the monastic order, he connected with a mountain tribe. He founded a monastery and converted many of the tribes to Buddhism.

Meanwhile, his two brothers met the eldest brother so that they could embark on yet another sea voyage in search of riches. Their inherited wealth was nearing its end. During this voyage, they found sandalwood trees on the shore. The merchants wanted to acquire the trees but the forest belonged to a *yakṣa*, who conjured a cyclone to destroy the ship. The elder brother reminded the others that Pūrṇa was a Buddhist monk and advised them to call out to him. Pūrṇa came to know through the deities that his brothers were in danger. Instantly, he emerged on board the ship and calmed the cyclone with his meditative powers. The *yakṣa* was impressed with Pūrṇa's abilities and donated the sandalwood trunks to build a monastery.

Pūrṇa himself supervised the construction of the monastery at Śūrpāraka. His brothers got the requisite royal patronage to send an invitation to the Buddha to visit Śurpāraka. In a miraculous way, Pūrṇa sent the offerings to the Buddha. The Buddha flew from Śrāvastī with his entourage. When they reached Śūrpāraka, they were respectfully welcomed by the king and the four brothers. There, the Buddha delivered a sermon, which led many citizens to his doctrine.

SOME NON-NARRATIVE THEMES

No. 42.4.[1] Bodhisattva kings in mountains (porch).

Just as in Cave 1 where this theme is better preserved, as seen on either side of the entrance of the shrine antechamber, so here, on the porch, the same setting was devised. And, why only here? Also flanking the main door of Cave 11 we have this theme in the same setting, on either side of the main door, which is sadly only partly preserved. It had become a standard composition in most other cave temples, not only in Ajanta, but also in the far distant places like Khambalida in western Gujarat. The theme was painted or carved on the walls flanking the doors. They are always along the central axes of the porch, rear walls of the hall, and antechambers. Unfortunately, due to such easily accessible locations the theme has been much easily vandalised, everywhere.

1 The numbers under the *non-narrative* themes including the captions refer to those assigned by Monika Zin to the *non-narrative* themes of the Ajanta paintings, vide Zin 2003a.

No. 42.4.-detail. *A* yakṣa *and a* kinnara *couple from the 'Bodhisattva King in a Mountainous Landscape' theme.* *Porch, rear wall, left side.*

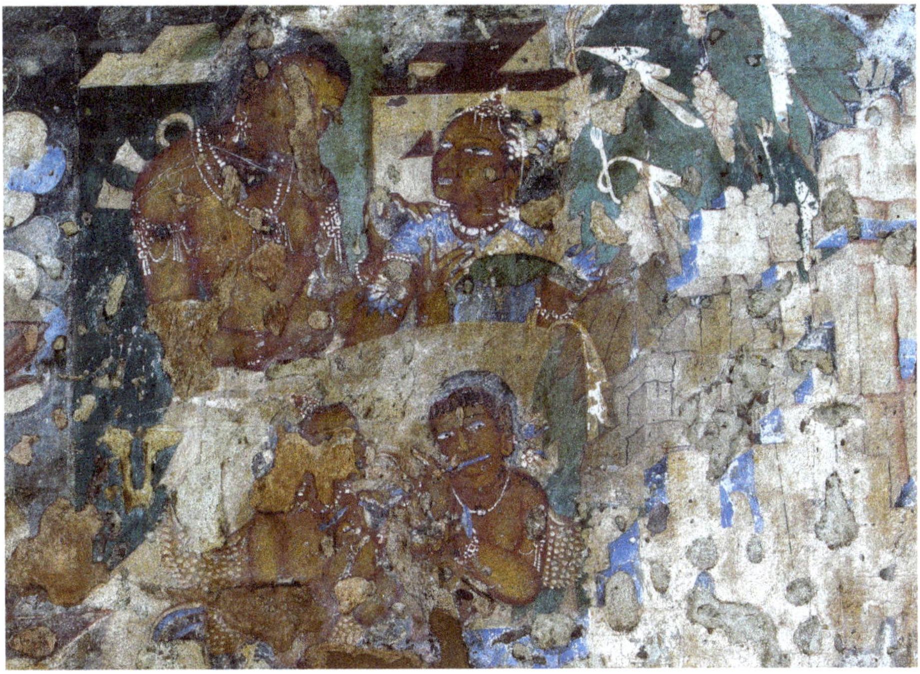

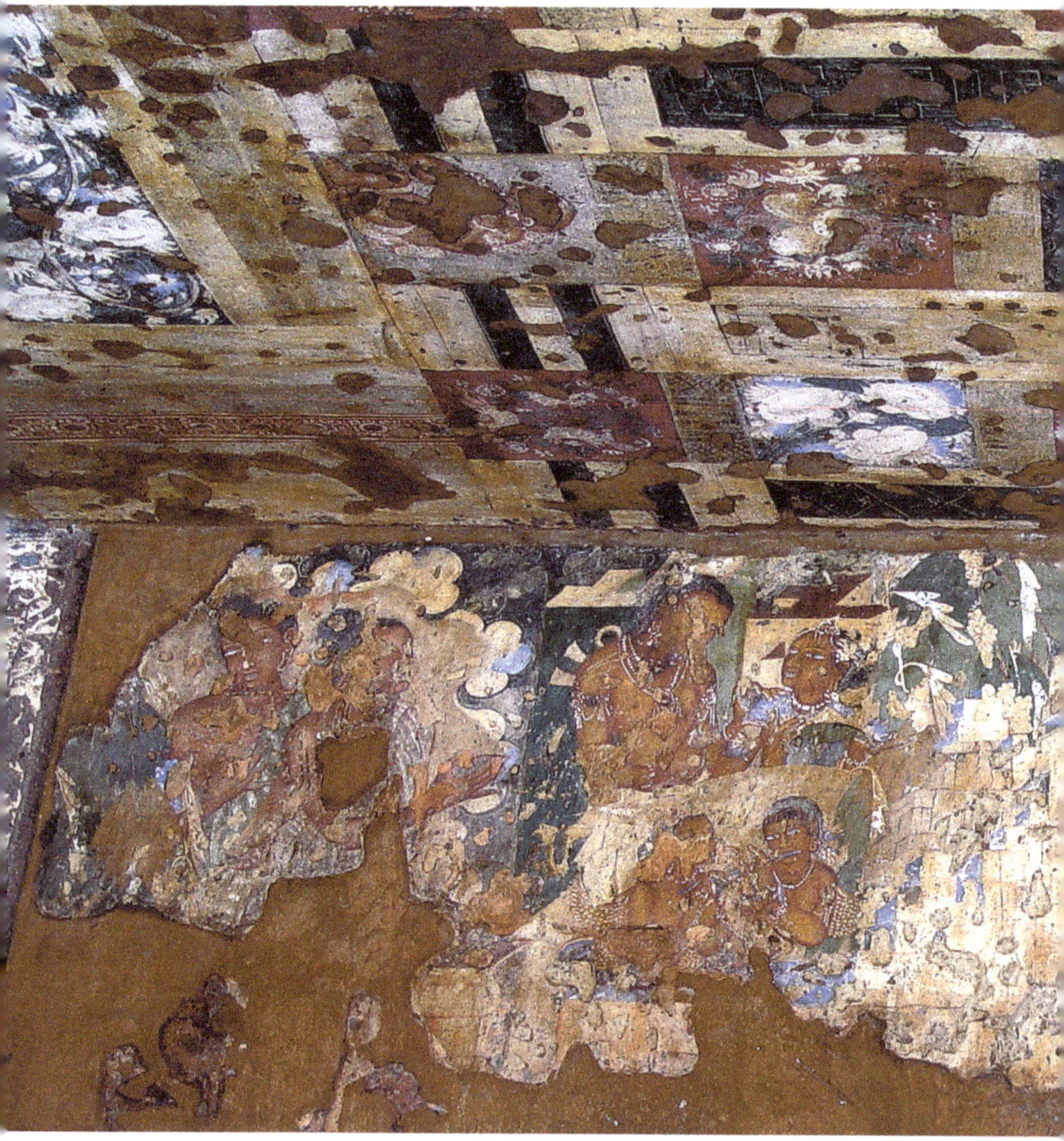

No. 42.4. *The upper parts of the 'Bodhisattva King in a Mountainous Landscape' theme.* *Porch, rear wall, left of main doorway.*

In this example too, we have permanently lost the Bodhisattva King, except the fragments of his crown. However, the upper portions are somewhat better preserved on the left side of the main door. Its counterpart on the opposite side of the main door has suffered greater damage so much so that only scant fragment are now extant.

The *brahmakāyikas* or the gods of the Brahmā Heaven can be spotted on the far left. To their right is a *yakṣa* couple. Below

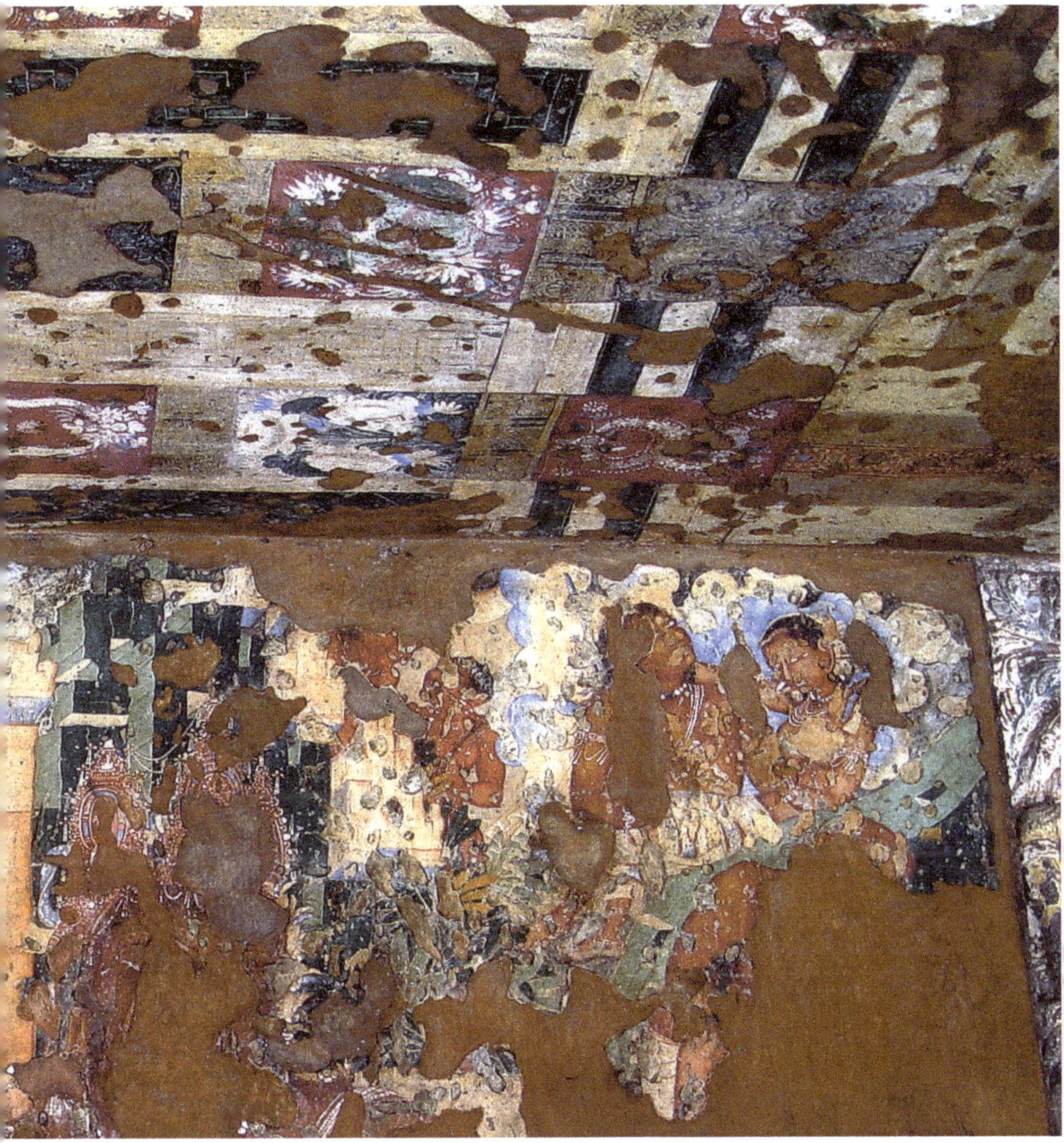

them is a *kinnara* couple (half-human, half bird creatures playing music). The backdrop of the Bodhisattva consists of a mountainous landscape. On upper right of the crown of the Bodhisattva inhabitants of the jungle are seen. On farthest right a handsome couple of *vidyādharas* (charm bearers) is seen.

No. 48. 'One thousand Buddhas.'

This scene is depicted on the walls of the shrine antechamber.

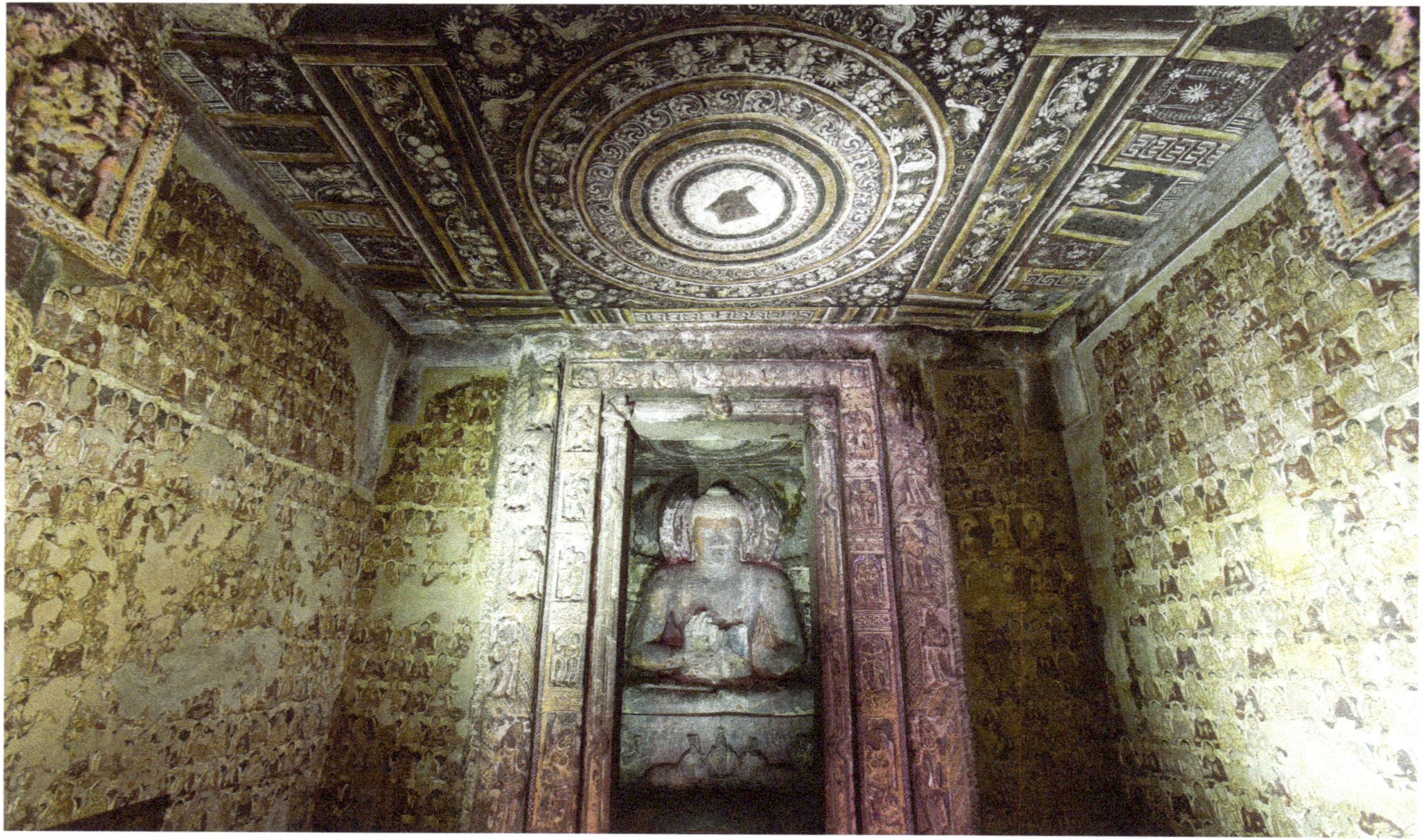

No. 48. *The depiction of 'One thousand Buddhas', is perhaps a variation of the Mahāprātihārya legend even if only a moment of the narrative is depicted here when the Buddha multiplied himself. According to the donative inscription, it was sponsored by one 'Ram[...].'* Shrine antechamber.

Essentially it seems to be a scene of the Mahāprātihārya (Miracle of Śrāvastī) theme, but since other episodes from the event are summarily absent here (save only the appearance of a multitude of Buddha figure) Schlingloff and Zin stopped short of calling it Mahāprātihārya. An inscription in place claims the depiction to be the donation of an *upāsaka* (lay devotee) whose name began with 'Rām...' He donated the One Thousand Buddhas for the benefit of his parents. The inscription confirms that it was not the part of the original plan, which must have consisted of scenes from the life of the Buddha, usual as such locations in other caves. The caves seem to have been abandoned by the original patrons, perhaps because of a sudden chaos (following the death or murder of King Hariṣeṇa). Thereafter, other individuals who were still around usurped the empty and prime locations for making their own donations, which Spink rightly calls 'intrusive' paintings and sculptures.

Zin has identified a central theme in the One Thousand Buddhas that indicates that it is meant to be the Mahāprātihārya theme. There is a centrally located Buddha figure flanked by Bodhisattvas holding attributes. 'This central scene shows that the entire picture consisting of a thousand Buddhas was conceived as portraying the Great Miracle in which the Buddha multiplied himself, so that the rows of Buddhas reached the sky.'

Similar Buddhas figures are also depicted inside the shrine. They are much bigger in size. They have no central scene.

No. 29. Māṇibhadra & Pūrṇabhadra Yakṣa Temple.

One of the most unique features of Cave 2 are the sanctum sanctora for *yakṣas* carved with sumptuous sculptures and beautiful paintings. The sanctum on the left is devoted to two male *yakṣas* whom Monika Zin identifies as Māṇibhadra and Pūrṇabhadra who are worshipped as a pair. Māṇibhadra looks like Kubera and holds a bag of money in his left hand that spills coins. In his right hand he holds a lotus, one of the *nidhis* (treasures) of Kubera. The left *yakṣa*, probably Pūrṇabhadra, is shown holding a mango. In front of these two *yakṣas* there are two piles of money on the ground -the resources they hold ready to give away to those who worship them. Māṇibhadra and Pūrṇabhadra were given an important task in Buddhism, charged by the god Kubera

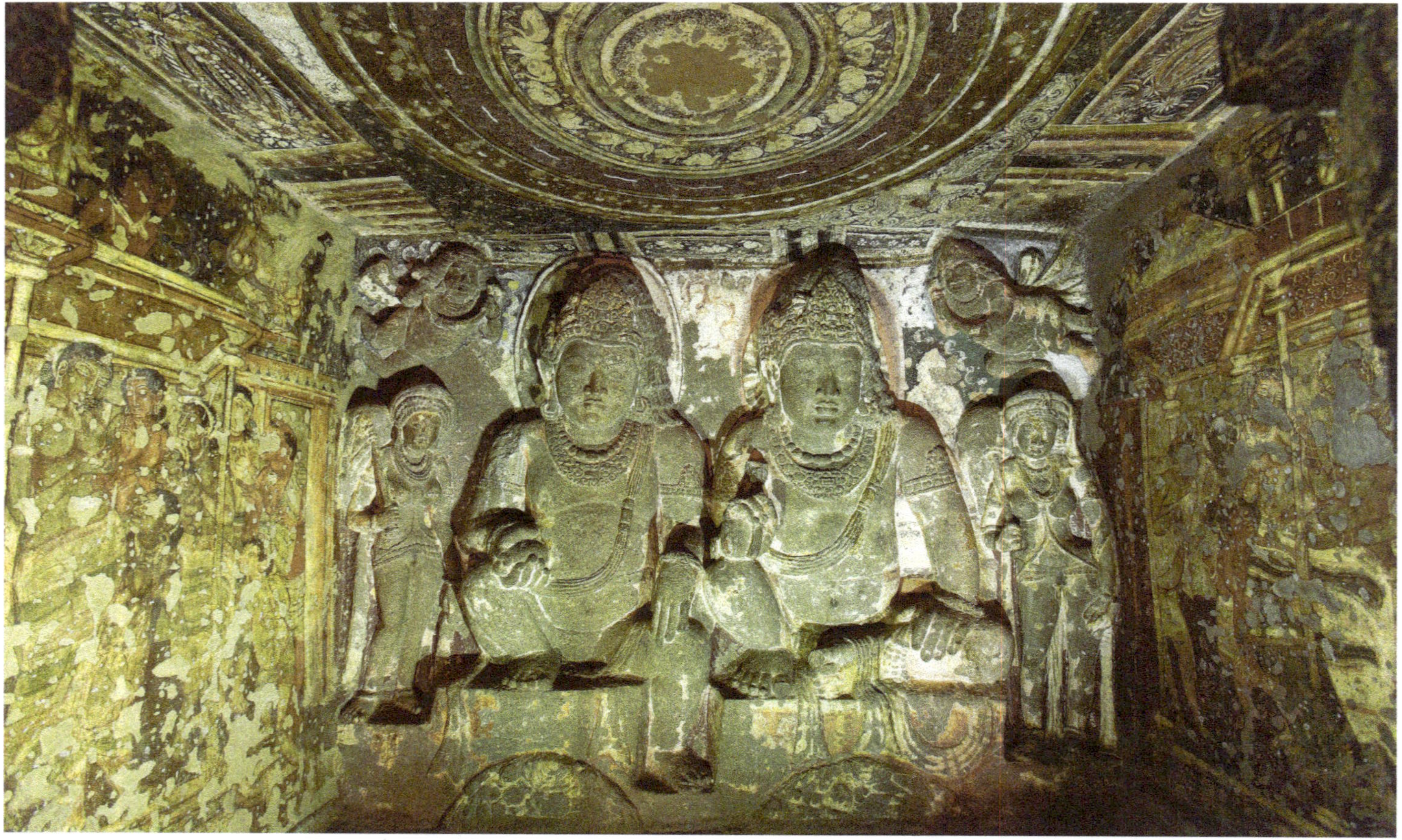

No. 29.1. *The shrinelet for Maṇibhadra and Pūrṇabhadra Yakṣa gods.* Hall, left rear.

to announce to mankind the appearance of the future Buddha Maitreya.

No. 29.1. Painted Yakṣa Temple (left).

The side walls of the *yakṣa* shrines depict painted versions of *yakṣa* temples. Two male figures are placed at both entrances to the depicted building, to the left a doorkeeper in sewn clothes and boots, to the right a bald brahman guarding the entrance to the interior of the *yakṣa* temple. In the middle, a beautiful woman is shown holding two bird chicks in her hands. The other women are observing the little birds and also showing them to a child. The picture is marked by a large number of the fat-bellied dwarfs with disproportionately long torsos and short, crooked legs. A *mithuna*

No. 29.1. *Zin identifies the painted scene as a yakṣa temple.* Left wall of the Maṇibhadra-Pūrṇabhadra shrine.

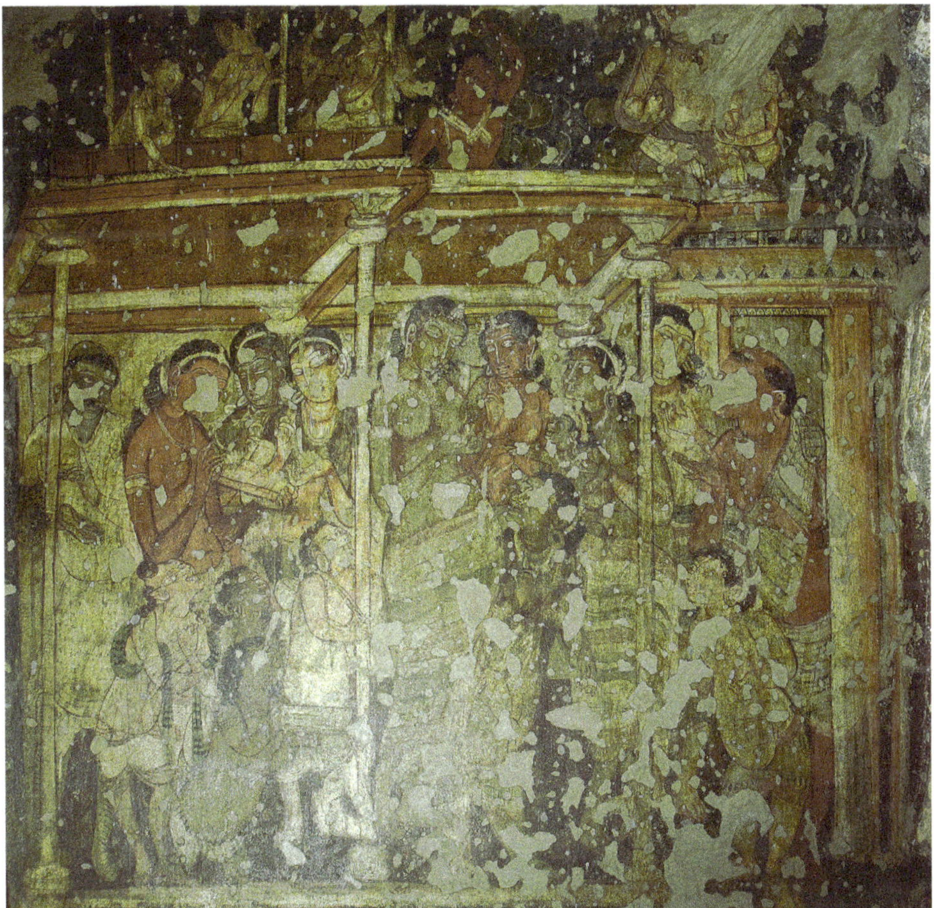

couple is depicted on the upper storey while *vidyādharas* ('charm-bearers') are seen in the clouds.

No. 29.2. Painted Yakṣa Temple (right).

This version too has a doorkeeper at the entrance armed with a stick while a brahmin stands on the other side. Here too women in the company of disproportionate, fat-bellied dwarfs, make up the scene. The offerings they are holding in their hands and on trays are probably meant for Māṇibhadra and Pūrṇabhadra as gods here. On upper level three genies float in the air. *Vidyādharas* can be recognised on the right above.

No. 29.2. *Zin identifies the painted scene as another yakṣa temple.* Right wall of the Maṇibhadra-Pūrṇabhadra shrine.

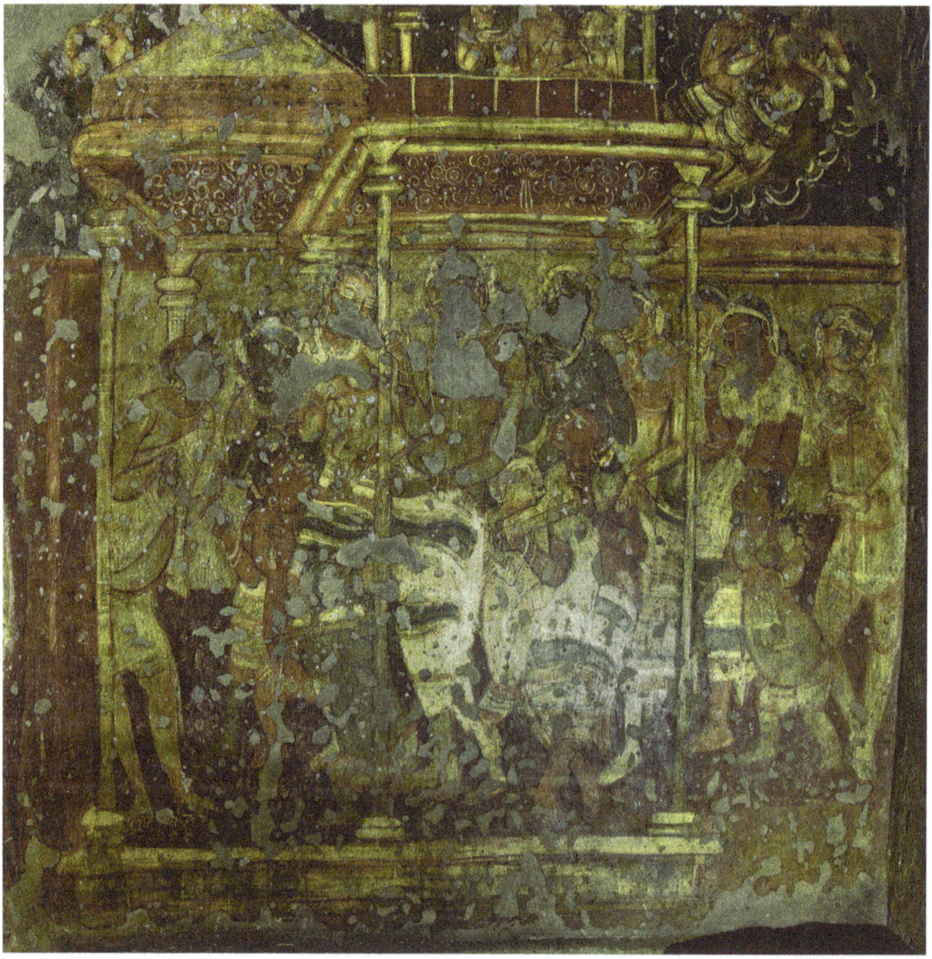

Nos. 25. Hārītī-Pañcikā Yakṣa Temple.

The Buddha converted Hārītī from a child eating demoness to a protectress of children. On the upper right corner Hārītī is seen a multi- armed demoness attacking the Buddha. On the upper left corner, she is seen together with her youngest son kneeling before the Buddha. Hārītī ('she who robs') stole the children of the town of Rājagṛha until the day the Buddha hid the youngest of her 500 children so that she would experience the pain of loss. The Buddha then extracted a promise that she would never again kidnap children, whereupon Hārītī became the protector of all children.

The male *yakṣa* is difficult to identify. In north Indian tradition Hārītī is depicted with her *yakṣa* husband Pañcikā, while in central India she is paired with Kubera or Jambhālā. Here Hārītī holds a child and several mangos by the stem while her consort's left hand is in the posture of a money donor and the right hand holds a fruit. A female figure with a parrot stands between them. The frieze below depicts on the right children sitting before a teacher, while the two in the middle are locked in a dispute. The left side shows the children romping around a pet ram during play time.

No. 25. *The shrinelet for Yakṣa Gods Hārītī and Pañcikā (or Kubera?).* Hall, right rear.

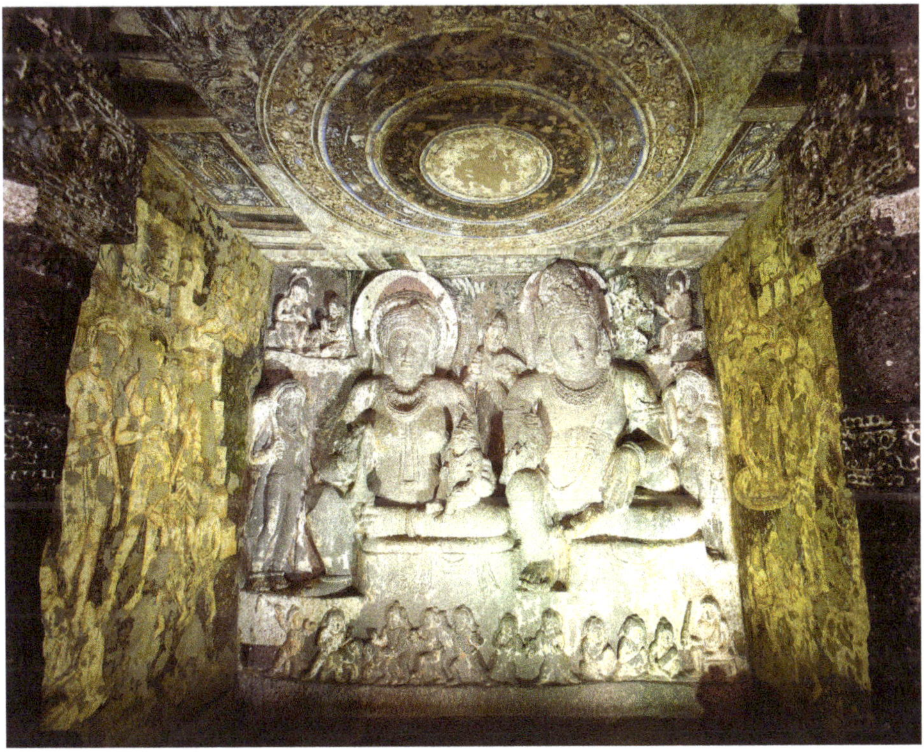

No. 25.1. Unidentified painting (left).

The scene has not been identified with certainty. Zin observes, it depicts a mountainous landscape inhabited by beautiful and extremely elegant women. Some of them have luxury goods in their hands: a richly decorated mirror, a tasteful box. These are

No. 25.1. *Unidentified.*
Hārītī Chapel, left wall.

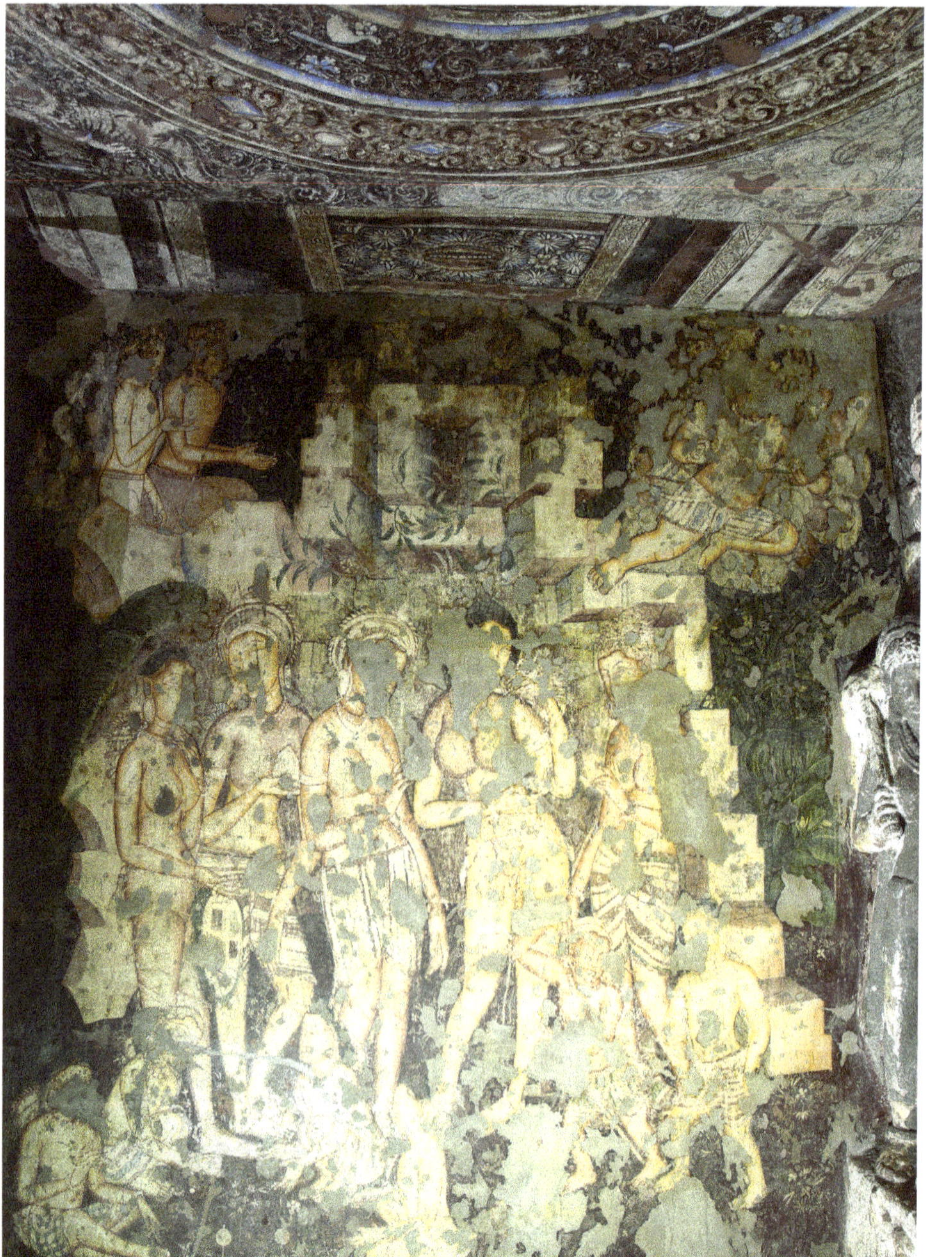

carefree and wealthy ladies with healthy and well-dressed children playing around. Four children are seated on the floor with a top. Two others are playing with hobbyhorses. Above the scene there are genies on the clouds lending a mythological dimension to the scene. In the upper left corner, there is a depiction of the *brahmakayikas*. The genie on the upper right corner is carrying gifts toward the devotional sculpture of the *yakṣa* couple.

No. 25.2. Unidentified painting (right).

This too is a mountainous landscape with women and six children. The three children on the left carry two pet chickens, the three on the right are moving towards a pile of money often shown alongside *yakṣas*. A *vidūṣaka* (jester) stands over the money pile, a funny figure. Such fools are frequently depicted in Ajanta paintings and sculptures often in the company of ladies. They can be identified by their round hair tufts and a stick with three curves, a theatrical attribute. The *vidūṣaka* is looking at her lady who is holding a tray of offerings for the *yakṣa* couple. She is accompanied by a female companion and two female fan bearers. Another beautiful figure, perhaps a *yakṣa*, is sitting casually on a cushion with a lotus flower in his hand. On the upper right corner a genie is seen with gifts.

No. 25.2. *Another unidentified scene. Hārītī Chapel, right wall.*

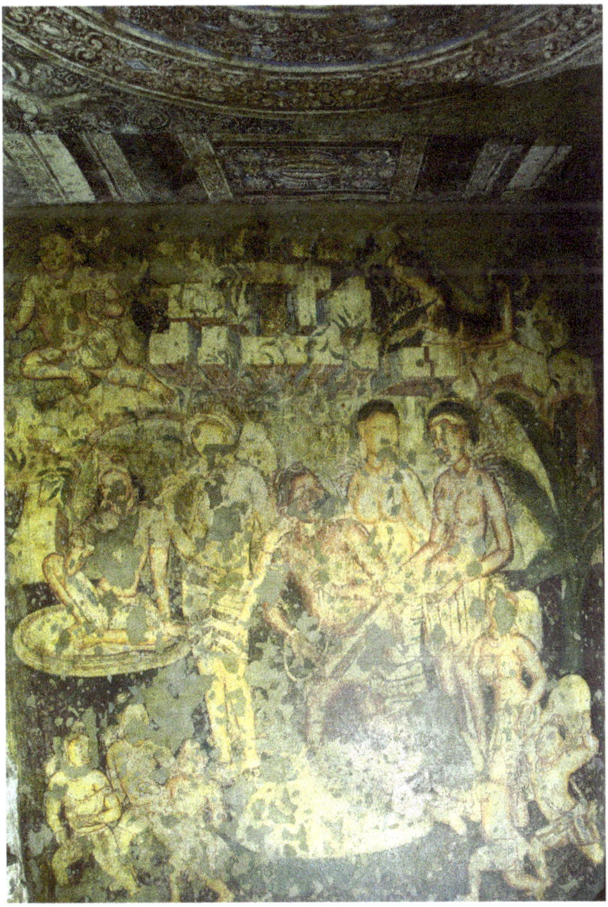

Nos. 42.6. Bodhisattva king in mountain (hall).

This richly decorated Bodhisattva King wearing an elaborate crown stands

No. 42.6. *The 'Bodhisattva King in a Mountainous Landscape' theme.* *Hall, right rear wall.*

barefoot between his court and the genies. In spite of the severe damage, a *yakṣa* couple, a flying couple, and a *vidyādhara* (charm bearer) couple have been identified. The latter holds a sword hanging across the shoulder and back.

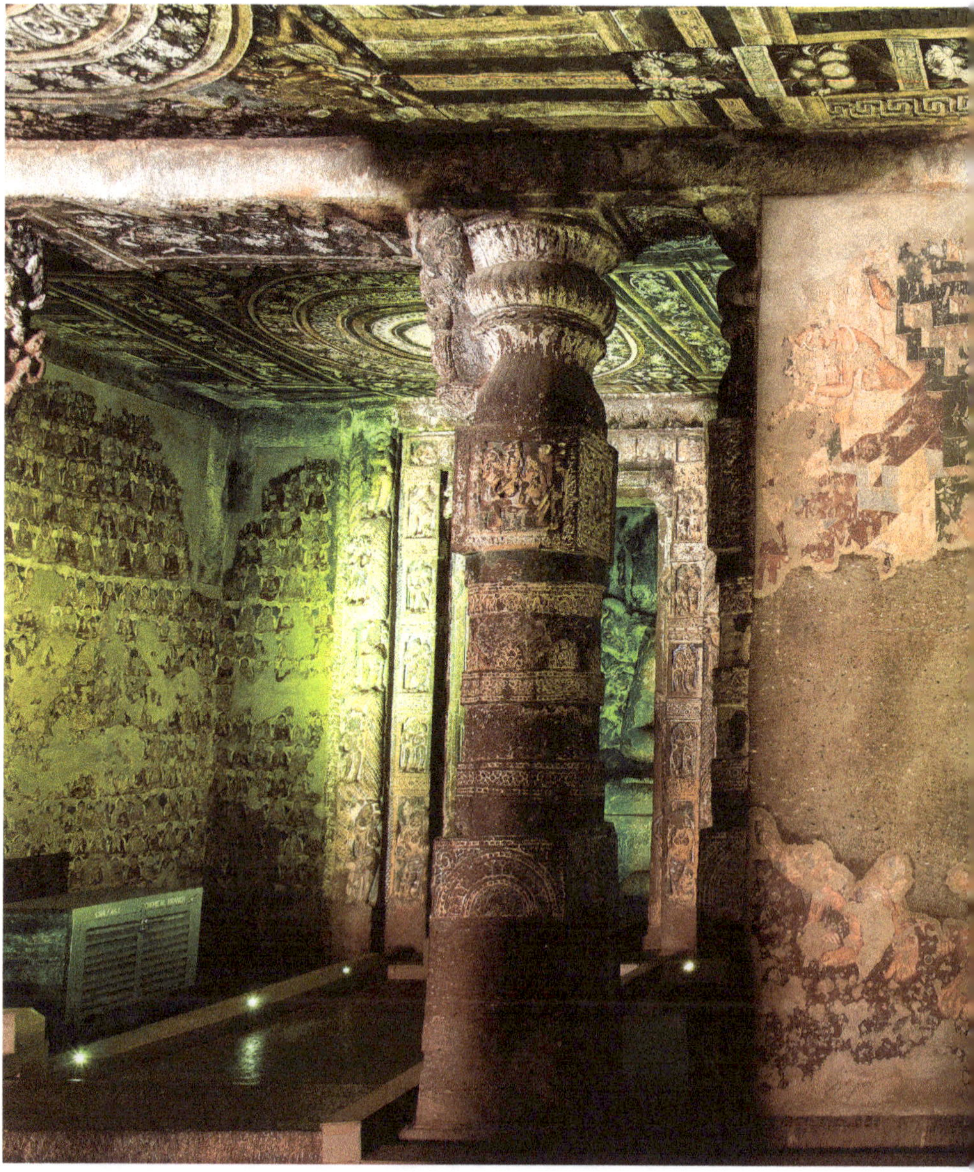

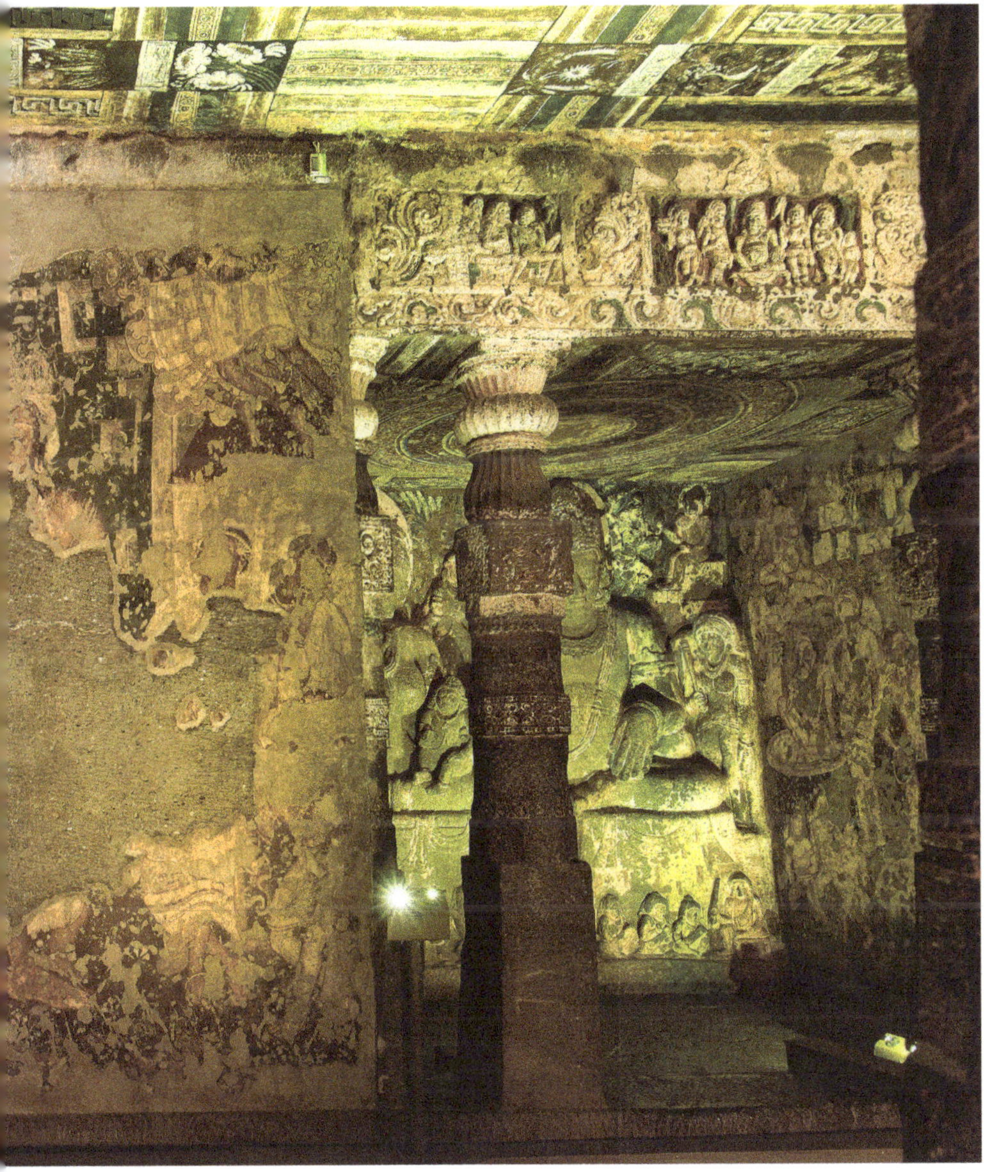

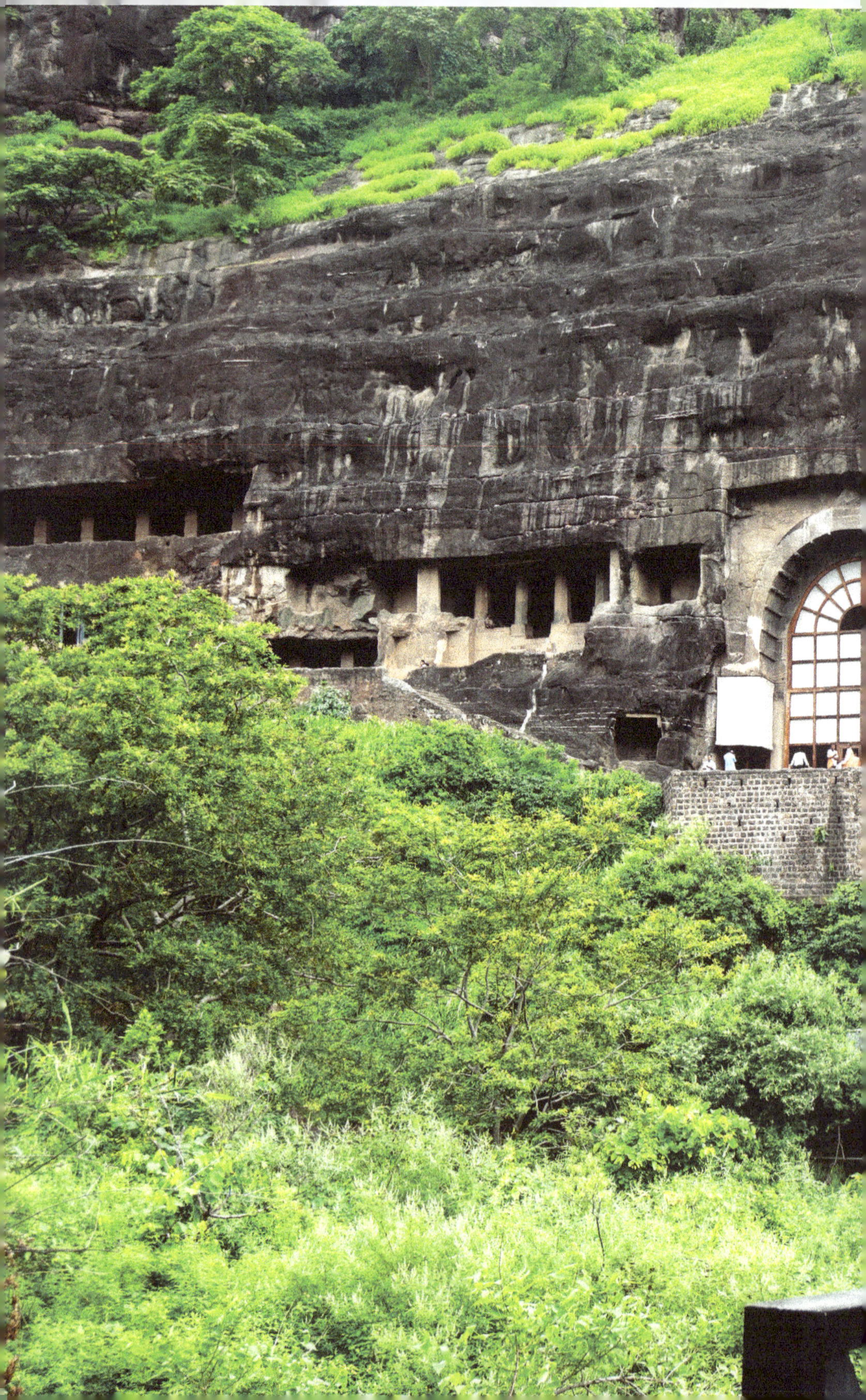

III. Cave No. 9

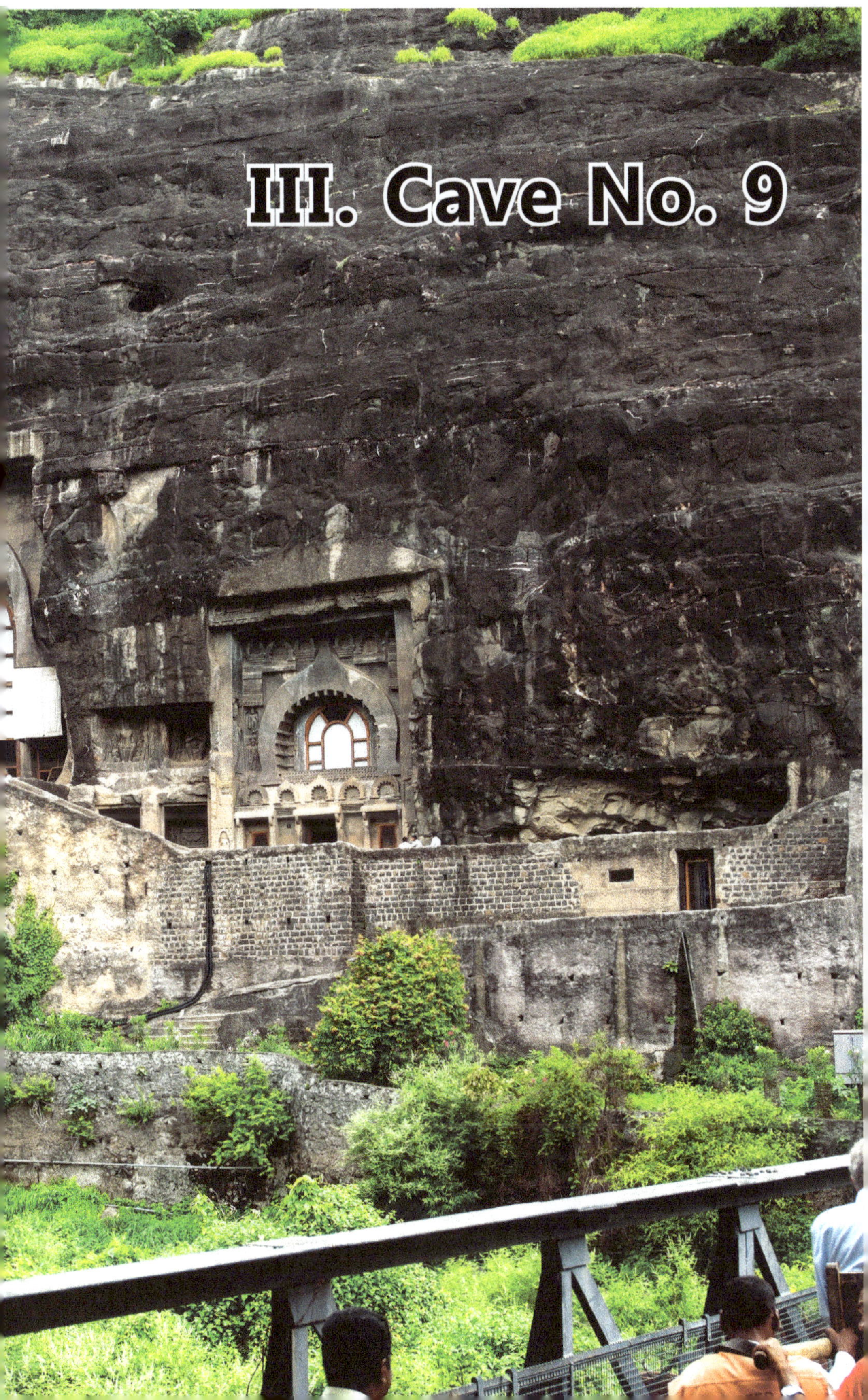

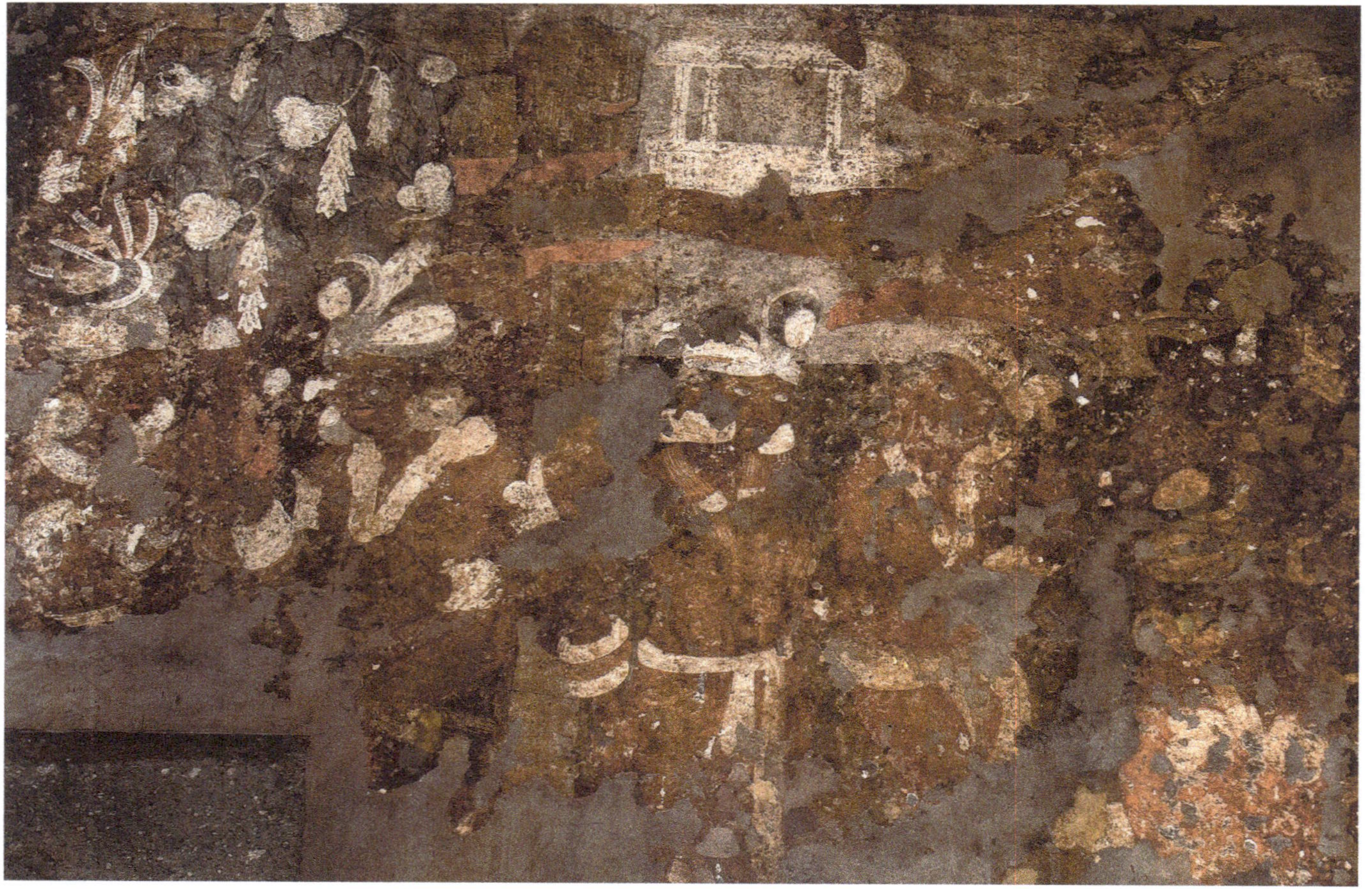

No. 1. Left: *the legend of the* nāga *(serpent) called Paṇḍara, scene 3.* Centre and right: *the legend of Mahāgovinda, scene 'a'.* Interior front wall.

NARRATIVE THEMES.

No. 1.[1] Paṇḍara.

Identification: episode 3 by Schlingloff (1993, p. 10 f.), 1 and 2 by Zin 2000.—Once a nāga (serpent) called Paṇḍara revealed the secret of guarding against the nāga-devouring *garuḍas* (eagles) to an ascetic friend. But the ascetic divulged the secret to the garuḍa. Hence, the garuḍa captured the nāga. When crying Paṇḍara narrated the false ascetic's betrayal to the garuḍa, the latter advised Paṇḍara never to share secrets with anyone. Thus, Paṇḍara's life was spared because garuḍa had already made him a disciple by imparting a teaching.—Paṇḍara, the serpent, was none other than the Buddha in his former existence.

No. 2. Mahāgovinda.

Identification: Schlingloff 2013.—A brahman named

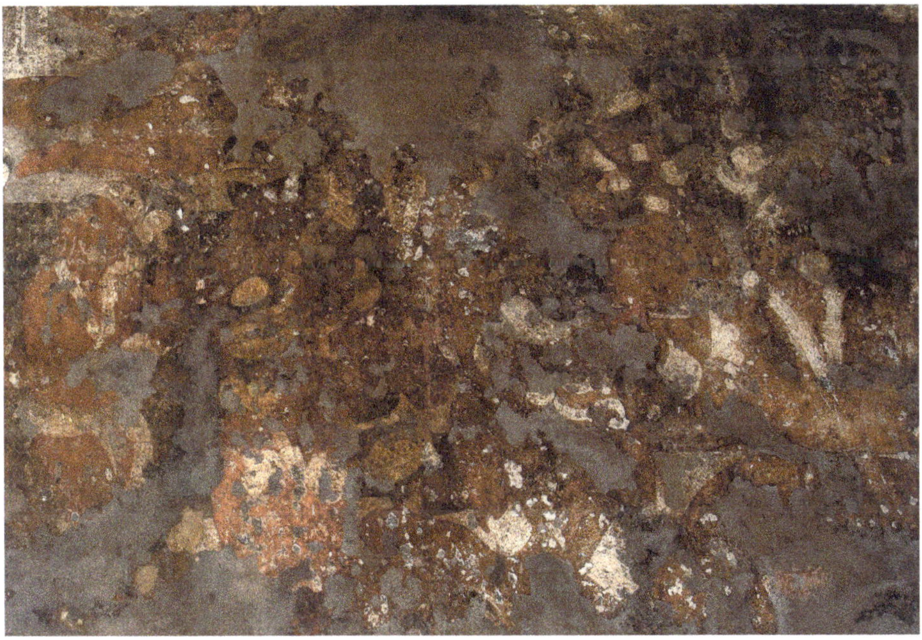

No. 2. *The legend of the brahman prime minister Mahāgovinda, scene* 'a'. *Interior front wall.*

1 The numbers under the narrative themes refer to those assigned by Dieter Schlingloff to the narrative paintings of Ajanta, vide Schlingloff 2013.

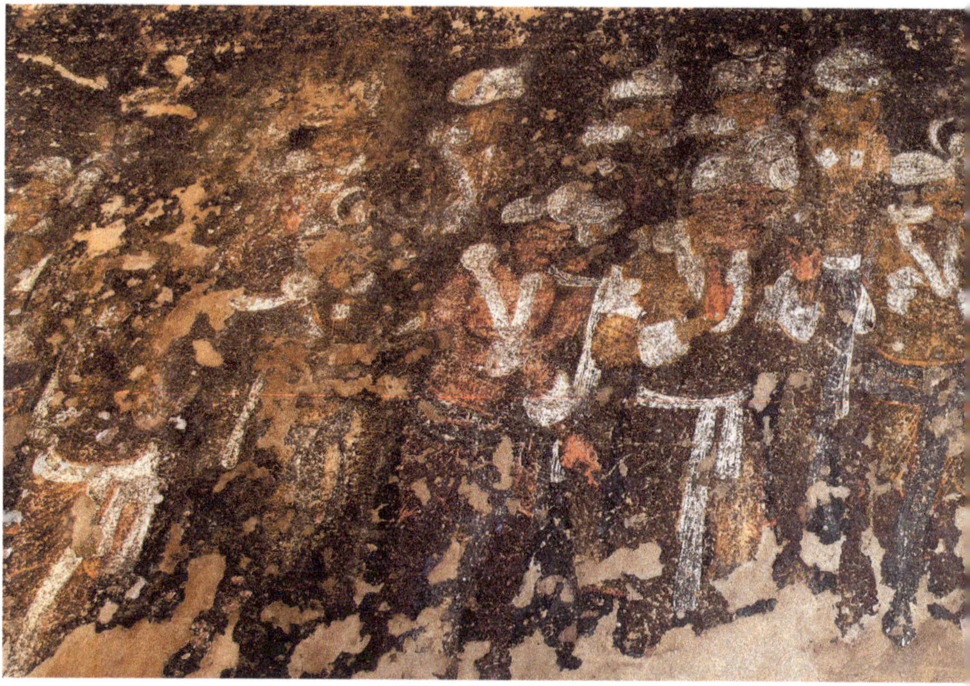

No. 3. *The legend of a śaśa (hare), scene 3? He hurled himself into the fire to feed a hungry hermit in drought. The photo likely shows the noblemen who have arrived to worship the stūpa erected as a memorial of the hare's sacrifice.* Left wall.

Mahāgovinda was the prime minister of a king. After the king's death, the king's son did not want the responsibility of ruling over the vast kingdom. Therefore, Mahāgovinda divided the kingdom among the son and six other princes while retaining the responsibility of superintendence. His skill in governance earned him a good reputation and even a relationship with God Brahmā. Soon, he embraced the path of seclusion and meditation, impelling Brahmā to come down and visit him. From Brahmā he sought answers to his queries about the other world. The event made Mahāgovinda renounce his office and the world; and the princes followed suit.—Mahāgovinda, the brahman prime minister, was none other than the Buddha in his former existence.

No. 3. Śaśa.

Proposed identification: Schlingloff 2013.—A hermit was planning to leave his forest habitation because of the ongoing drought. To make him stay back, four animals offered gifts of food to him. An otter gave him seven Rohita breed of fish. A jackal gave a stolen dinner consisting of two skewers of meat, a cup of curdled milk, and a lizard. A monkey gave him mangoes and water. A *śaśa*

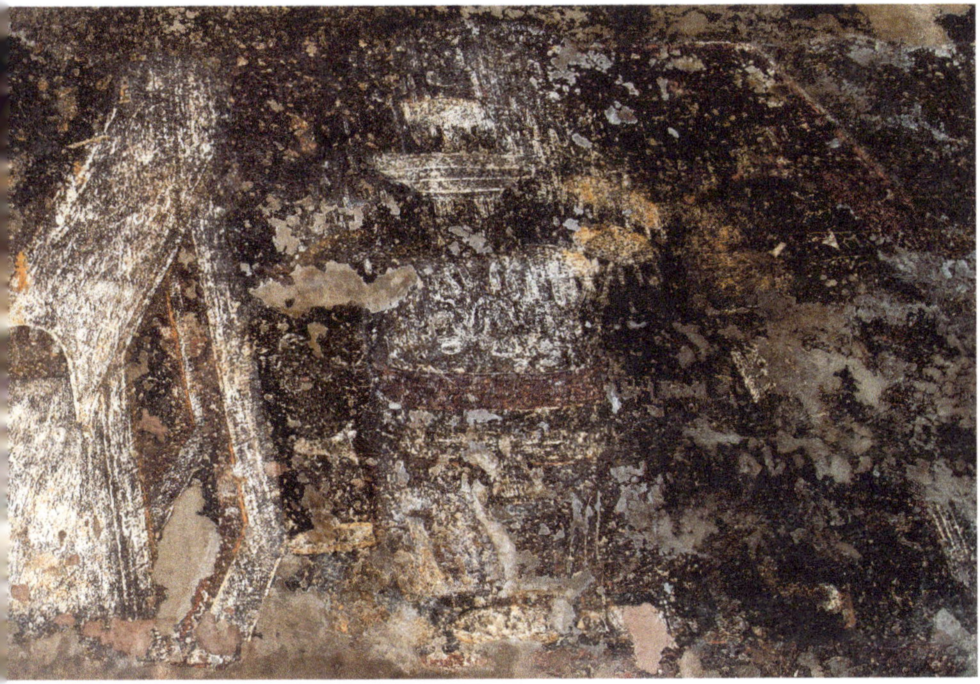

(hare) had nothing to offer. So, it hurled itself into the fire and gave him the roasted body. To commemorate the hare's sacrificial death, a stūpa was erected over its remains.—The hare was none other than the Buddha in his former existence.

No. 4. Kuṇāla.

Identification: Schlingloff 2013.—Once, there was a king of the glossy cuckoos, named Kuṇāla, who despised the female sex. His friend, a king of the speckled cuckoos, fell ill and was abandoned by his female entourage. After his recovery, Kuṇāla delivered to him a sermon while seated on a stone form under a Śāla tree in the Himalayas. Nārada and the king of the vultures also attended the sermon with their retinues. In the sermon, Kuṇāla explained about the depravity of the female sex by citing many examples.—Kuṇāla, the cuckoo, was none other than the Buddha in his former existence.

No. 5. Udaya. (No photo.)

Identification: Schlingloff 1995.—A prince named Udaya was reborn as a *yakṣa* (a class of semi-divine being marked by genius).

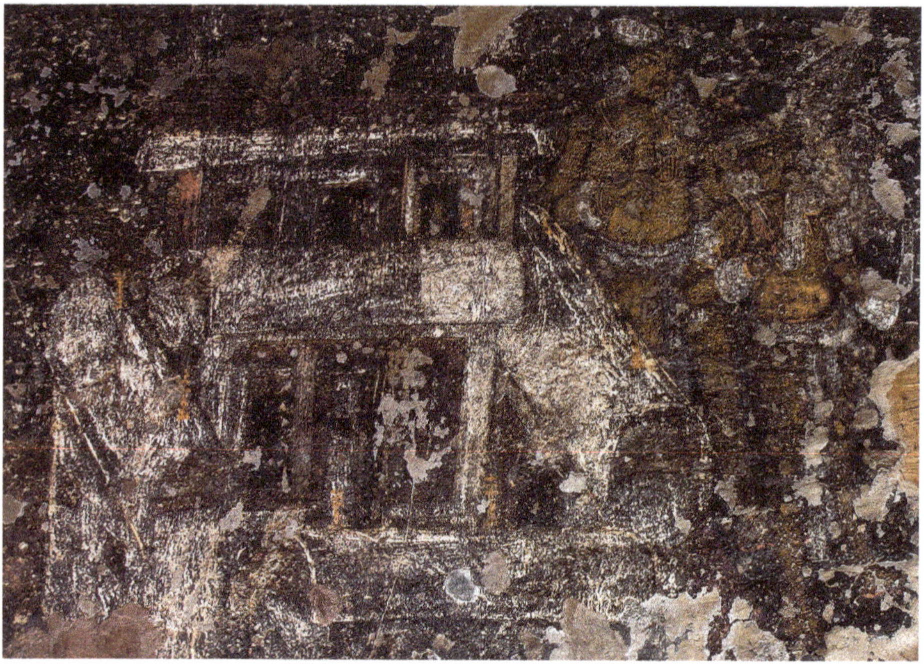

No. 4. *Kuṇāla. Atrium hall as scene divider and the Kuṇāla narrative on right.* Left wall.

To keep his promise to his wife, he visited her in the palace and asked for some favours. The princess, not recognising him, wondered how he had entered the well-guarded palace. Udaya told her that he was a yakṣa and offered a pot full of gold. The princess refused the gift, saying that she only longed for her husband, and entreated him to leave and never return. However, the yakṣa came again, this time with a pot full of silver. Surprised, the princess asked him why he had downgraded the value of gift from gold to silver. The yakṣa explained that as the span of her life decreased with time, so did the value of his object of love; and that celestial beings alone are exempted from ageing. Revealing his identity as her former husband, he told her that only a virtuous life could promise rebirth in heaven and can free the humans from the fear of ageing and death; and that earthly pleasures are short-lived. After his departure, the princess decided to leave the palace and become an ascetic.—Prince Udaya was none other than the Buddha in his former existence.

No. 67. Kāśyapa.

Identification: episodes 1 to 3 by Foucher (1921, narrative no. 53), 4 to 8 by Schlingloff (2013). The legend is from the life of the Buddha.— As the Buddha began teaching his sermon and accepted his first disciples as monks in his doctrine, he thought of converting an ascetic. Thus, he went to Magadha, where an old brahman named Urubilva-Kāśyapa, belonging to Kāśyapa lineage, lived with his disciples near the river Nairañjana. Once, Kāśyapa invited the Buddha to stay awhile. The Buddha expressed his wish to spend the night in the brahman's fire house. Kāśyapa informed the Buddha about a poisonous snake which dwelt in that house, but the Buddha entered the fire house and sat in meditation. The enraged snake spewed smoke and fire, but the Buddha, deep in meditation, produced such a bright light that Kāśyapa thought the fire house was ablaze and the Buddha had turned to ashes. The Buddha forced the snake into his food bowl and took the animal to Kāśyapa. Kāśyapa was surprised and deeply impressed by the power of his meditation.

Next, the Buddha demonstrated to Kāśyapa his control over the fire. Kāśyapa's disciples attended to three fire pots and tried to light a fire. Kāśyapa correctly assumed that because of the Buddha's power, they failed to do so; on Kāśyapa's request, the Buddha lit the fire. Once, when Kāśyapa's hut caught fire, no one could extinguish the blaze. Only the Buddha could do so with his magical power. Kāśyapa observed the nightly visits of the deities to the Buddha. First came the Four Kings of Heaven followed by Indra; then came Brahmā who appeared like columns of fire. Later, the Buddha accepted Kāśyapa's invitation for some lavish entertainment. He repeatedly offered delicious fruits to Kāśyapa and filled his bowl with food derived from different plants.

On another occasion, Kāśyapa sat down beside the Buddha to eat a meal. The Buddha wanted water to clean himself. Indra appeared and produced a stream of water from the earth's cleavage. The Buddha, after his ablutions, bathed in that water; the branch of an Arjuna tree bent low, so that he could seize it. When the Buddha wanted to clean his patched robe, Indra provided him with a big stone to thrash his wet clothes on and another slab for drying them.

The people of Magadha would come to Kāśyapa to pay their respect during a seven-day festival. Kāśyapa feared that the people would pay respect to the Buddha rather than to him; the Buddha read his mind, and departed. After the festival, he came back on Kāśyapa's secret bidding. Once, the river Nairañjana flooded, but the Buddha walked on a dry ground. Kāśyapa thought that he might drown and went in a boat to rescue him. When Kāśyapa saw him walking on the ground, he asked the Buddha to come

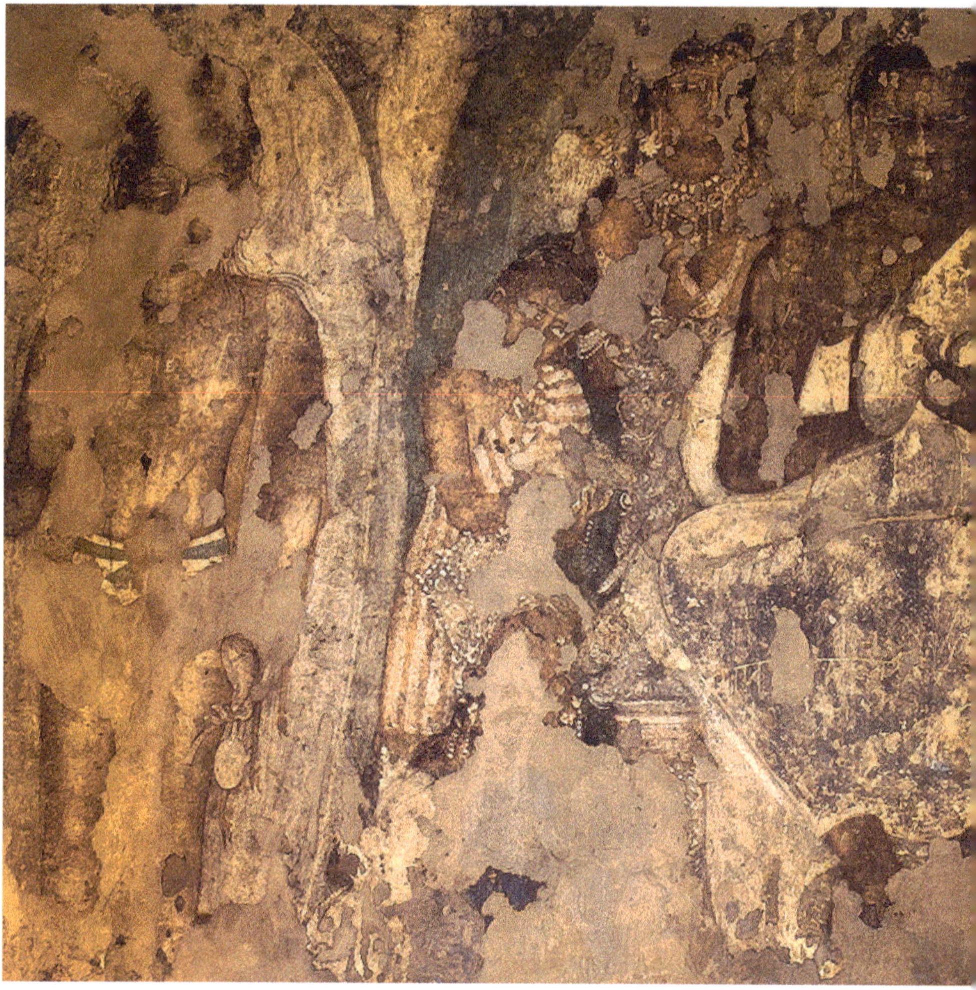

No. 67. Left: *Avalokiteśvara as the scene divider.* Centre and right: *the legend of the brahman Kāśyapa, scene 4. The Buddha at night is preaching to the gods of various heavens. On the right is a stūpa as the scene divider.* Rear wall.

on board. The Buddha rose above the water and stepped into Kāśyapa's boat. Kāśyapa was amazed at all these miracles but still considered himself to be a saint. The Buddha again read his mind and told him that he had not attained sainthood. When Kāśyapa became aware of his weakness, he asked the Buddha to let him become a monk. The Buddha admitted Kāśyapa, and later, his two brothers into his doctrine. The Buddha went to Gaya from Urubilva, where he manifested his spiritual powers to his newly converted disciples with three miracles; that of his magical power, of his authority and of his persuasive power. Thus, the Kāśyapa brothers and other disciples became saints.

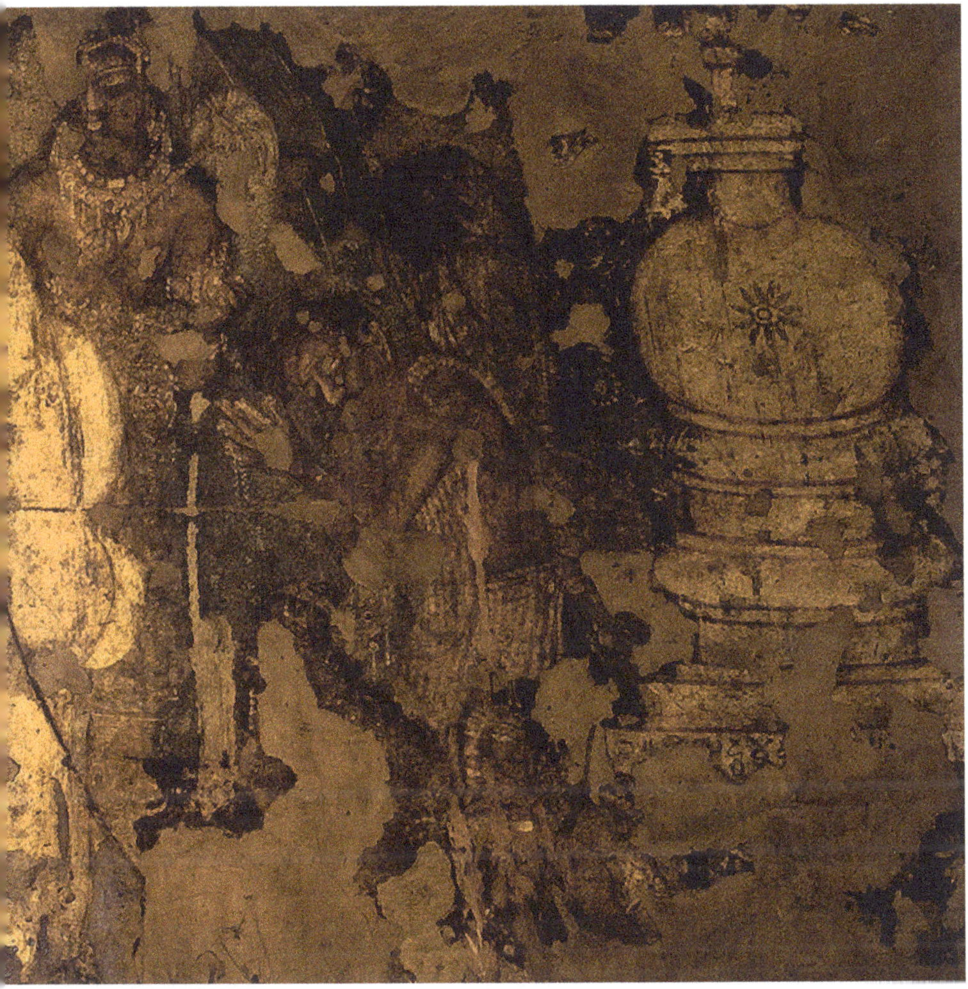

No. 10. Elapattra. (No photo.)

Identification: Zin 2000. The legend is from the life of the Buddha.—Elapattra, the nāga king, found his way to the Buddha with great difficulty. The Buddha asked him to assume his original form. Elapattra then assumed his huge body of a serpent.

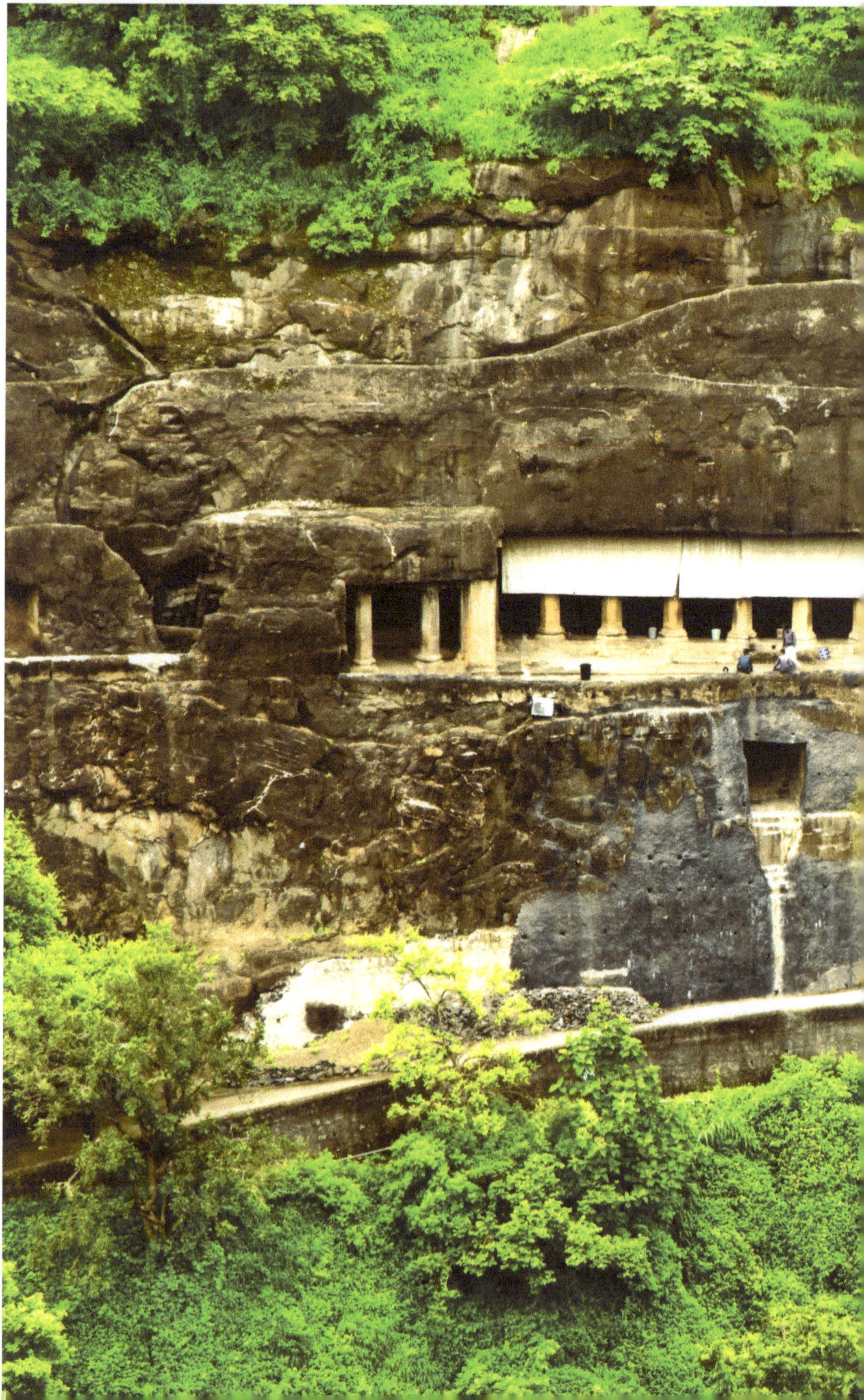

IV. Cave No. 16

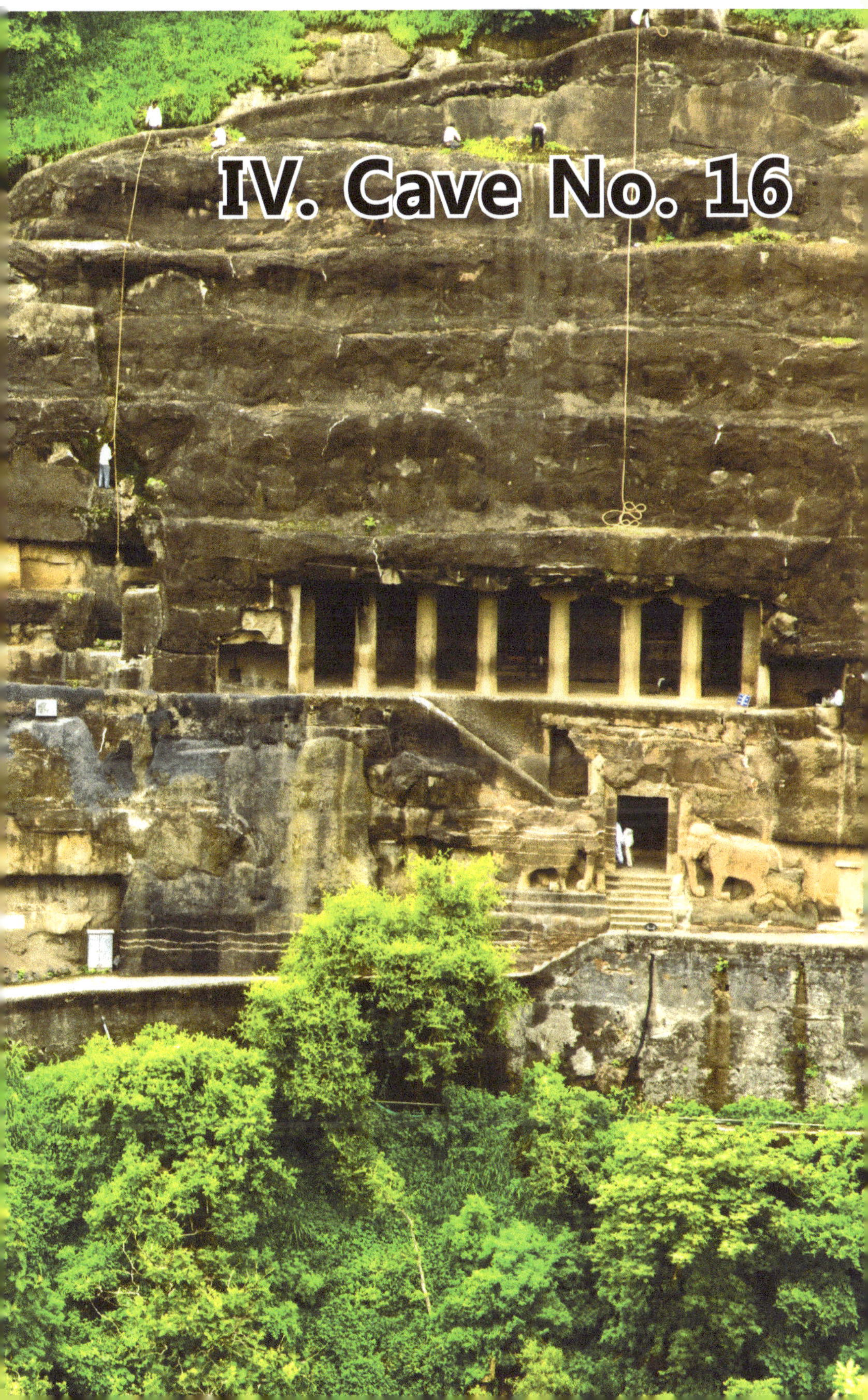

NARRATIVE THEMES.

No. 84.[1] Devāvatāra.

Identification: Foucher (1921, narrative nos. 58–60). The legend is from the life of the Buddha.—After defeating the ascetics with his superhuman powers, the Buddha went to Indra's heaven. He spent three months there and preached the doctrine to his mother,

No. 84. *Devāvatāra (much vandalised).* *Porch, rear wall, left side.*

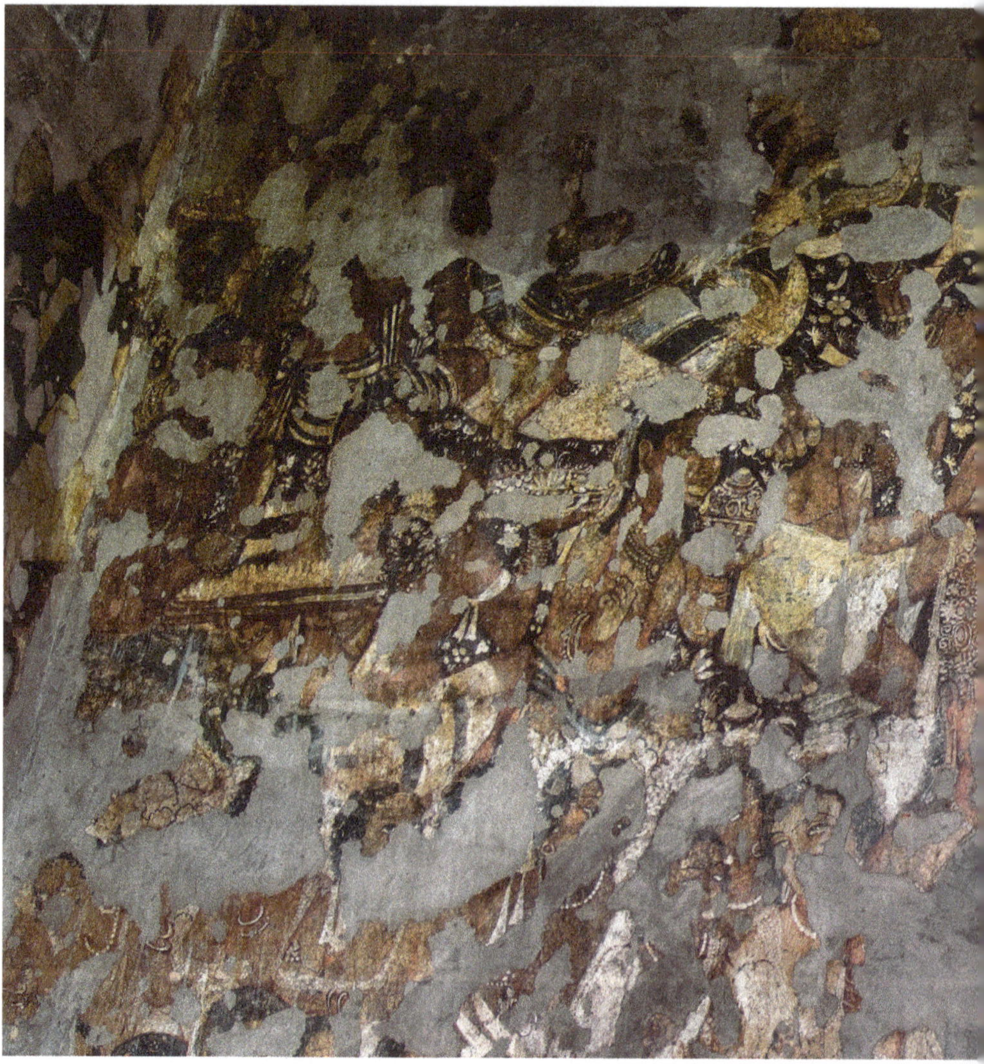

1 The numbers under the *narrative* themes refer to those assigned by Dieter Schlingloff to the *narrative* paintings of Ajanta, vide Schlingloff 2013.

who was reborn as a goddess, besides other gods and goddesses. On earth, the monks were yearning for the Buddha's return. Therefore, the monk, Maudgalyāyaṇa, flew to Indra's heaven and received the Buddha's promise to descend to earth after a week. For the Buddha's departure, the gods made three staircases of precious material, ending near the city gates in a grove of fig trees at Sāṃkāśya. The Buddha was escorted by Brahmā and Indra. He descended to the middle staircase while Brahmā and Indra,with their entourage, joined on the right and left staircases,

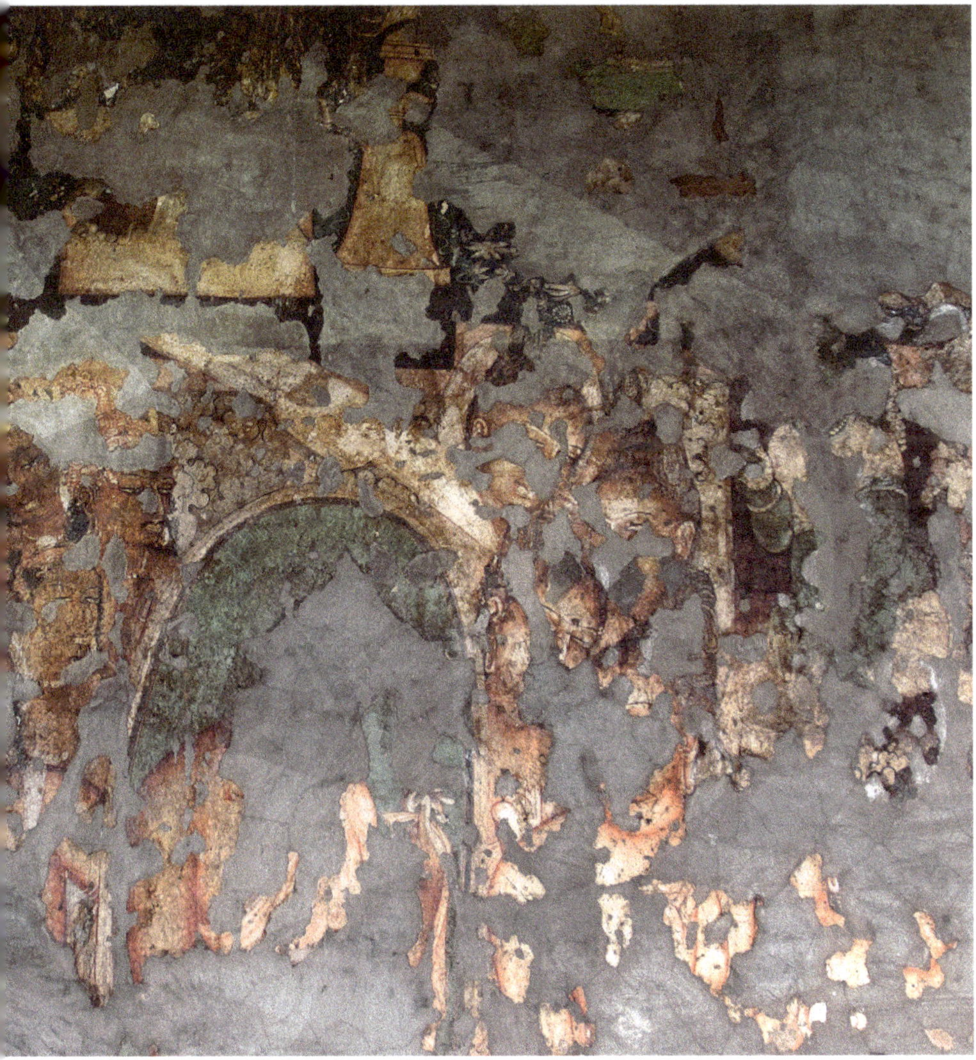

respectively. On his return, the monk, Śāriputra, welcomed him. There was a huge crowd waiting to honour the Buddha. The monk, Subhūti, chose to meditate in isolation. The nun, Utpalavarṇā, arrived late and missed the Buddha's reception. She edged close to the Buddha's throne in the form of a great king and attended his sermon from the first row, but was recognised by the monk, Udāyin by her female smell. Subsequently, the Buddha issued a rule that one should not use one's superhuman powers for personal advantage.

No. 56. Sutasoma. (No photo.)

Identification: Foucher (1921, narrative no. 20). For the story, vide Cave 17, No. 57.

No. 12. Vartakāpota. (No photo.)

Identification: Schlingloff (1977a, p. 458 f.)—There was a little *vartakā* (Hindi/Gujarati *baṭér;* Eng. quail). It had eaten only the vegetative leftovers of the food brought to the nest by its parents. Once there was a forest fire, which soon approached the nest. All the birds flown away except the little quail. The quail spoke a truth spell that he had never hurt any being, and implored the fire to recede. Miraculously, the fire spared the nest.—The quail was none other than the Buddha in a former existence.

No. 17. Ruru. (No photo.)

Identification: Schlingloff (1987, p. 144). For the story, vide Cave 2, narrative no. 16.

No. 21. Mahiṣa. (No photo.)

Identification: Begley (1966, p. 141). For the story, vide Cave 17, narrative no. 22.

No. 36. Vyāghrī. (No photo.)

Identification: Begley (1966, p. 125, n. 9).—Once there was a tigress in a jungle. A brahman was passing by. He saw her starving. He feared that she might eat her own cubs. So, he climbed a hillock and jumped to death in front of her so that the tigress can eat his dead body and spare her cubs.—The brahman was none other than the Buddha in his former existence.

No. 42. Viśvantara. (No photo.)

Identification: Chakravarti in Yazdani (vol. III, 1946, p. 96).—Prince Viśvantara practised extreme form of charity. He never refused donation to anybody. He owned an esteemed elephant and rode often to inspect the donation halls. Once, brahmans from a hostile neighbouring kingdom asked the elephant in donation. Viśvantara gave away the elephant without much ado. But, his subjects did not like the extremity of his generosity. They feared that the royal coffers will get emptied soon, which could be fatal for the kingdom's welfare.

The citizens issued a warrant of exile to the prince. Viśvantara's wife, Madrī, insisted that she will too follow him with the children. Viśvantara gave away all his personal belongings to the beggars and bade farewell to the king and the queen. He departed from the city on a chariot accompanied with wife, son, and daughter.

On reaching the forest, they came across other brahmans, who asked for his horses in donation. The prince gave away the horses. As he was to pull the chariot himself, four yakṣas disguised as deer put themselves to the yoke.

On the way, another brahman appeared and begged for the chariot. The was only too happy to oblige. The prince now walked on foot carrying the kids in the arms. They reached a hermitage in a forest. They spent half an year there in solitude.

One day, when the princess had gone away to gather food, a brahmin came to Viśvantara. He begged for the kids saying that he needed some slaves. The prince begged for some time to let his wife return. But the brahmans were not willing. So, the prince poured water, thus giving legal sanction for his children as alms. The wicked brahmin happily whisked them away.

Madrī had the premonition. She got weird visions. She wanted to return home as soon as possible. But she was held back by a lion on the way. Somehow when she managed to reach home she found her children missing. She began weeping. Viśvantara attempted to calm her down by explaining the motive. It was when the earth trembled. But Lord Indra now decided to test the true limits of Viśvantara's charity. He descended from the heaven as a brahman

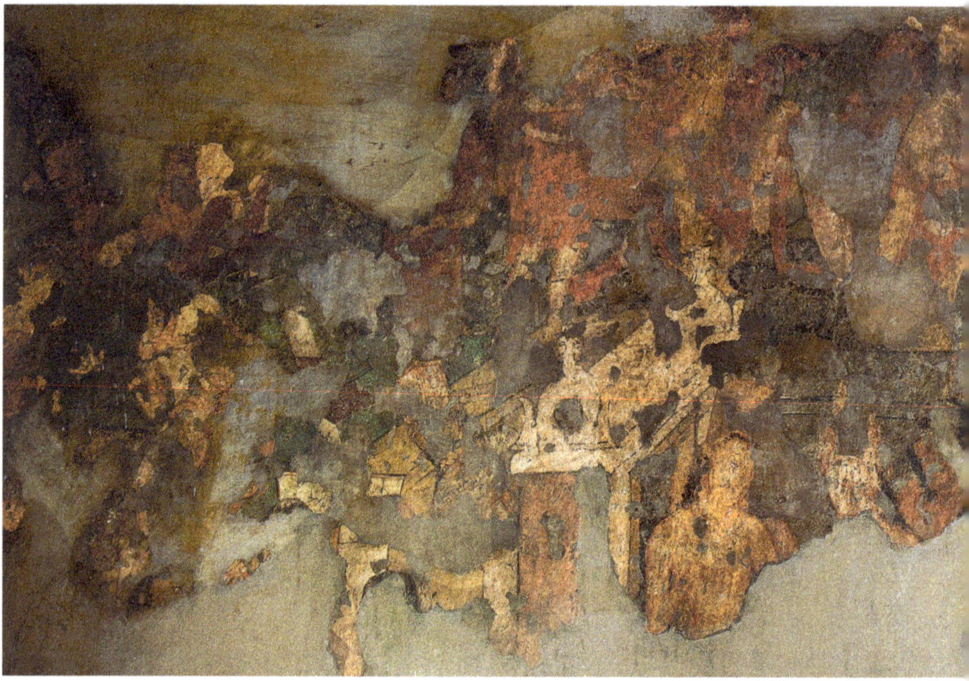

No. 33. *Bisa (left of gateway).*

No. 62. *Kumbha (right of gateway).*
Hall, front wall.

and demanded the hands of Madrī in donation. Without the slightest hesitation, Viśvantara poured water over the brahman's hand and legally sealed the donation of the last of what belonged to him.

Deeply moved, Indra assumed his real form. There was rain of flowers from the sky. Indra returned Madrī to him. Other brahmans too appeared there urged by Indra. They returned the children back. Overcome by Viśvantara's magnanimity, the king and the subjects reinstated him as the crown prince.—Prince Viśvantara was none other than the Buddha in a former existence.

No. 33. Bisa.

Identification: Schlingloff (1977a, p. 466 f.)—Along with his six brothers, a sister, a friend, and servants, a brahman and his family had renounced the worldly life. They dedicated their lives to meditation. Each lived alone in a hut and met once in five days to receive spiritual discourse from their eldest brother. The maid collected lotus stalks (*bisa*) on a lotus leaf for each of them every day. To test their virtue, Indra stole the lotus stalks kept for the eldest brother on five successive days. When the ascetics met on the fifth day they were surprised by the eldest brother's physical

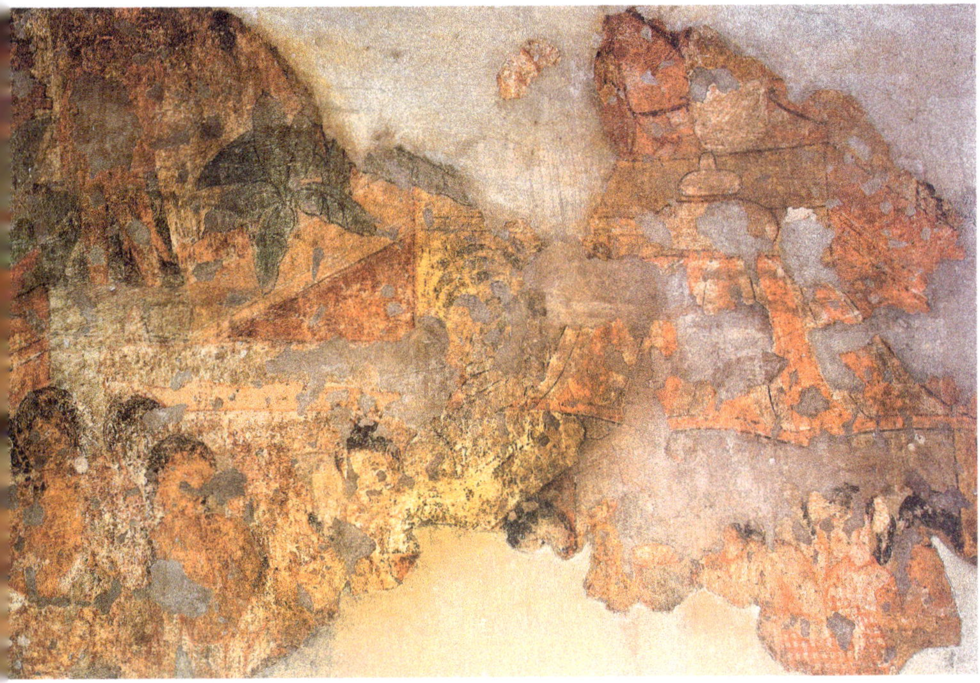

decay. When he told them about the theft, each brother pleaded innocence. They swore in front of a forest yakṣa, an elephant, and a monkey. It was when Indra appeared and confessed that he was responsible for the theft. He had done it to test their virtues and asked for forgiveness.—The brahman ascetic was none other than the Buddha in a former existence.

No. 62. Kumbha.

Identification: Schlingloff (1977a, p. 467 f.)—At a time when alcoholic drinks did not exist, a hunter found a cut in a tree from which came drop by drop an intoxicating drink for natural fermentation. With the help of an ascetic, he produced and sold the beverage in the royal cities with a great success. This is how the world came to know about the magic of intoxicating liquor.

Indra noticed from the heavens above that a king had become a hopeless addict. His kingdom had landed in chaos. To save the kingdom from annihilation, Indra disguised himself as a forest-dwelling brahman and went to the alcoholic king's court. He offered a *kumbha* (jug) of intoxicating potion, which was only sold to those who were willing to accept the disastrous results of liquor consumption. The king was surprised at the seller's behaviour. It was then that Indra revealed his identity. He explained to the king about the evil effects of alcoholism. He persuaded the king and his men to give it up and returned back to his heavenly abode.—Indra was none other than the Buddha in a former existence.

No. 52. Maitrībala.

Identification: Schlingloff (1972, p. 63–65). For the story, vide Cave 1, narrative no. 50.

No. 25. Hastin.

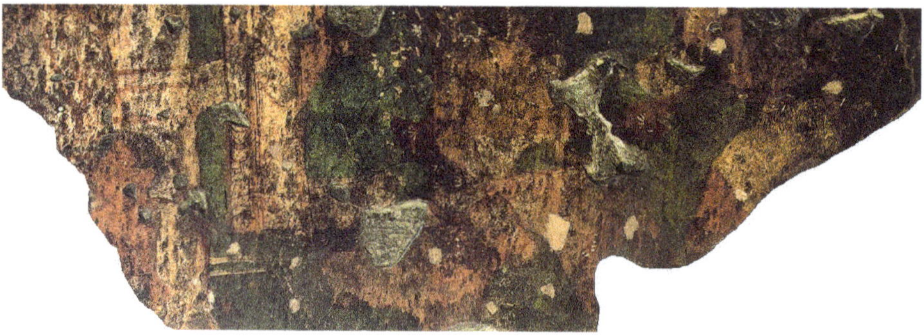

No. 52. *Maitribala, extant part. Hall, front wall, left side.*

Identification: Foucher (1921, narrative no. 22).—Once a group of travellers got lost in a forest. They were exhausted and almost close to death, when they met a *hastin* (elephant) and pleaded with him for help. The elephant, knowing that they would not find food in the oasis, directed them to a rock-bed, where they could find water and a dead elephant's body. The men went to the place directed by the elephant and found a dead elephant near the water. The travellers realised that the dead elephant was none other than the one they met before; he had sacrificed himself for them. The

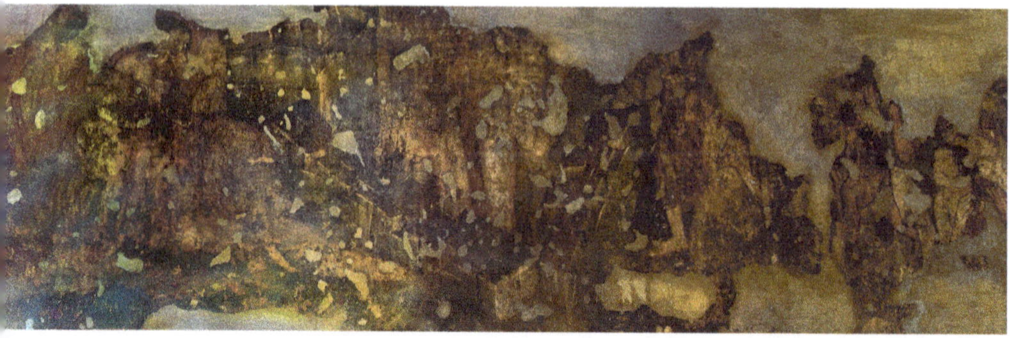

No. 25. *Hastin. Hall, front wall, left side.*

travellers cremated the elephant with due respect. They concluded that they should not reject his sacrifice and appeased their hunger and refilled their provisions. They made water containers with the elephant's skin, filled them with water, and were able to cross the desert.—The elephant was none other than the Buddha in a former existence.

No. 39. Mūkapaṅgu.

Identification: Schlingloff (1977a, p. 472–476).—When Prince Udaka (Water) grew up, people would call him Mūkapaṅgu, meaning 'Dumb and Numb.' He had seen his father pronouncing death sentences. So, he feigned an incapacity to become a king. Nobody could make him utter a sound or move a limb. The doctors diagnosed that he was physically and mentally normal, and that he was feigning it. They counselled the king to give him a death threat. The king accordingly ordered his execution. At the time of his said execution, the prince uttered a mysterious verse. So, he was presented back to the king, but remained dumb and numb. This happened twice. In the third attempt, he got scared by his imminent execution; he broke his silence and faked inability to move. The executioners reported this to the king. The prince explained that the reason for his strange behaviour was that in his previous life he had failed to carry out the duty of his royal office and suffered in hell for a long time. To avoid a similar fate, he faked his disabilities, which he hoped would relieve him from the duty of pronouncing death sentences to prisoners. He requested his father to allow him to become an ascetic. His father granted him his wish. After revealing the meaning of the mysterious verses, the prince left the palace with other like-minded men.—Prince Mūkapaṅgu was none other than the Buddha in a former existence.

No. 30. Mahākapi. (No photo.)

Identification: Schlingloff (2013, p. 139–143). For the story, vide Cave 17, No. 31.

No. 73. Nanda.

Identification: episodes 7, 8, 10, 11 by Foucher (1921, narrative no. 55).—After the enlightenment, on his first visit to the hometown of Kapilavastu, the Buddha convinced many to follow his doctrine.

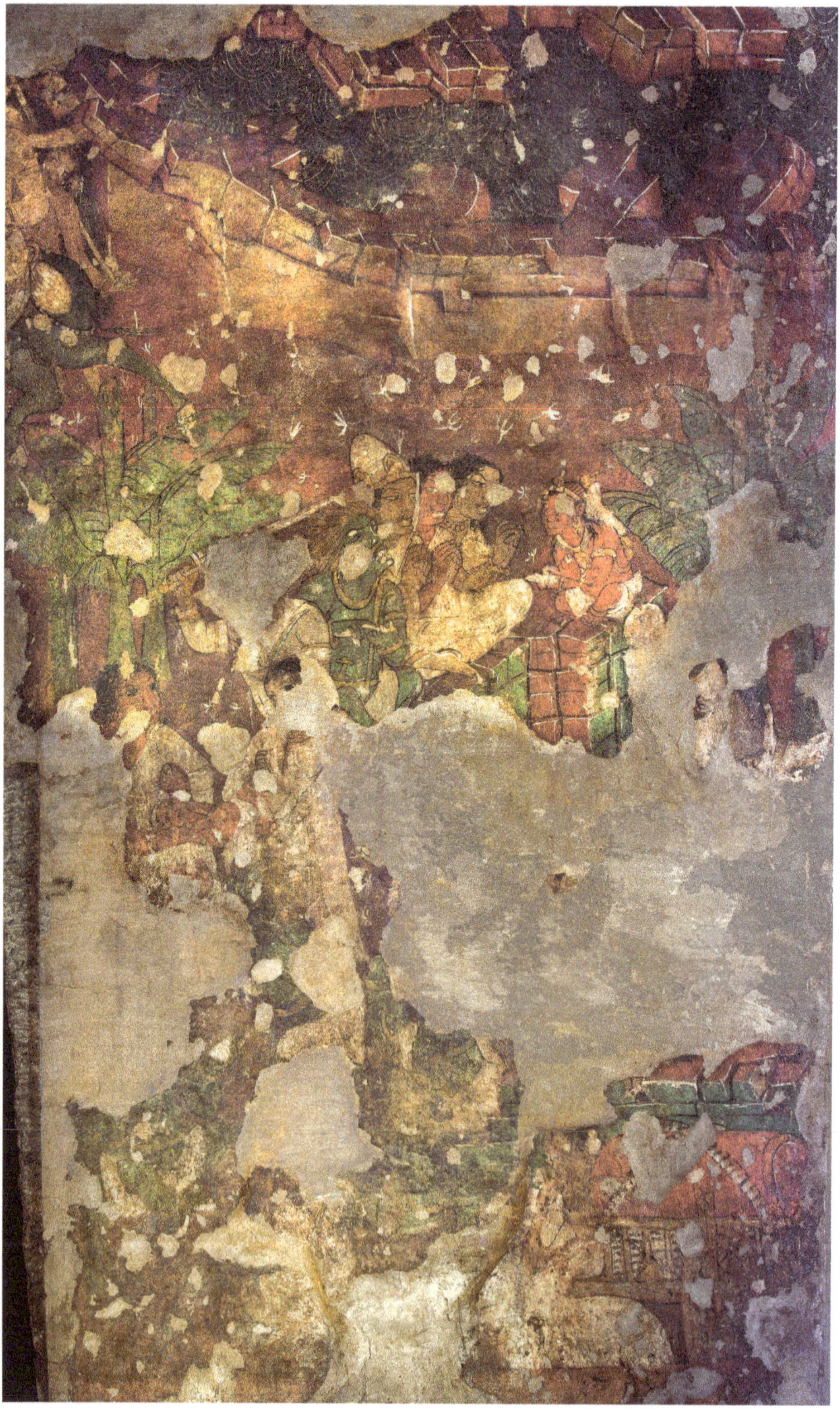

His half-brother, Nanda, immersed in passion for his wife, Sundarī (Beauteous), missed that sermon. While the Buddha went from house to house for food, Nanda spent time with Sundarī, helping her with her make-up and holding the mirror for her. When the Buddha reached the palace, he went unnoticed as Nanda and Sundarī were busy in the make-up room. So, the Buddha quietly left. When a lady saw him and informed the prince, Nanda left the house in a hurry to repair the damage and offer his respects to the Buddha. He saw the Buddha addressing many people in the street, surrounded by disciples.

No. 39. Opposite. *The legend of Mūkapaṅgu. Hall, front aisle, left wall.*

Unable to go anywhere near him, Nanda decided to return home. However, after the crowd had dispersed, he managed to meet his brother alone in the street. The prince respectfully bowed and wanted to take his leave. The Buddha handed his food-bowl to him and Nanda had no choice but to carry it till the monastery. Once in the monastery, the Buddha convinced him about the virtues of a monastic life, to which Nanda halfheartedly agreed. He allowed his head to be shaved and dressed in a monk's robe.

Meanwhile, Sundarī kept waiting for her husband. When a maid servant informed her about Nanda becoming a monk, she was engulfed in intense sorrow. Nanda too pined for his wife and thought about giving up the monastic life. When the Buddha came to know about Nanda's distress, he flew him to heaven. He drew Nanda's attention to a one-eyed female monkey in the Himalayas, to contrast her ugliness with his wife's beauty. In Indra's heaven, they met celestial nymphs who were far beauteous than Nanda's wife. So, Nanda went back to his ascetic life to be reborn in Indra's heaven. But the monk, Ānanda, convinced him about the

No. 73.1. *The legend of Nanda.* On left: *scene 7, in the presence of the Buddha, Nanda's head is being tonsured while a servant of Nanda is trying to stop the barber (damaged).* On right: *scene 9, the Buddha observes Nanda who has kept his head on his hand, as he cannot forget his wife.*

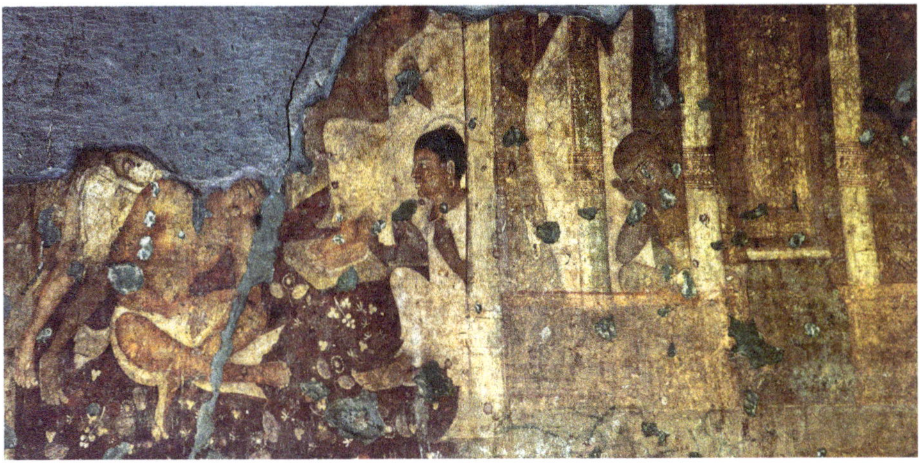

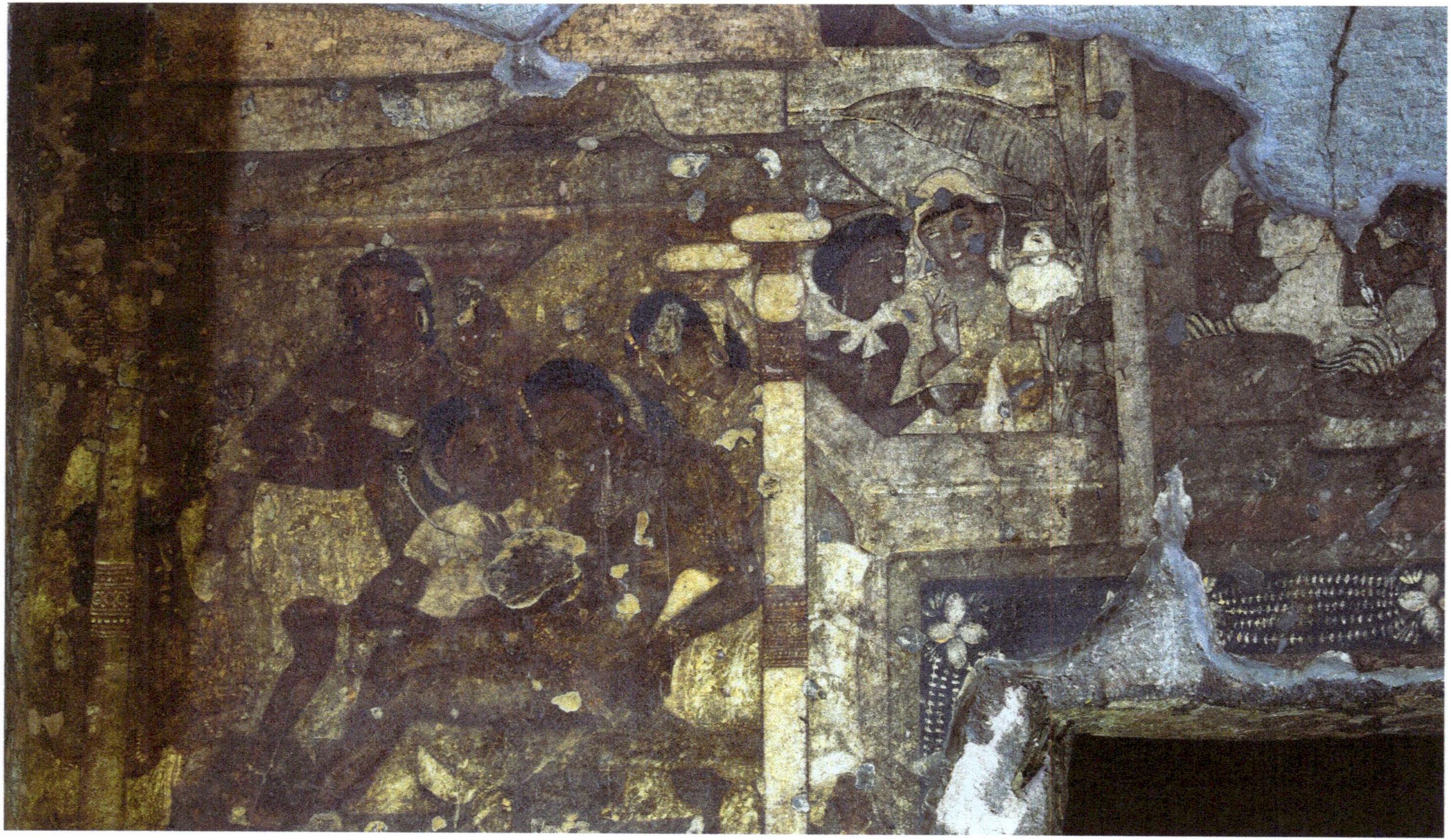

No. 73.2. *Scene 8: After Nanda's servant returns with the crown of Nanda, the princess seeing the crown falls unconscious, as she realises that Nanda has become a monk.*

importance of enlightenment over the heavenly sphere. After the Buddha's teaching, he devoted his life to meditation and attained sainthood.

No. 91. Mahāprātihārya.

Identification: Vogel (1948, p. 157). For the legend, vide Cave 1, No. 88.

No. 82. Mahāsamāja.

Identification: Foucher (1921, narrative no. 61).—Near Kapilavastu, the Buddha delivered a sermon to the monks before the *Mahāsamāja* (Great Assembly) of gods. The four Brahmā gods too moved from heaven, each pronounced a verse and left. The Buddha recognised and disclosed the presence of the deities to the monks: the Four Great Kings of the world regions, the leaders of the hosts of *yakṣas*, the *nāgas*, the *garuḍas*, the *asuras*, the gods and goddesses of the pantheon, and the *rākṣasī* Hārītī with her sons. Māra with his army attempted to disturb the sermon but in vain.

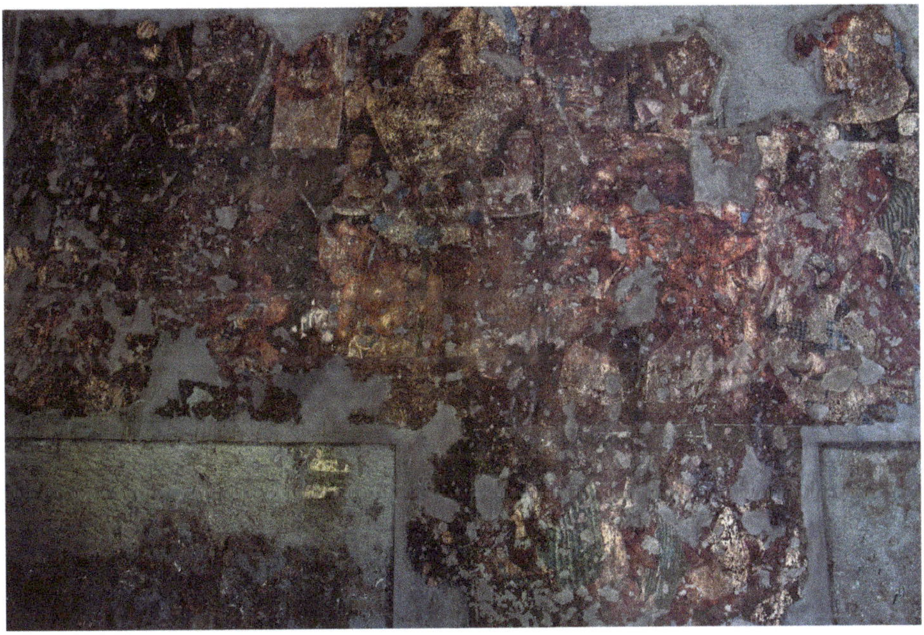

No. 91. *Mahāprātihārya (severely damaged).* *Hall, rear wall, left of shrine.*

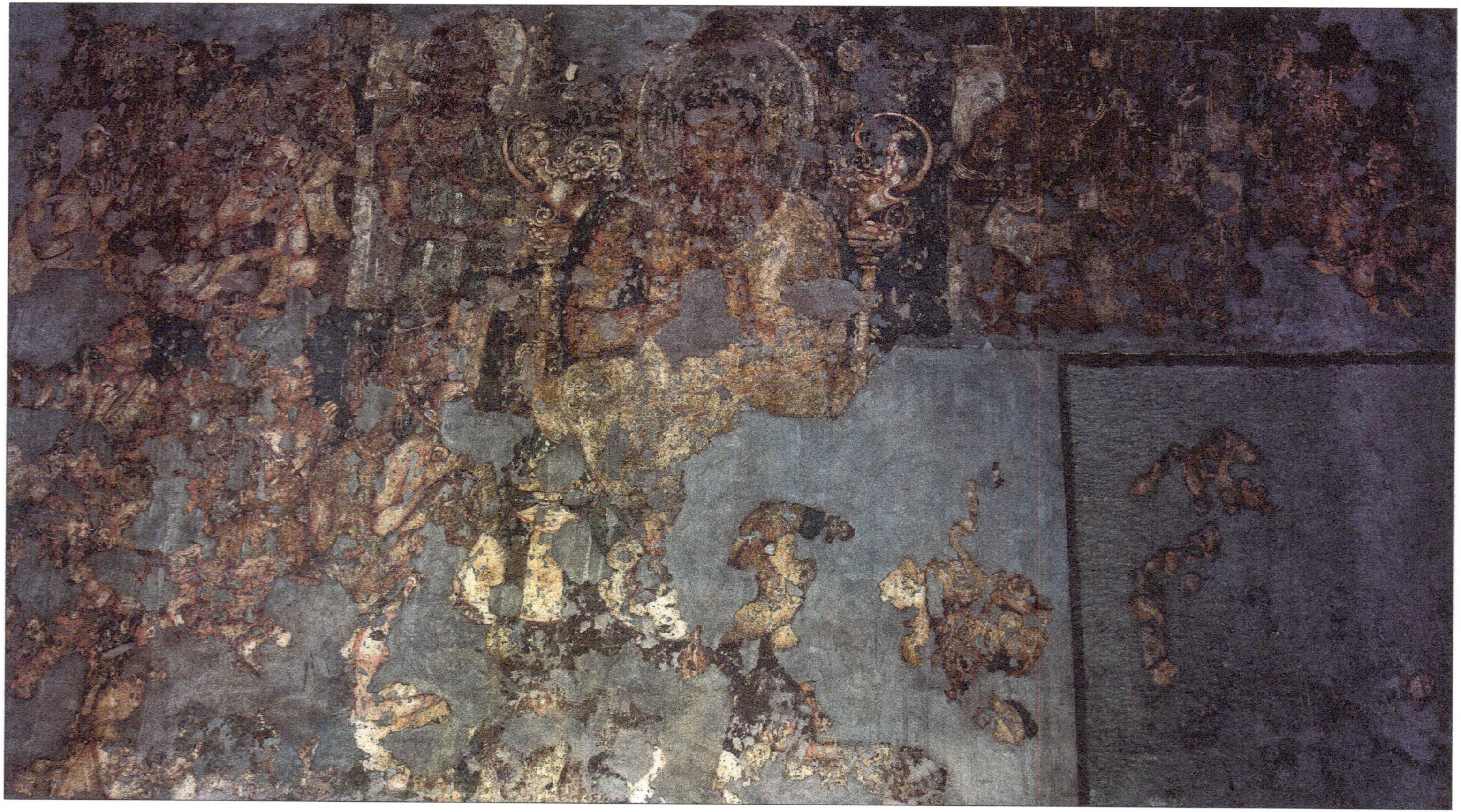

No. 82.2. *The Buddha preaching to the monks in the presence of a Great Assembly (Mahāsamāja) of gods.* Hall, rear right wall.

No. 64. Bhagavān.

Identification: episodes 1–5, 8–15, 19–20, 23, 25, 28–29, and 31 by Schlingloff (1983, p. 119–122, 127–131, 135–136, 140, 142–144,

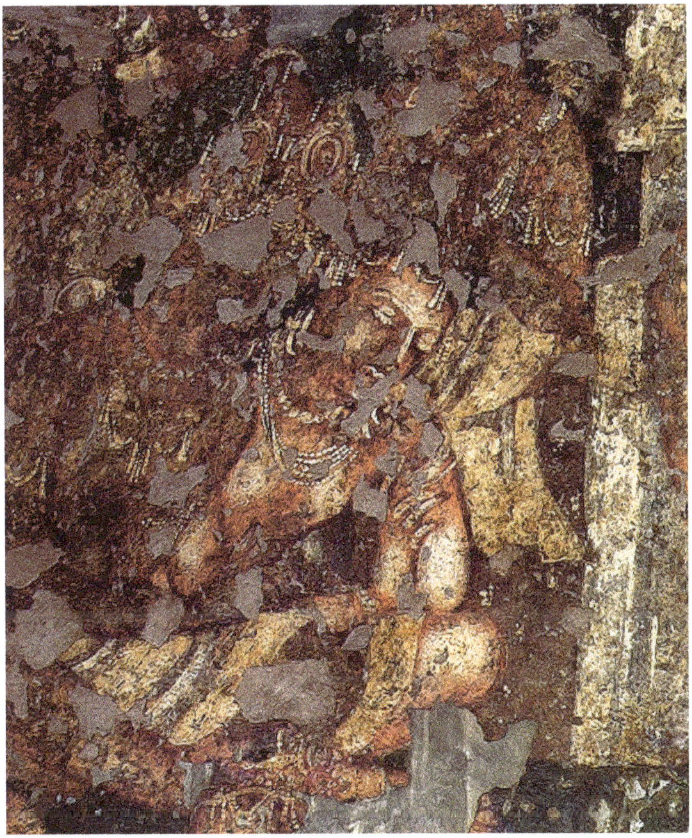

No. 82.3. Detail from previous: *Māra is despondent after he failed to disturb the Buddha's sermon.*

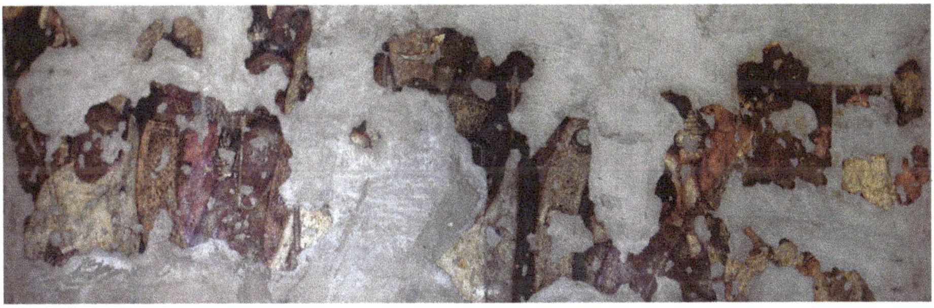

No. 82.1. *Māra retreats with his warriors.*

146), episodes 6 and 7 by Yazdani (III, 1946, p. 67, 167), episodes 16, 18, and 24 by Burgess (1879, p. 60 f.), episode 17 by Griffiths (1896, p. 33), and episodes 21–22, 26–27 and 30 by Foucher (1921, p. 224–225). The legend is from the life of the Buddha.—

The Bodhisattva chose Māyā, King Śuddhodana's wife, for his last rebirth in Kapilavastu. In the midnight hour, the Bodhisattva entered Māyā's womb in the form of an elephant. Māyā saw four dreams relating to this, which she narrated to the king. On the king's request, the brahmans explained to the queen that she would give birth to a son who would become either a universal monarch or an enlightened Buddha.

At the time of delivery, Māyā expressed her desire to visit her father's place, Lumbinī, where she went with her retinue of maids. She clung to an Aśoka tree to give birth to the Bodhisattva. After the birth, the Bodhisattva took seven steps in four directions and announced his redemption. After the Bodhisattva's birth,

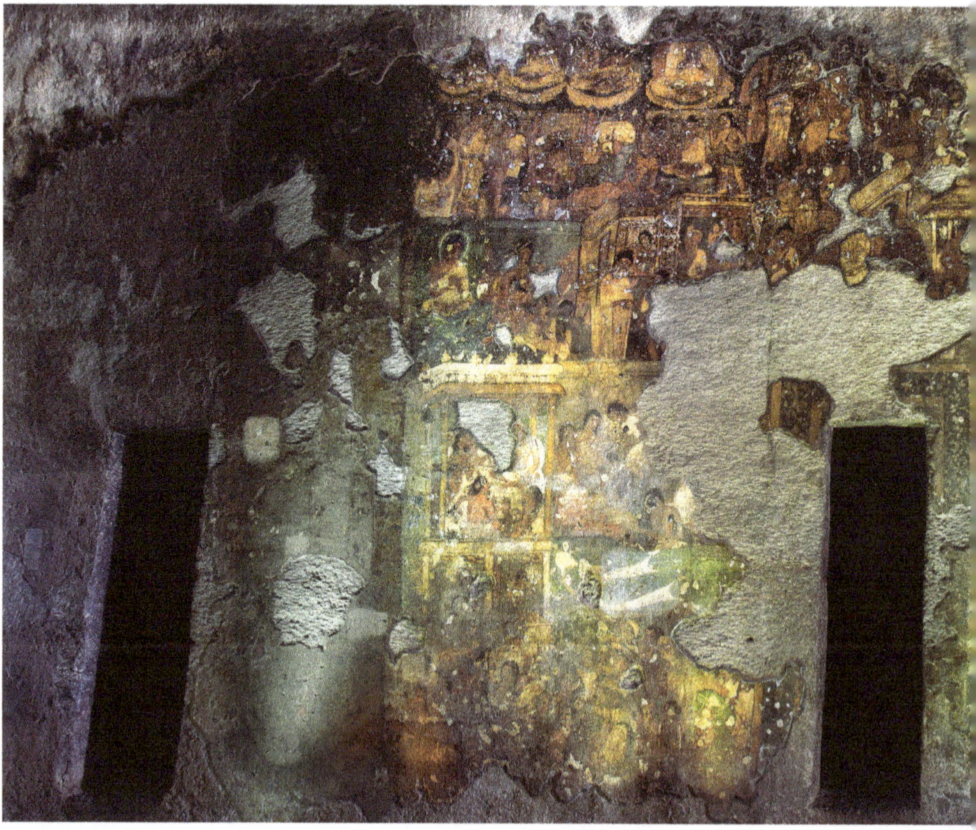

No. 64. *The wall with the Bhagavān narrative. Hall, right wall.*

successors of a neighbouring kingdom were born. Then the Bodhisattva was taken to a *yakṣa* temple. A foster-mother was entrusted to look after the child. The brahmans and experts recognised 32 signs of a great personality and predicted that the child would become either a great emperor or an enlightened Buddha.

One week after the Bodhisattva's birth, the queen died and was reborn in Indra's heaven. Saint Asita, escorted by Śuddhodana, saw the sleeping child with open eyes and heard the prophecy of the brahmans from the king.

The Bodhisattva demonstrated amazing strength by holding a food bowl against 500 elephants. His teachers found that he already knew all the scripts. Further, he showed the Brāhmī script, which became known at the appearance of the Buddha. Everybody was surprised by his strength and skills. He flung away a dead elephant killed by his cousin, Devadatta. He broke thick bamboo smoothly

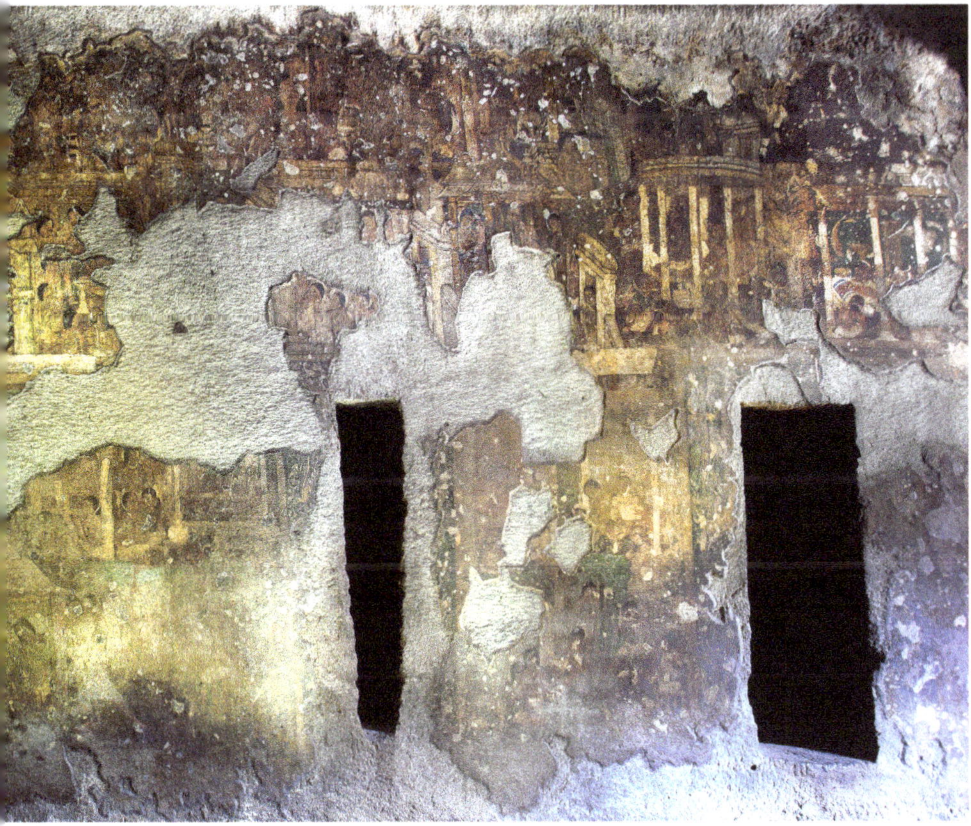

and shot seven palm trees with a single arrow. The Bodhisattva married Yaśodharā, the daughter of the Śākya Daṇḍapāṇi.

When the water management system was disrupted by a massive tree, which fell into the river, the Bodhisattva helped to lift and remove the tree. He healed a goose wounded by Devadatta's arrow and released him. In the same outing, a youth, Udāyin, killed a snake which was about to attack the Bodhisattva. Udāyin turned black and was thus called Kālodāyin (Black Udāyin). On his return, people noticed the chemistry between the Bodhisattva and a girl, Gopikā, and informed the king about it. The king suggested that the Bodhisattva wed Gopikā.

Once the Bodhisattva, accompanied by his charioteer saw an old man, a sick man, and then a funeral procession. On his fourth outing, he saw a monk. The king tried to divert the attention of the prince and asked the Bodhisattva to inspect a village of the royal estate. He saw a pitiful sight there and sat under a rose-apple tree to meditate and completed the first degree of contemplation. In the evening, the shadow of the tree had not left the Bodhisattva's body uncovered. Seeing this miracle, the king bowed in front of his son, returned to Kapilavastu and told his brothers about the brahman's prophecy.

The king and his brothers kept a watch over the prince but the Bodhisattva's mind was set on renouncing the world. When his wife became pregnant and he saw the ugliness of the exhausted court ladies in their quarters, he left the city under the cover of night on instructions from Indra, Brahmā and other gods. The Bodhisattva met Saint Bhārgava, who welcomed him, but he moved on. He crossed the river Ganges and reached Rājagṛha, collected food in his bowl, begging from house to house. King Biṃbisāra noticed him and asked him the reason for renouncement. The Bodhisattva explained the reason and promised the king that he would visit his palace after achieving enlightenment.

When the Bodhisattva moved to Gṛdhrakūta, he realised that his path to redemption was not the right one. He met two yoga teachers, Ārāḍa Kalāma and Udraka Rāmaputra, but he was not satisfied. He started practising extreme asceticism. He remembered his first meditation exercise and understood that he was on the correct path. Once, he visited a village, where the maidens had made a special milk-pudding for the Bodhisattva. The ascetic, Upaga, wanted to taste this pudding but the maidens refused to give it to him. When the gods arrived, the maidens wanted to know who had the highest rank. The gods named the Bodhisattva. Two maidens went to the Bodhisattva and offered him the pudding. This was his last meal before he became the Buddha. When Upaga asked him about his teacher, the Buddha informed him that he had attained enlightenment without a teacher. Then he headed for Benaras to preach his sermon.

No. 85. Devāvatāra. (No photo.)

Identification: Begley (1966, p. 141). For the story, vide Cave 16, No. 84.

A NON-NARRATIVE THEME.

No. 30.[2] Kubera.

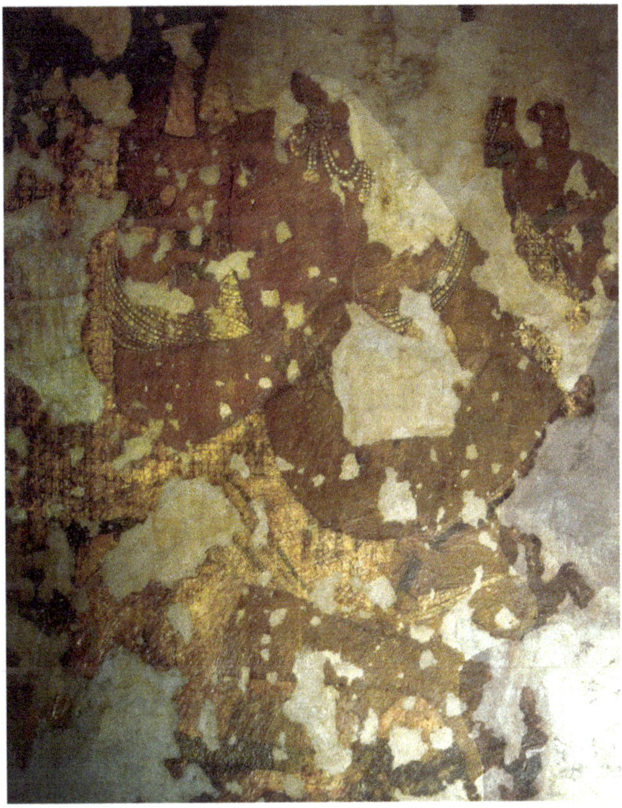

No. 30. *A genius (yakṣa), guarding a monk's cell, produces coins from a purse.* *Hall, front aisle, right wall.*

2 The numbers under the *non-narrative* themes including the captions refer to those assigned by Monika Zin to the *non-narrative* themes of the Ajanta paintings, vide Zin 2003a.

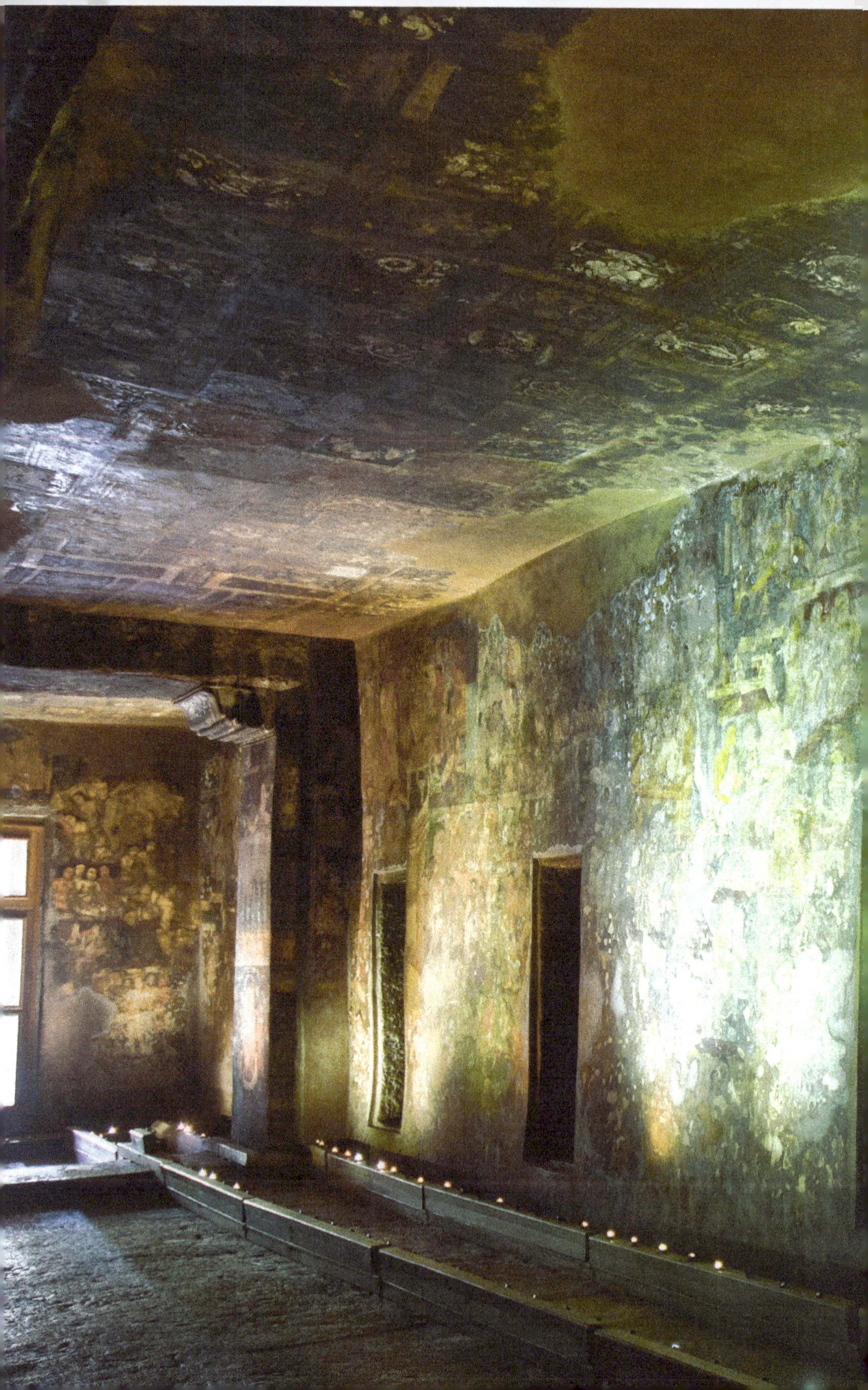

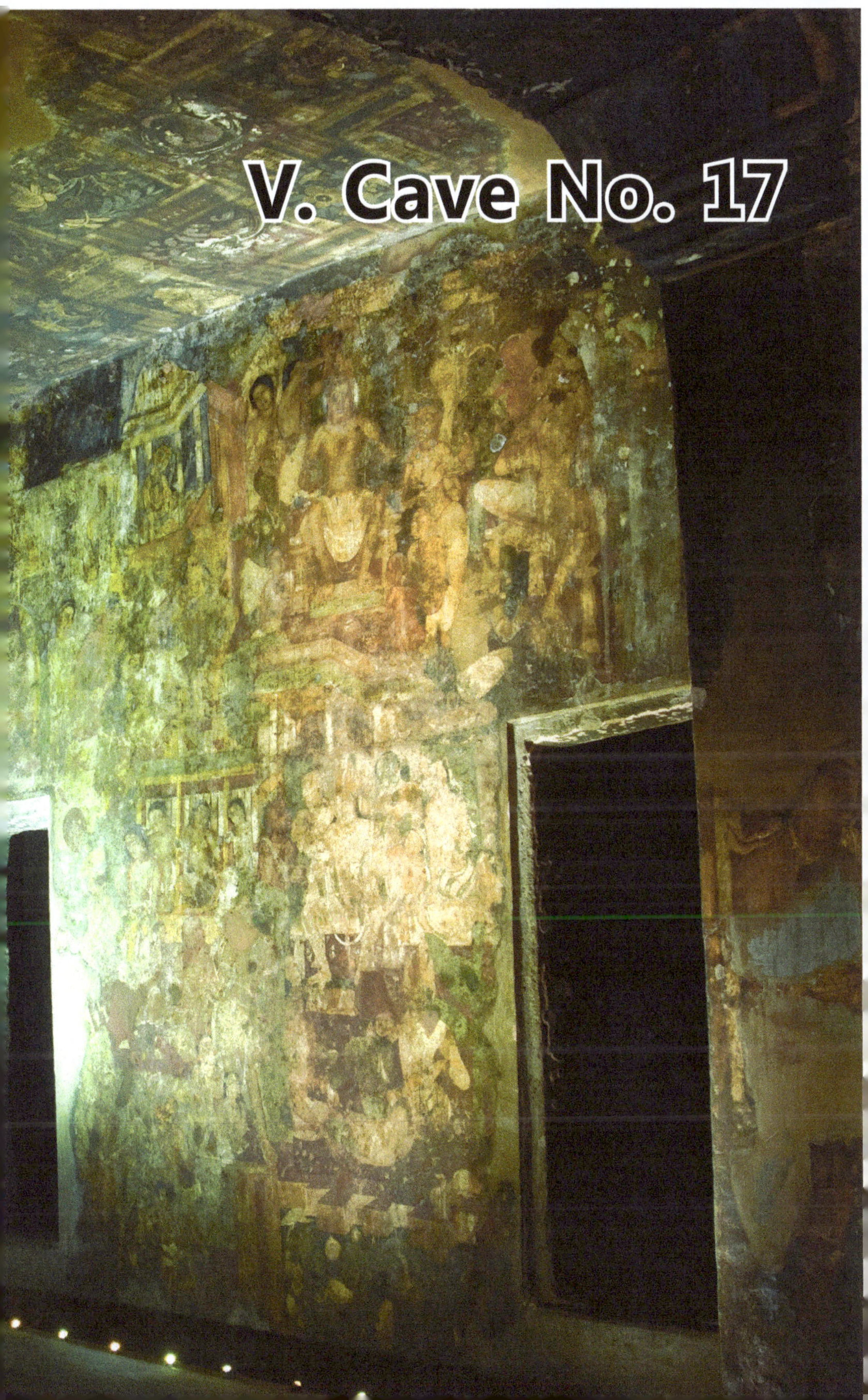

V. Cave No. 17

NARRATIVE THEMES.

No. 24.[1] Siṃha.

Identification: Foucher (1921, narrative no. 29).—A *siṃha* (lion), on hearing the loud wails of merchants caught by a giant snake in a jungle, came running with his elephant friend to help them. From atop the elephant's head, he jumped on the snake and killed it. The elephant, however, died as the lion's hind claws accidentally pierced its head. The lion too did not survive the venomous breath of the snake.—The lion was none other than the Buddha in a former existence.

No. 24. *The legend of a* siṃha *(lion). Porch, left side.*

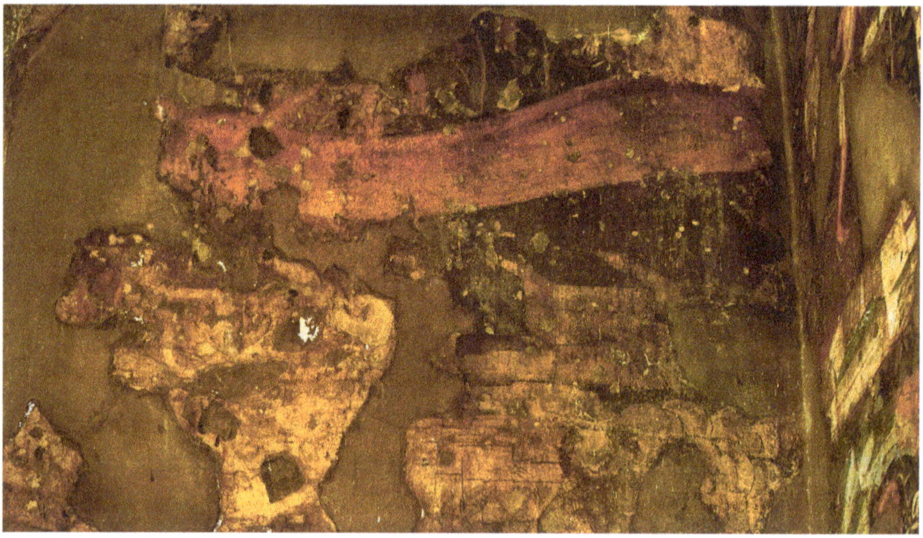

No. 68. Śuddhodana.

Identification: Schlingloff 2013. It is an episode from the life of the Buddha.—Māra, the king of the world of desires, spread the rumour that in his quest for enlightenment, the Buddha had succumbed to his severe lifestyle. However, well-wishers quickly dispelled the rumours and asserted that the prince was now an enlightened Buddha. On hearing this, along with the news

1 The numbers under the *narrative* themes refer to those assigned by Dieter Schlingloff to the *narrative* paintings of Ajanta, vide Schlingloff 2013.

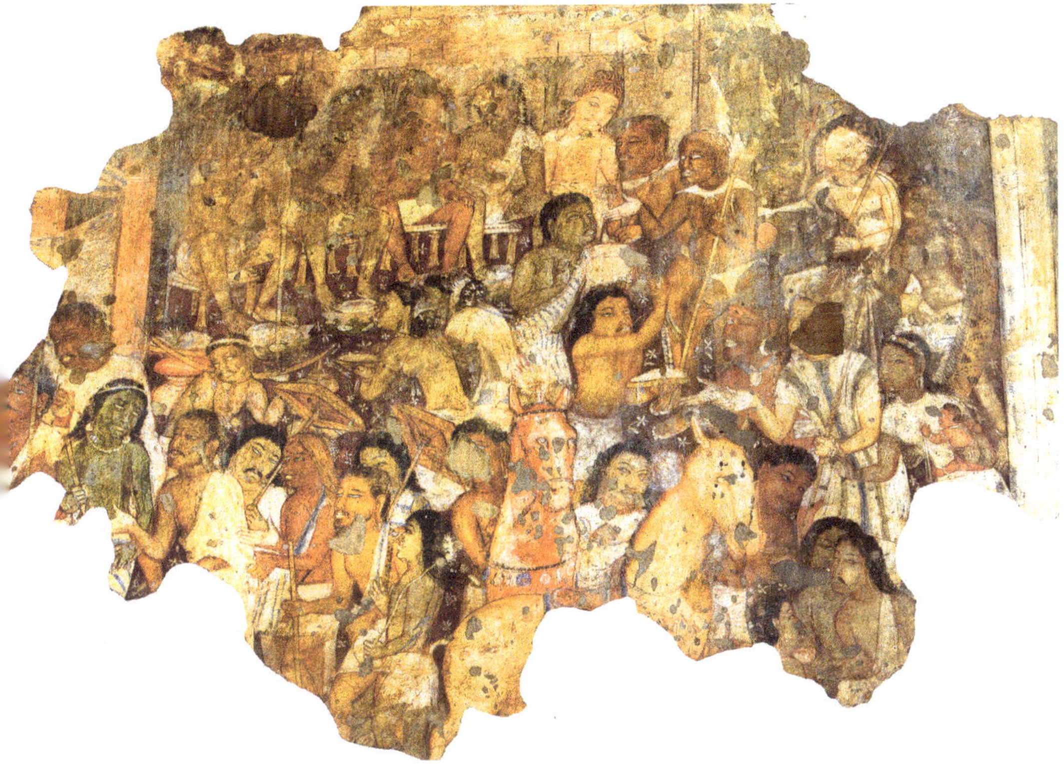

No. 68. *The legend of King Śuddhodana.* *Porch, rear wall, far left.*

that Buddha's wife had given birth to a boy, King Śuddhodana, Buddha's father, organised a great celebration at Kapilavastu. He had the city cleaned and decked up, and halls set up at the gates where one and all were showered with gifts, and beggars were served with food and drink.

Śuddhodana decided to invite the Buddha, now residing near Śrāvastī, to Kapilavastu. However, all the messengers ended up becoming monks at the behest of the Enlightened One, and stayed back at Śrāvastī. Finally, the king sent Udāyin, the son of the royal priest, with a promise of returning at any cost. Udāyin returned, but as a monk, with the message that the Buddha had accepted the king's invitation.

No. 69. Udāyin.

Identification: Schlingloff 2013. It is an episode from the life of the Buddha.—Udāyin, the son of the court priest at Kapilavastu that was the kingdom of King Śuddhodana, was called Kālodāyin as he was dark-complexioned. Śuddhodana had close ties with

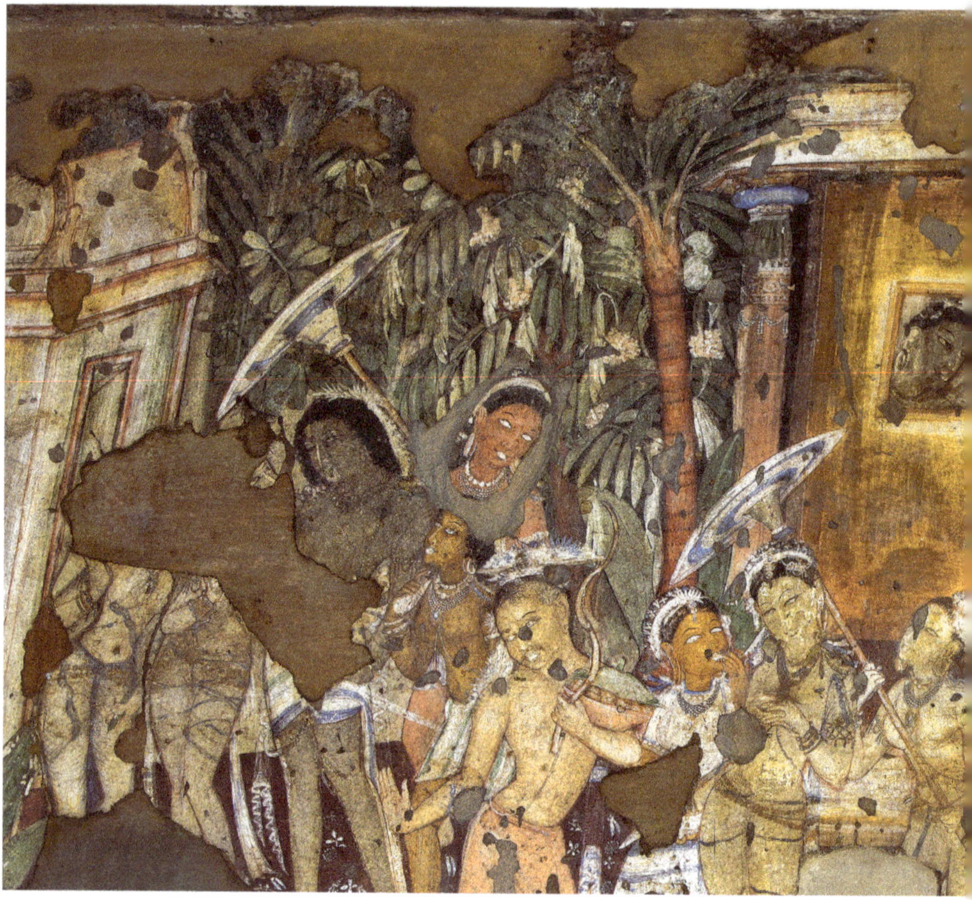

No. 69. *The legend of Udāyin. Porch, left of the rear wall.*

Prasenajit, the king of Śrāvastī. Udāyin would carry Śuddhodana's messages to Prasenajit and the latter conveyed his missives through a minister's son, Guptā. In due course, Udāyin became a great friend of Guptā and stayed at his palace whenever he was in Sravasti. By and by, Udāyin fell in love with Guptā, his friend's beautiful wife. After Guptā's sudden death, and with no heir in the scene, Prasenajit prepared to seize the widow's assets. In this distressful hour, Guptā turned to Udāyin for help. Udāyin, made a deal with the king, became the administrator of Guptā's assets, and settled down to domestic bliss with his beloved. One day, King Śuddhodana wanted to invite the Buddha to visit Kapilavastu and sent Udāyin as a messenger. Udāyin left Guptā's home, but became a monk after meeting the Buddha. Guptā plunged into grief, but later accepted her destiny. Finally, she too left her home in order to join the Buddha's order of the nuns.

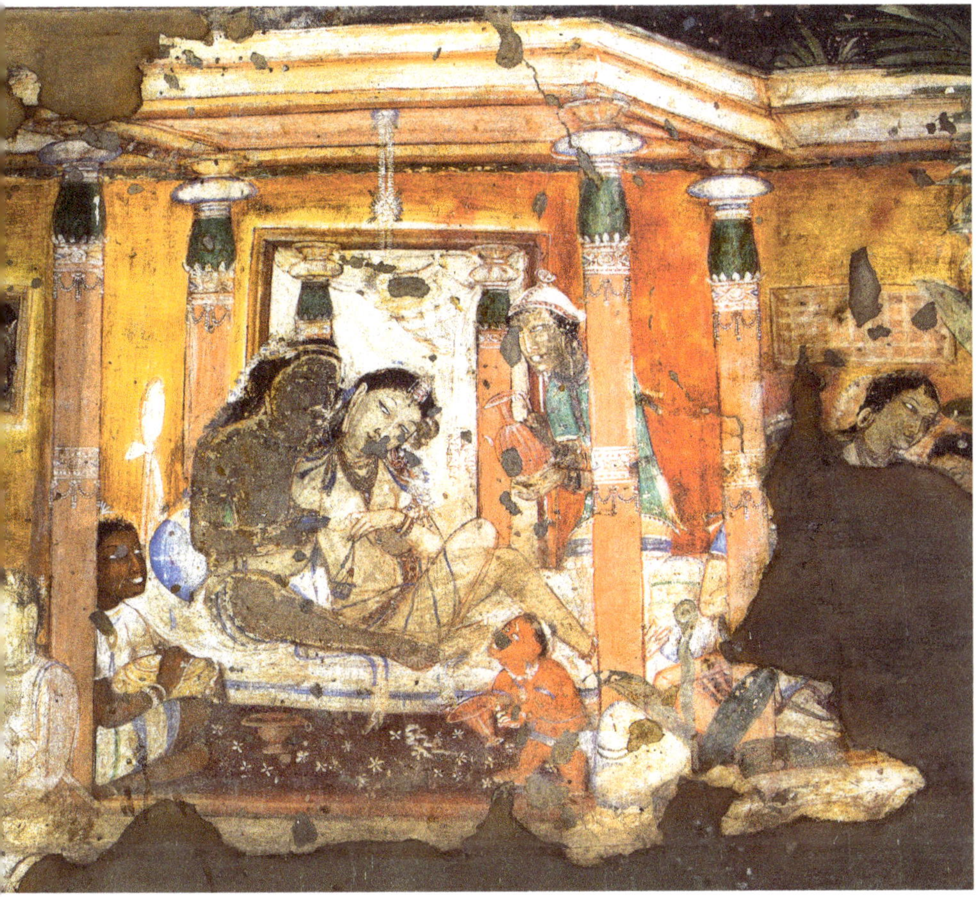

No. 77. Dhanapāla.

Identification: episodes 1, 3, 4, 5 by Griffiths (1896, p. 36). It is an episode from the life of the Buddha.—King Ajātaśatru had an angry elephant, Dhanapāla, at Rājagṛha, who was often involved in rampages. So, whenever Dhanapāla went on his rounds in the town, the public was given prior notice. Once, when the Buddha was staying at a monastery near Rājagṛha, a citizen invited him home for a meal. Monk Devadatta, seeking a chance to kill the Buddha, went to Ajātaśatru and requested him to release the elephant in town on that day around lunchtime. Hesitantly, the king announced the elephant's outing. The host, disheartened, wondered how he was going to rustle up the lunch for the Buddha, what with the elephant advisory in the town. He thus had food delivered to Buddha in the monastery and also informed him about the adversaries. The Buddha calmly told him to carry on

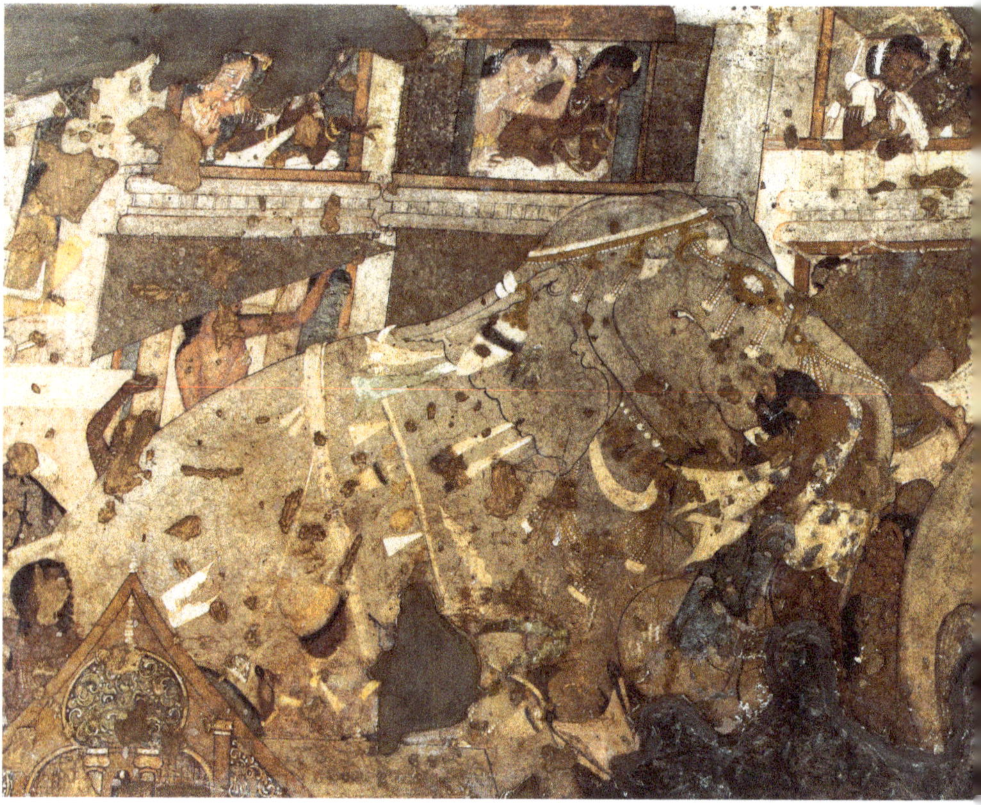

No. 77. *The legend of Dhanapāla, the elephant.* *Porch, right of the rear wall.*

with his plans to host him. The following day, the elephant was let loose as the Buddha and his monks walked into the city street. The animal went on a rampage in the street and rushed to the Buddha even as Devadatta and king watched the scene from the palace. All, except the faithful Ānanda, the Buddha's attendant, fled. The Buddha produced five lions on his palm, followed by blazing fire seen everywhere except at his feet. The Buddha tamed the elephant by the power of his benevolence, and the elephant bowed for him. The Buddha then proceeded to finish his lunch. The now docile elephant waited at the door till he was done. After that the elephant followed the Buddha wherever he went till he was taken away by the royal keepers. Eventually depressed over the separation from the Buddha, Dhanapāla ended its life.

No. 71. Rāhula. (No photo.)

Identification: Yazdani (1955, IV, p. 70 f.). It is an episode from the life of the Buddha. Another depiction of the narrative is in the

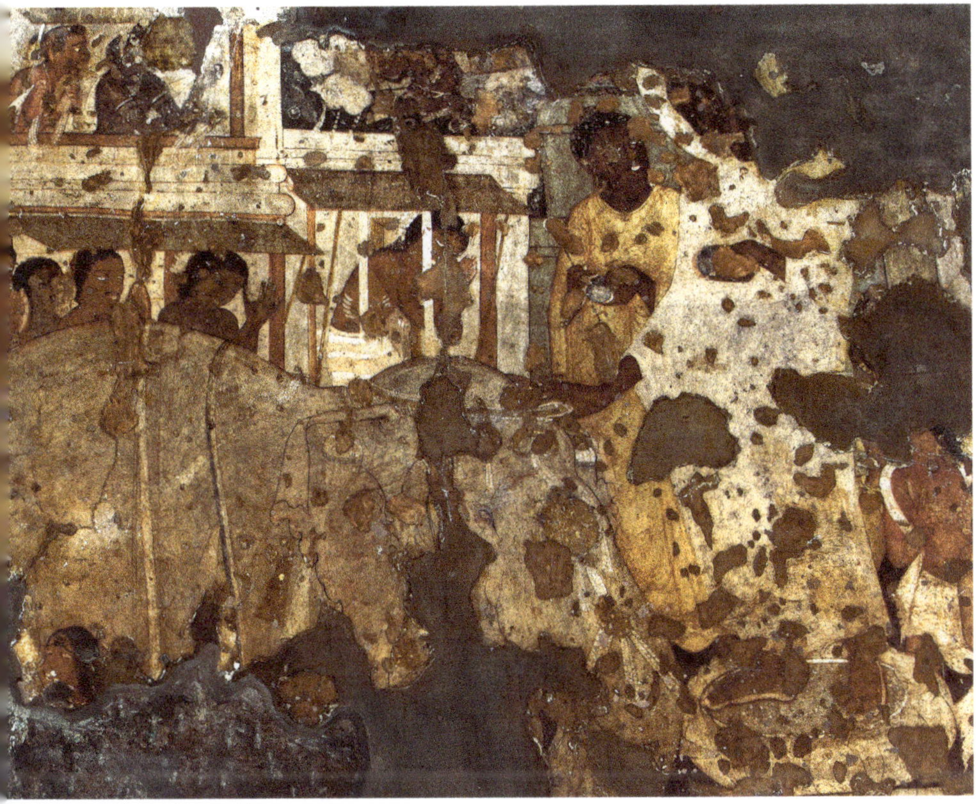

interior of the temple, which is much bigger and more elaborate, vide No. 70, ahead.

No. 72. Sumati. (No photo.)

Identification: ? It is an episode from the life of the Buddha.—When the Buddha Dīpaṃkara was residing near King Dīpa's palace, a brahmin student, Sumati, received gifts from the neighbouring king on account of his exceptional acumen in Vedic studies. The gifts were a walking staff, a water bottle, a golden food bowl, a jewelled bedstead, 500 gold coins, and an adorned maiden. The youth graciously accepted the gifts but refused the maiden, who sadly traded her ornaments to a garland maker in return for lotuses being delivered daily to her for her worship activities.

Sumati gave his gifts to his teacher, who accepted all but the 500 coins. Then, he eagerly walked towards the capital, which was getting festooned for the arrival of the Buddha Dīpaṃkara. The king had ordered that all the flowers should be reserved for the Buddha.

Now, the garland maker, left with no flowers for the aforementioned maiden, gave her seven blue lotuses from his own pond. Hiding the lotuses in a jug, the maiden came across Sumati, who, unable to get any flowers, announced that he was willing to give away his 500 coins for a bunch. Initially resentful, the maiden decided to give five of her flowers to him when she learnt that he was going to offer them to the Buddha, on the condition that he would include her wish to be his wife for all further births in his prayers. As the Buddha approached the city, King Dīpa along with kings from neighbouring kingdoms and their entourage, escorted the Buddha to the gates where a huge crowd surged to welcome him. Suddenly, a downpour set in, driving the crowds away, and Sumati, who was unable earlier to get near, threw his five lotuses towards the Buddha. Miraculously, the flowers formed an aureole round the Buddha's head; while the two flowers of the maiden formed a canopy over his ears.

Sumati kowtowed, fanning out his hair, so that the Buddha could walk on it thus avoiding the sludge left in the aftermath of the sharp shower. Sumati pronounced his wish to become a Buddha someday. The Buddha stepped on his tresses, enraging Sumati's co-student, Mati. Buddha promised Sumati that he would be reborn as Buddha Śākyamuni, hearing which Sumati flew up to the skies. People witness to this miraculous event prayed to be the disciples of Buddha Śākyamuni. The smitten maiden, who wished to be Sumati's wife in all subsequent lives, became the disciple of the Buddha in his last birth.

No. 83. Mahāsamāja.

Identification: Foucher (1921, narrative no. 61). It is an episode from the life of the Buddha. For the legend, see Cave 16, No. 82.

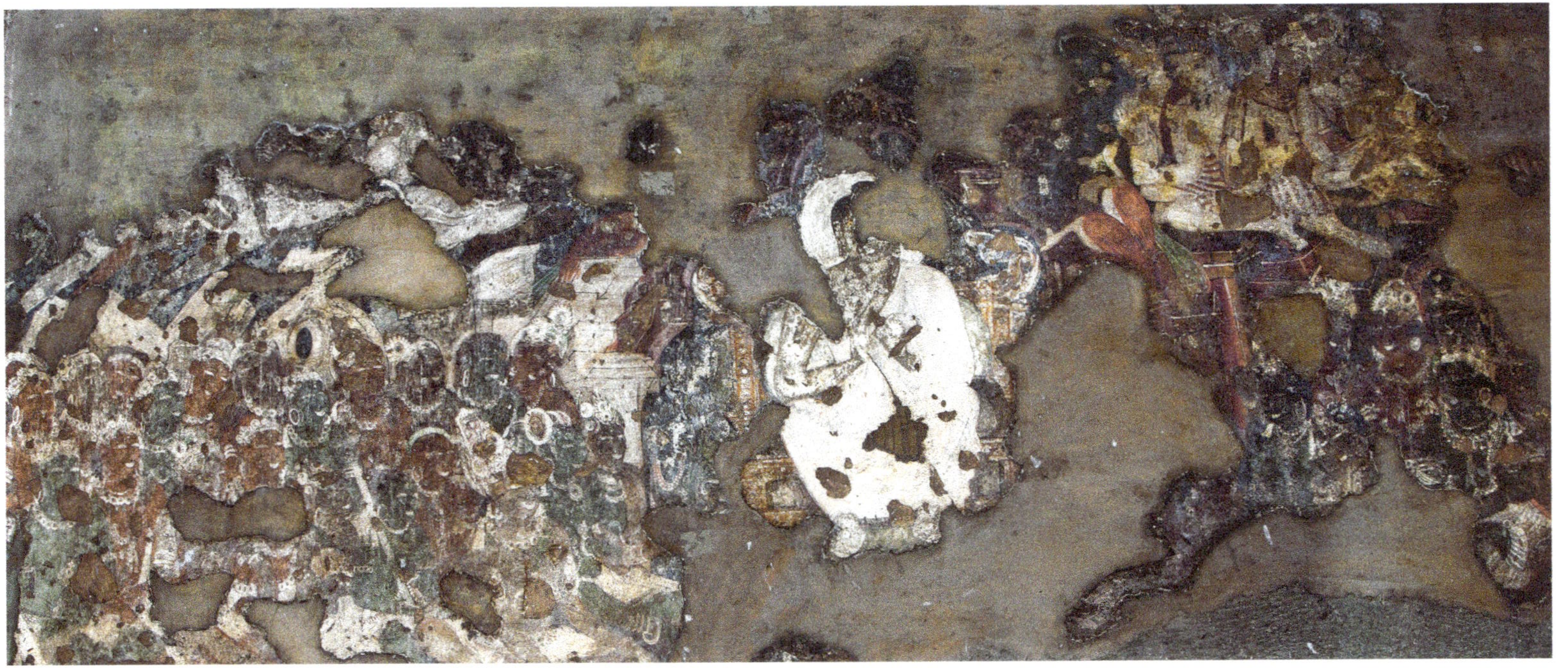

No. 83. ***The Mahāsamāja narrative.*** *Porch, right wall.*

No. 78. Indrabrāhmaṇa.

Identification: Schlingloff 2013.—Indra was very proud of his stature and beauty and was curious to know if the Buddha could surpass him. He attempted to measure the Buddha's stature but was not successful; despite climbing high on a pedestal he could not see the Buddha's head. The Buddha then explained that no one could look down at him, even from the peak of Mount Meru. And if he wanted to measure the Buddha's stature, he could do so with the help of a sacrificial stake buried beneath his fire altar. Indra found the stake and, converted by the Buddha's omniscience, became an ardent follower. Then, taking the sandalwood stake, he measured the Buddha's height. The brahmans and the rest resolved to hold a festival for goodness and blessings for all future generations.

No. 49. Śibi.

Identification: Burgess (1879, p. 75 f.). It is an episode from the life of the Buddha.—King Śibi was renowned for extreme generosity. He provided for all needy persons even if they were from faraway places, having built donation halls in his palace. One day,

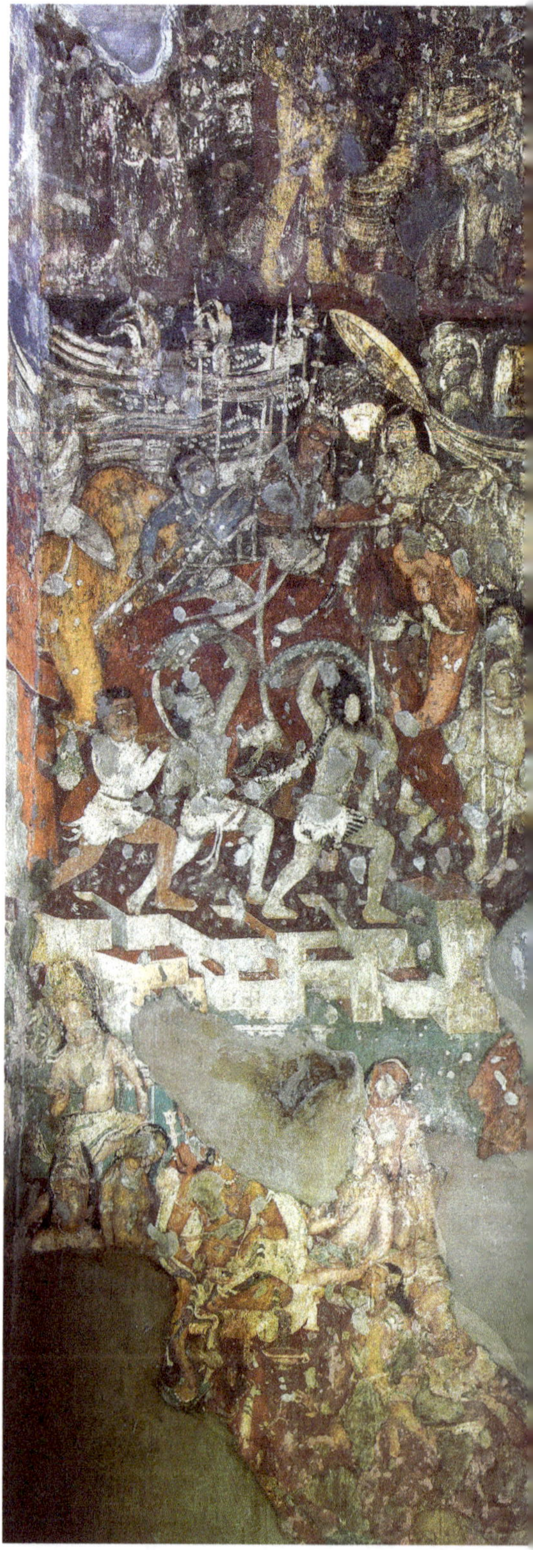

No. 78. Upper part: *the legend of Indra as a brāhmaṇa measuring the greatness of the Buddha.*

No. 49. Middle and lower parts: *the legend of King Śibi.*

Hall, front aisle, right wall.

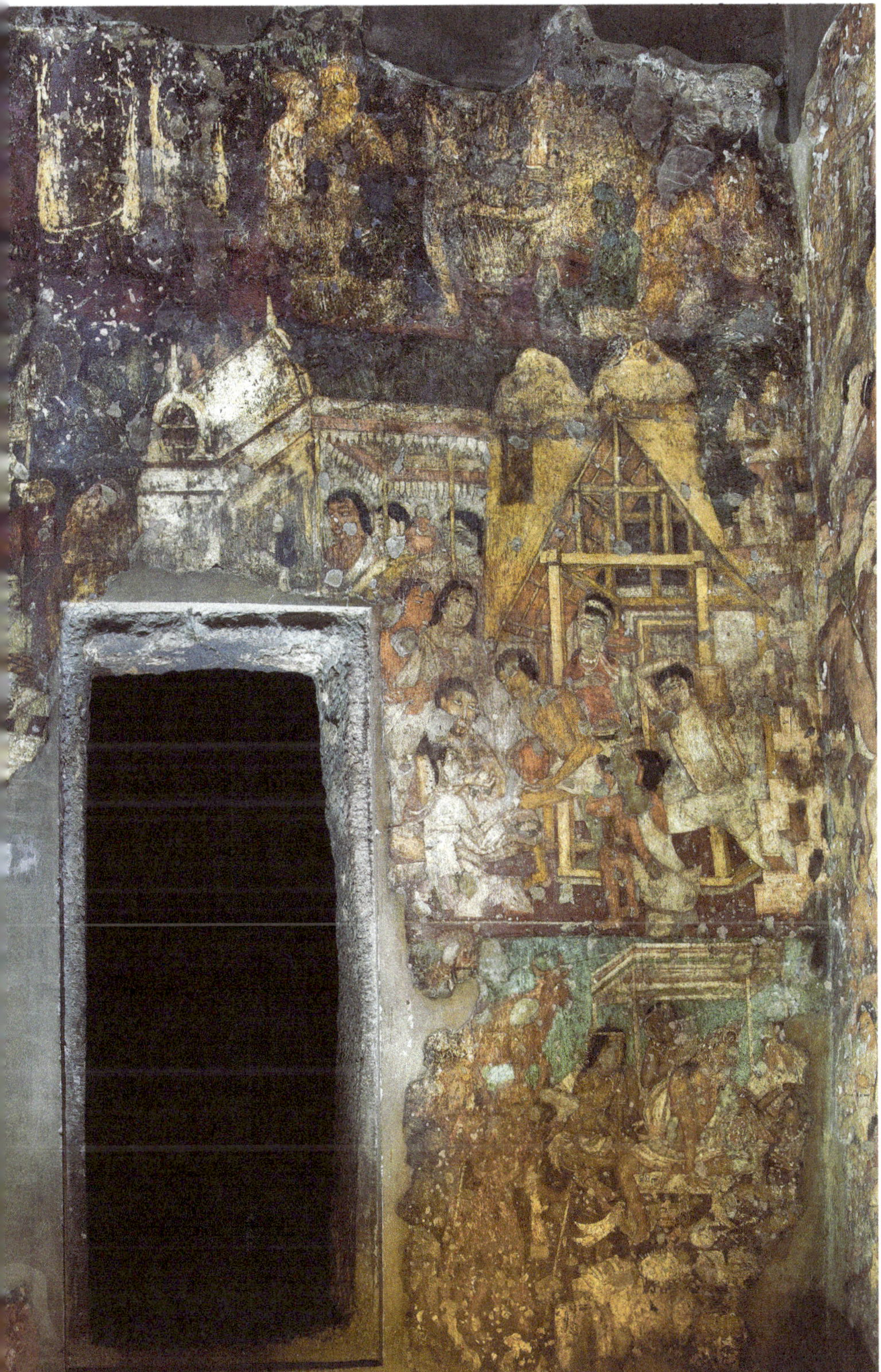

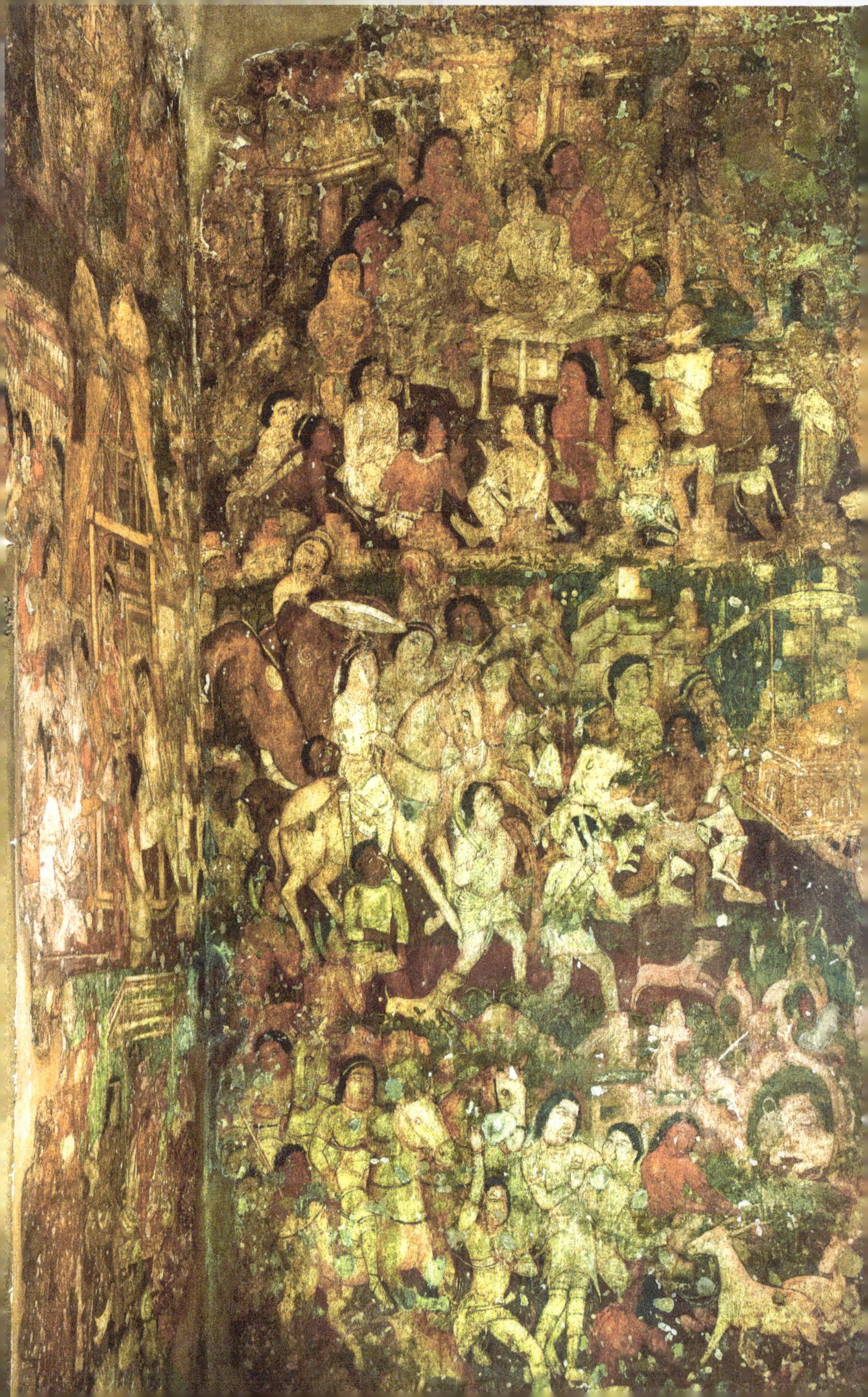

the king observed that few people were interested in material gifts as the needs of the people were so fulfilled that they did not need any more. King Śibi then proclaimed that he would give anything to the needy, even his body parts. The heavens shook over the proclamation. God Indra decided to test the word of King Śibi. So, at one such grand donation, among carts full of supplies and trunks full of jewels and precious stones, Indra came disguised as a blind beggar. He begged for an eye of the king. Amid frantic protests from his horrified subjects, the king had, not one, but both of his eyes, removed and fitted them into the beggar's sockets.

Time went by. As the blind king relaxed by a lotus pond outside the city gates, Indra appeared and offered to grant him a boon. The king wished to die as he was now deprived of the pleasure of seeing the faces of his people who were satisfied with his donations. Indra inquired if the king still experienced pleasure in giving, and the king told him that the voices of the needy were the dearest to him. On this pronouncement, sight returned to one of his eyes. In the next spell, he pronounced that he had felt immense joy when he donated both his eyes. In a trice, he could see with his other eye as well. The universe shook at the significance of the event and the gods came down from all directions to heap praises on the king. The king was welcomed to the city amid great pomp and splendour.

No. 18. Opposite. *The legend of a* rúru *(stag). Hall, front wall.*

No. 18. Rúru.

Identification: Oldenburg (1895, narrative no. 2). For the legend, see Cave 2, No. 16.

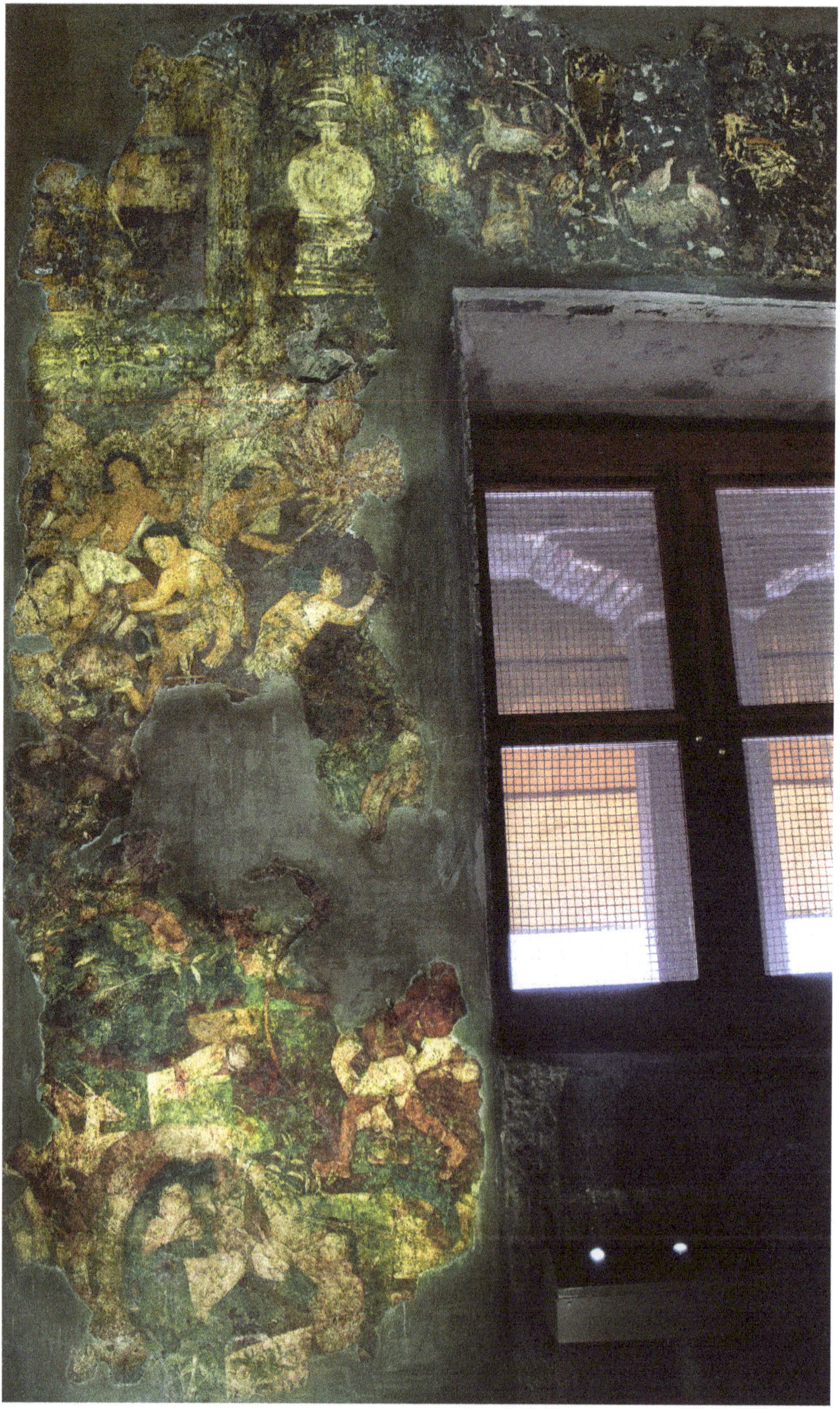

No. 23. Ṛkṣa.

No. 23. Opposite. *The legend of a* ṛkṣa *(bear). Hall, front wall.*

Identification: episode 2 by Lalou (1925, p. 335 f.); other episodes Schlingloff 2013 (?)—A poor woodcutter was caught in a storm while on his way to work. Shivering with cold, he took refuge in a mountain cave, where he came across a bear. He was terrified, but was soothed by the bear, who gave him warmth and food to sustain himself during the week-long tempest. The woodcutter thanked him. The bear just requested him not to betray him. On his way back, the woodcutter met a hunter friend and shared his experience with him. The hunter coaxed him to disclose the whereabouts of the bear, and promised him double the share of his bear-meat. The woodcutter, hesitant at first, ultimately gave into temptation and took him to the cave. The hunter burned a big fire in front of the cave. The bear perished in the smoke. The hunters then cut the meat into their respective shares. As the traitor was about to take his share, his hands fell off, seeing which the hunter ran in alarm. Reports of the incidence reached the king. A Buddhist monk recognised the bear as a Bodhisattva. The king cremated the bear on a pyre of precious wood. A stūpa was also erected.

No. 19. Mṛga.

No. 19.1. *The legend of a* mṛga *(deer). Hall, front wall.*

Identification: Foucher (1921, narrative no. 9).—There lived a

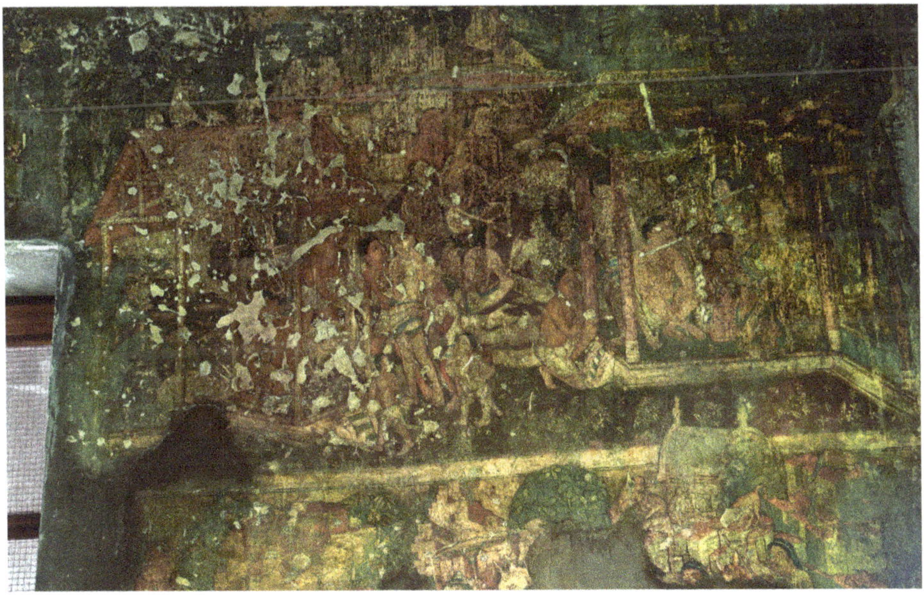

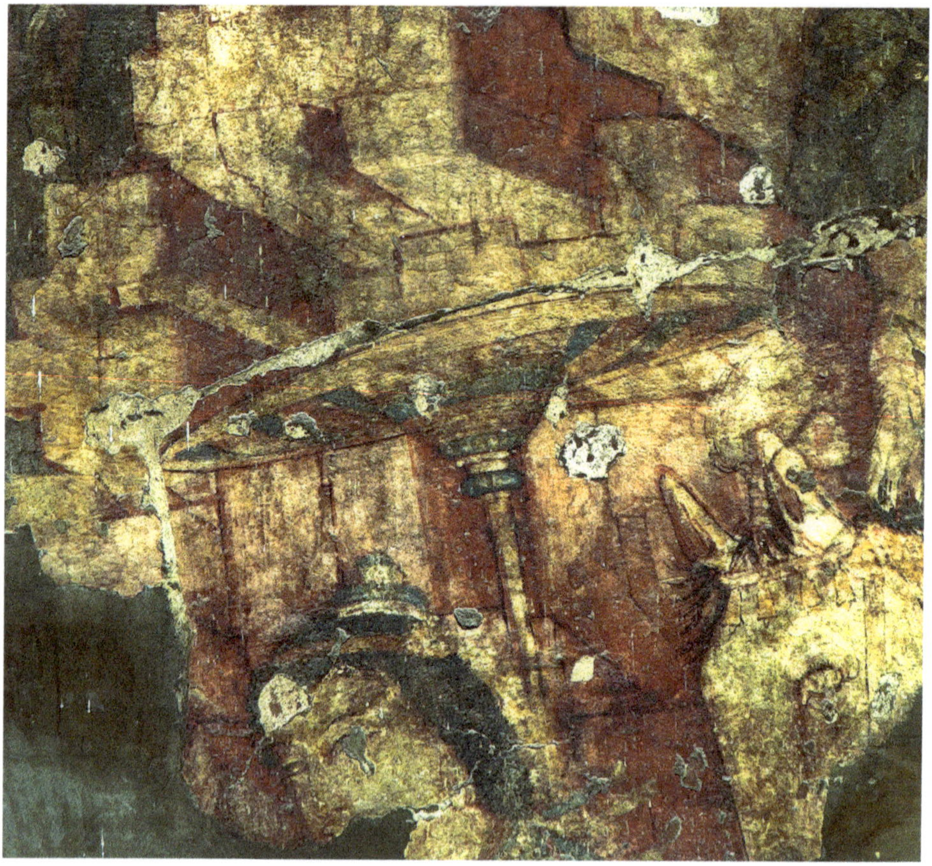

No. 19.2. *Detail of an umbrella from the Mṛga narrative showing the painter's knowledge of retinal perspective*

king of the *mṛgas* (antelopes) with his herd in a Himalayan forest. One day, in a battle with the king of that country, his herd and a few neighbouring herds were encircled and could not escape. In order to prevent a mass slaughter, the antelope king visited the king and struck a deal; an antelope would be sent daily to the royal kitchen, with each herd taking turns. After a while, the head of the second herd selected a pregnant antelope for the king, in spite her request to be spared ill the birth of her child. The pregnant one thus went to the antelope king with her plea. As he considered it unfair to place a substitute from his own herd out of turn, he presented himself at the royal kitchen. The cook, recognising him, reported it to the king. The king, amazed, himself went and asked him whether his herd had already perished, to which the antelope king reverted the plea of the pregnant antelope. The king was so stirred that he banned antelope hunting in his kingdom and gave a lifetime assurance to all antelopes.—The antelope king was none other than the Buddha in a former existence.

No. 28. Ṣaḍdanta.

Identification: Foucher (1911, p. 234).—There lived an elephant called Ṣaḍdanta (Six-tusked), the king of a herd, in the Vindhya ranges. One day, a beautiful lotus fell from a flying nymph at the elephant's feet, which he offered to his second wife, who appeared before him first. The first wife flew into a jealous rage and left her husband. Out of her mind with envy, she wandered and came across a Pratyekabuddha. She offered him a flower to ensure a good rebirth and jumped off a rock to her death. Born as a queen, she pretended to have an ailment that could only be cured with the tusk paste of a six-tusked elephant.

The king found a hunter, and the queen advised him to disguise himself as a monk and go on the expedition. As he reached the Vindhyas, he was caught by the elephant herd, but the elephant king asked them to calm down as a human in a monk's robe was supposed to be harmless. The hunter shot a poisonous arrow at the elephant's forehead, who in turn protected him from the herd's attack. The elephant swore love for his murderer, and uttered a wish that the virtue of his truth may neutralise the arrow's poison. No sooner had he uttered the spell, the lethal venom receded. The hunter, having seen this, threw himself at his feet and narrated the motive behind the shot. The elephant, using his trunk, pulled out

No. 28. *The legend of Ṣaḍdanta (six tusked elephant). Hall, front wall, left side.*

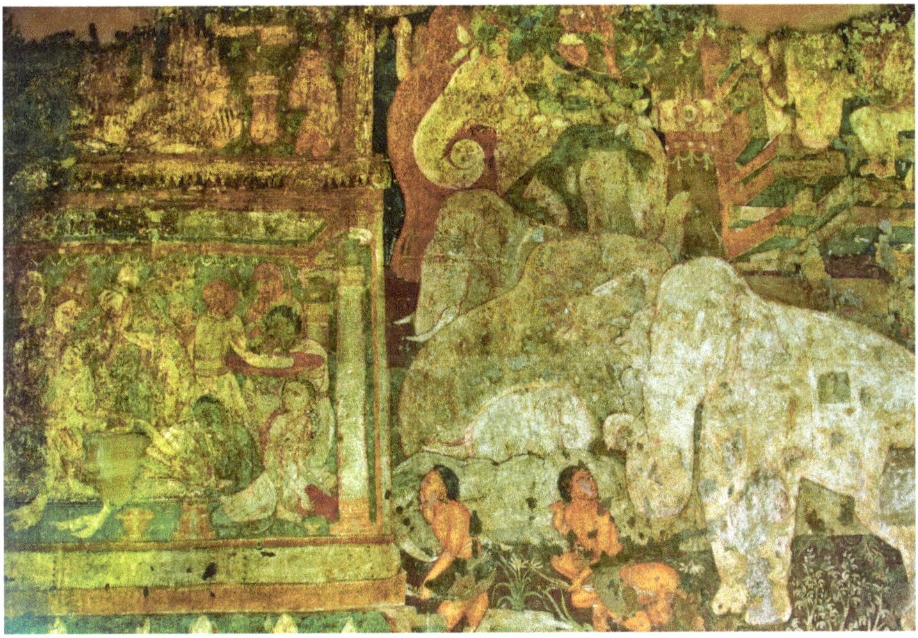

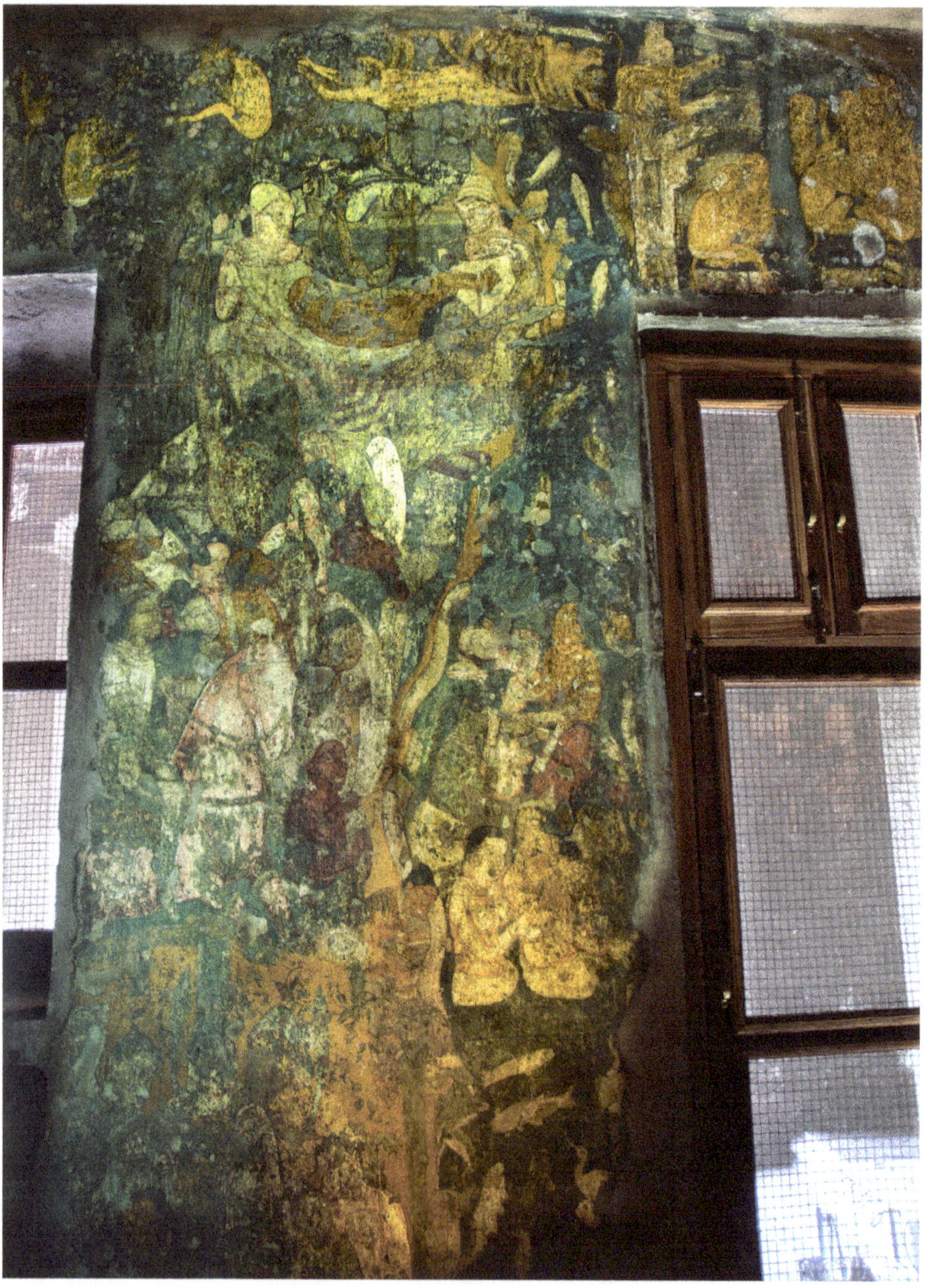

No. 31. *The legend of Mahākapi (the Great Monkey). Hall, front wall, left side.*

his tusks and gave them to the hunter. The power of his oath healed the wound and the new tusks grew back. The hunter took the tusks to the queen. On seeing the tusks, she felt great remorse for her actions and confessed her motives to the king. The hunter calmed her down, telling her about the miraculous healing.—Ṣaḍdanta, the elephant king, was none other than the Buddha in a former existence.

No. 31. Mahākapi.

Identification: Foucher (1921, narrative no. 5).—There lived a Great Monkey ('Mahākapi') with his herd on a fig tree, beside a river in the Himalayas. Once, a ripe fig from the tree fell into the river, where a king with his female attendants was bathing downstream. The king ate the fig and loved its taste and flavour. He had his men search the fig tree and found that it was full of monkeys. He ordered the tree to be vacated by shooting the monkeys. The great monkey, the only one capable of jumping across the stream, leapt across and tied a creeper to his feet. Then he jumped back so that a creeper bridge could be slung across, allowing his herd to escape. The creeper, however, fell short by a body length. So the great monkey selflessly used his body to complete the bridge, letting the others jump on his back, which they had to do to cross the stream. The king was amazed at the way he bore his pain to save his herd. He arranged for a safety net below the monkey and ordered his men to shoot through the creeper at his legs and also at the branch of the tree. The monkey fell down in the safety net, almost unconscious. The king had his wounds treated and treated him with honour and respect. Once recovered, the monkey instructed the king on a ruler's duty towards his subjects.—Mahākapi, the monkey king, was none other than the Buddha in a former existence.

No. 26. Hastin.

Identification: Foucher (1921, narrative no. 22).—Once a group of travellers were lost in a forest, tired and exhausted to death. They met an elephant (*hastin*) and pleaded with him for help. The elephant, knowing that they would not find food in the oasis, directed them to a rock-bed, where they could find water and a dead elephant's body. The men went to the place directed by the elephant and found a dead elephant near the water. The travellers realised that the dead elephant was none other than the one they met before; he had sacrificed himself for them. The travellers cremated the elephant with due respect. They concluded that they should not reject his sacrifice and appeased their hunger and refilled their provisions. They made water containers out of

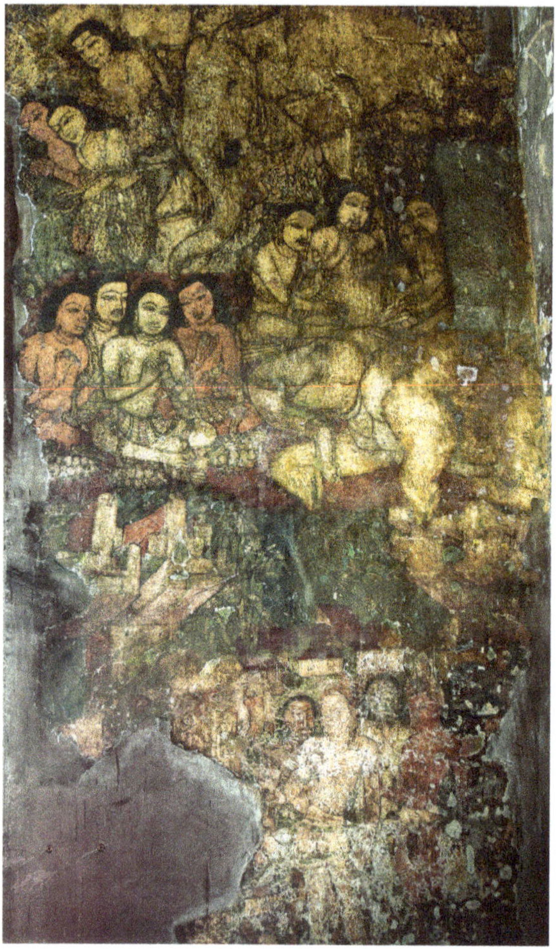

No. 26. *The legend of a* hastin *(elephant). Hall, front wall, left side.*

the skins, filled them with water, and were able to cross the desert.—The elephant was none other than the Buddha in a former existence.

No. 35. Bodhi.

Identification: Schlingloff (1986, p. 305 f.).—A brahman, named Bodhi, and his beautiful wife, lived in the seclusion of a forest, leading an ascetic life. Once, the king of the land came across them and started lusting after the brahman's wife. After assurances that the brahman would not curse him, the king had the wife taken away to his palace. The king was surprised at the calm reaction of the brahman, as the latter advised him to rein his natural instincts. The brahman's tranquillity had its effect, the king was filled with remorse and he returned the lady back to her husband and begged for his forgiveness.—The brahman ascetic Bodhi was none other than the Buddha in a former existence.

No. 48. Sarvadada.

Identification: Schlingloff (1986, p. 305–308).—A king, titled *Sarvadada* (Giving Everything) for his generosity, once went to his audience hall to address his subjects' welfare. Just then a scared pigeon flew in pleading for life. The king promised to grant him security. The pigeon had escaped a bird-catcher, who was actually Lord Indra in disguise. The bird-catcher asked the king for his rightful catch, since his family would starve without the pigeon's meat. To do justice to both the hunter and the pigeon, the king

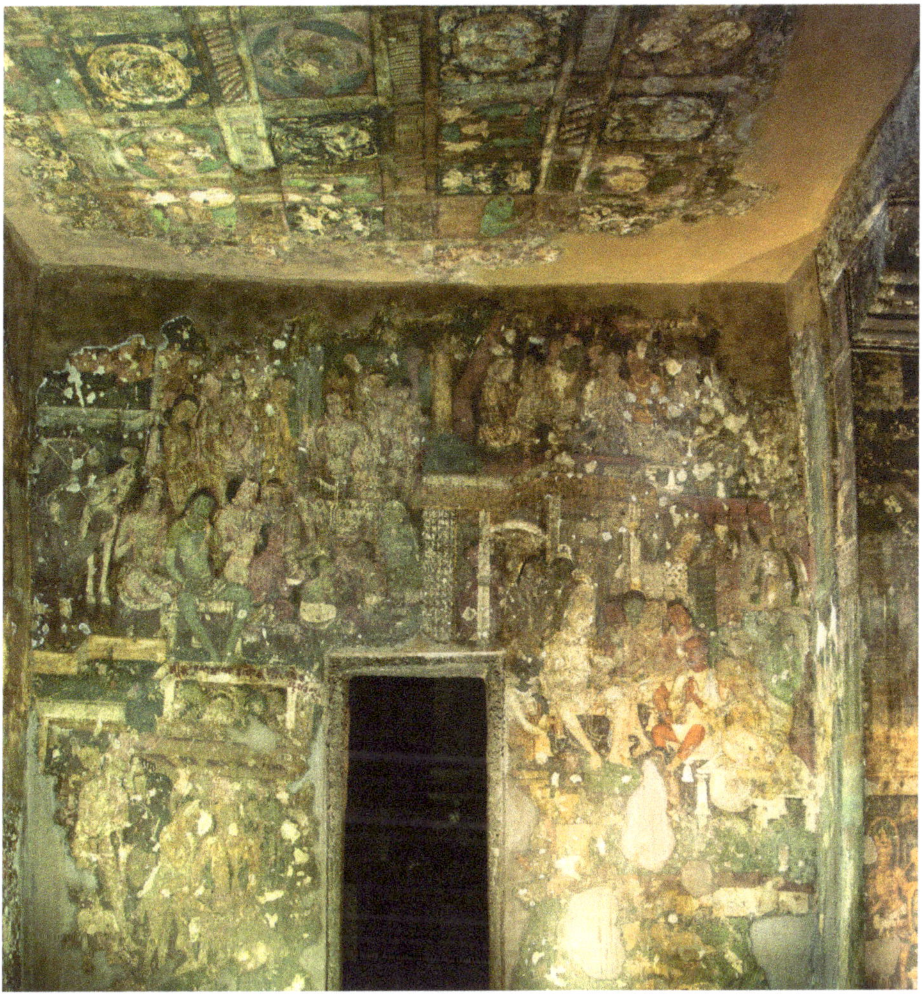

decided to give his own flesh as compensation. He had a balance brought in and cut flesh from his thigh which was equal to the pigeon's body weight. The pigeon, however, kept getting heavier and the king too kept adding his flesh, till finally he himself stepped on the balance. Questioned by Indra, the king made a truth spell. He said he did not sacrifice for his own good but for the good of all beings. By the power of this spell, the king was restored to his previous health.—King Sarvadada was none other than the Buddha in a former existence.

No. 35. Upper left: *the legend of a brahman named* ***Bodhi***.

No. 48. Lower left: *the legend of a king named* ***Sarvadada***.

No. 14.1. Right, vertical half: *the legend of a* haṃsa *(goose)*.

Hall, front aisle, left wall.

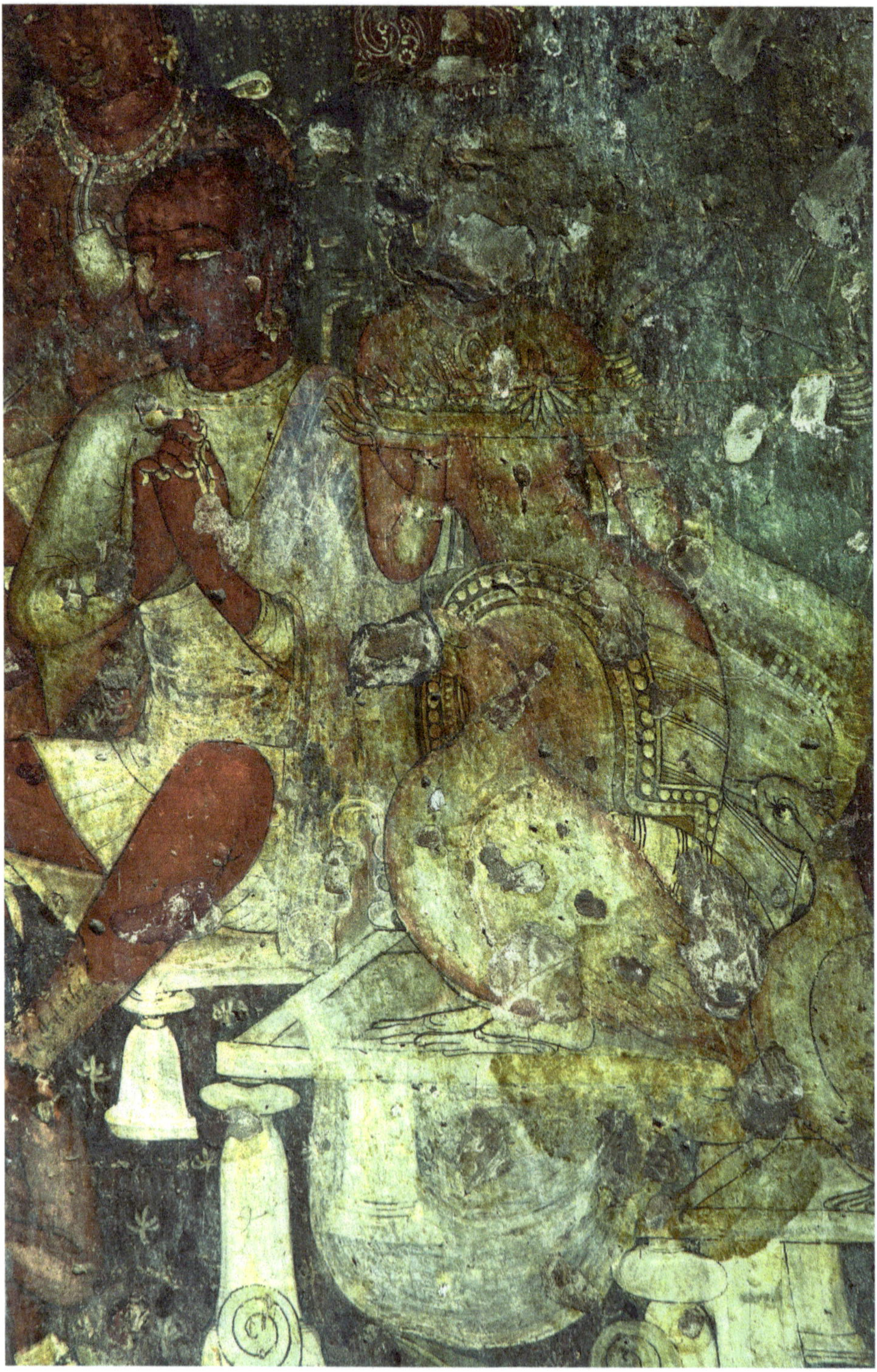

No. 14.2. Haṃsa *(Goose). Detail from previous photo. The goose seated on a throne is giving a sermon to the kings on the merits of loyalty.*

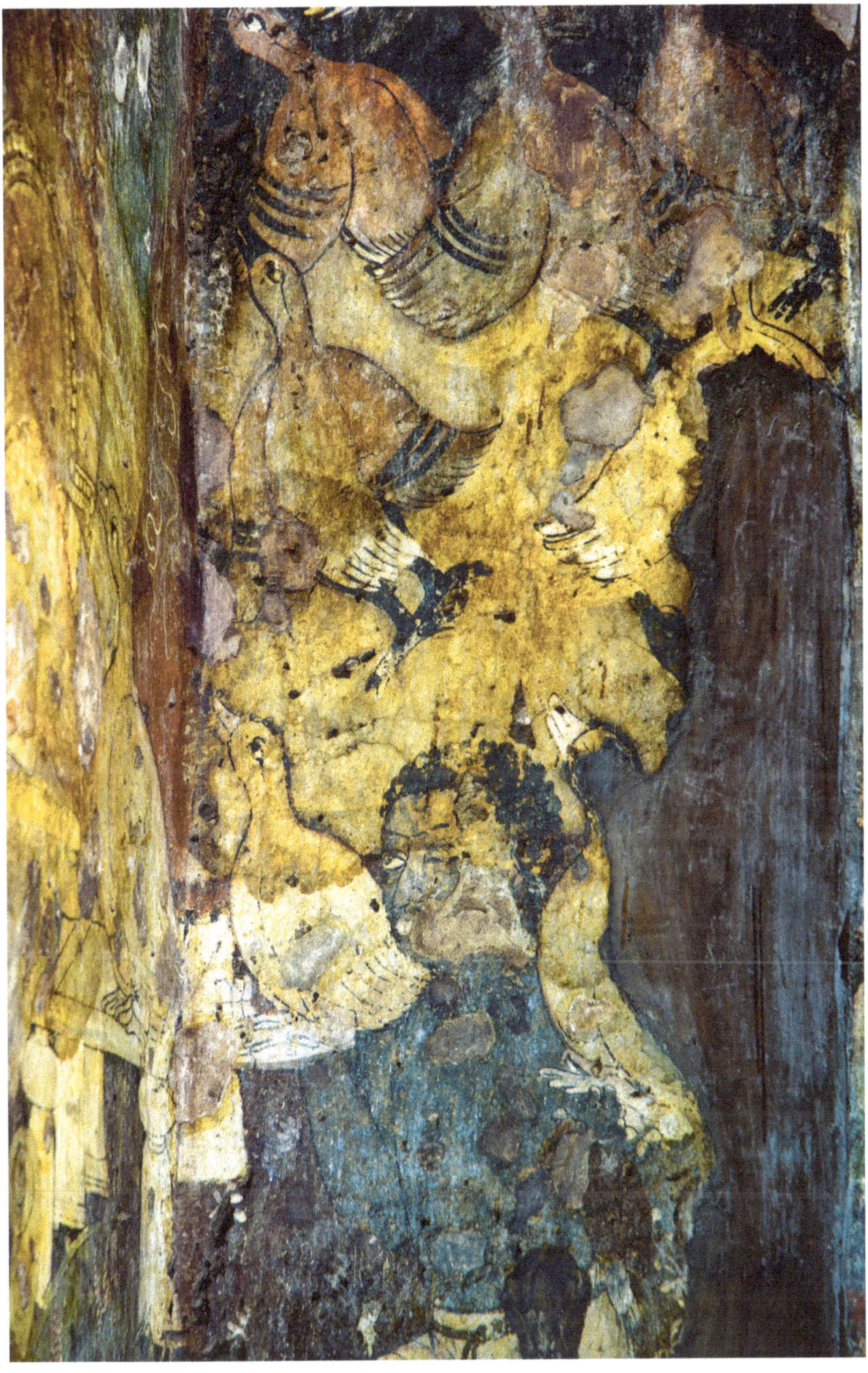

No. 14.3. *Haṃsa. Detail of the bird catcher carrying the two* haṃsas *(geese) on his shoulders.*

No. 14. Haṃsa.

Identification: Oldenburg (1895, narrative no. 5). For the story, vide Cave 2, No. 13.

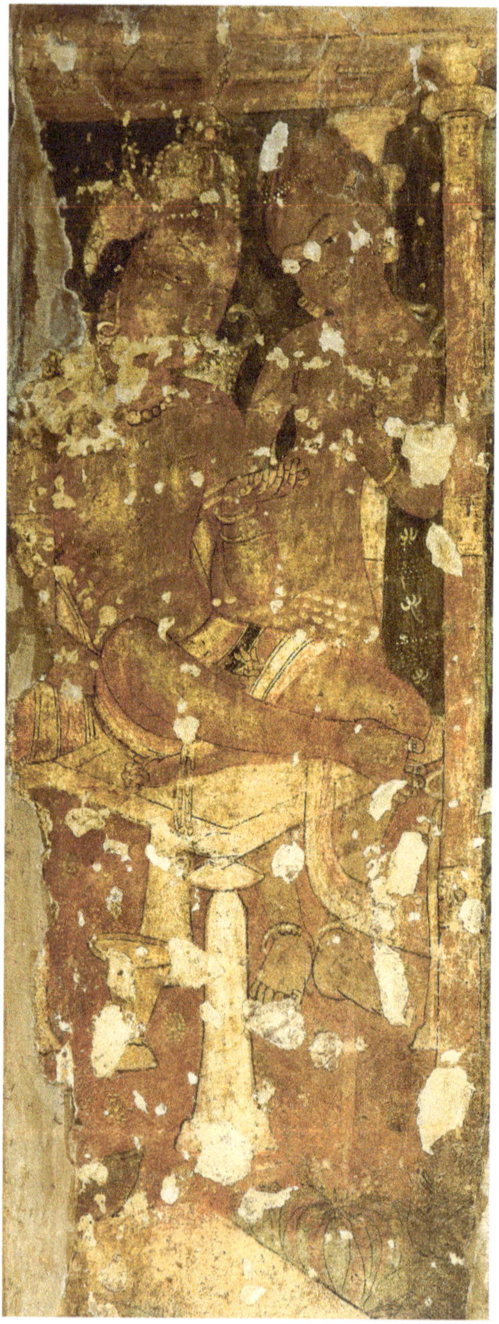

No. 43.2. *Scene 2. Prince Viśvantara in his palace is thinking about the citizens who have issued a warrant of his banishment from the kingdom due to his extreme generosity.*

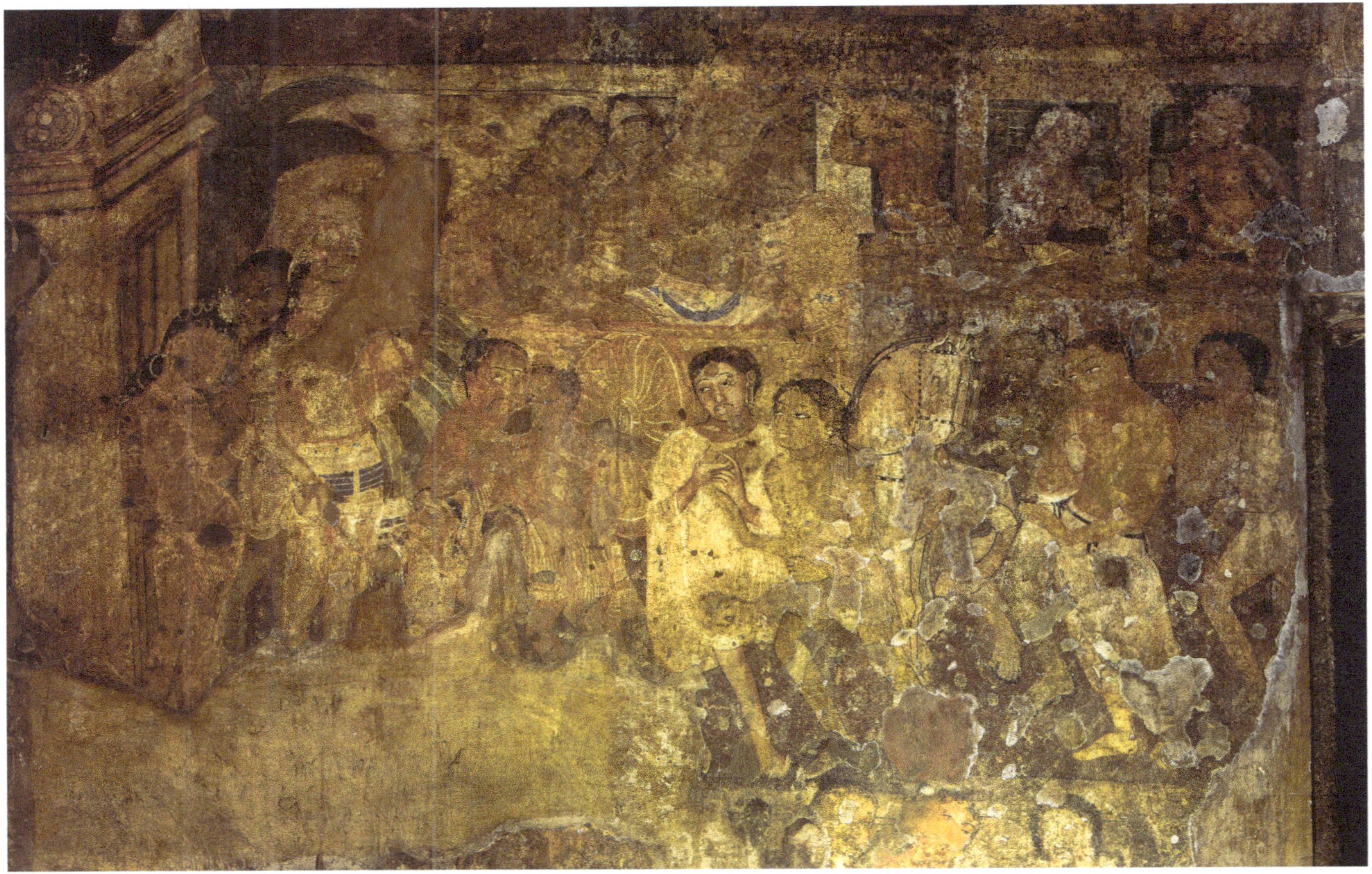

No. 43.1. *Scene 6. Outside the palace gates, prince Viśvantara riding a chariot with his wife and children is bidding farewell to the citizens.*

No. 43. Viśvantara.

Identification: Oldenburg (1895, narrative no. 6). For the story, see Cave 16, No. 42.

No. 63. Indra.

Identification: Schlingloff (1973, p. 196–203).—Once, the *asuras* (demons) attacked Indra, the king of gods, because they begrudged

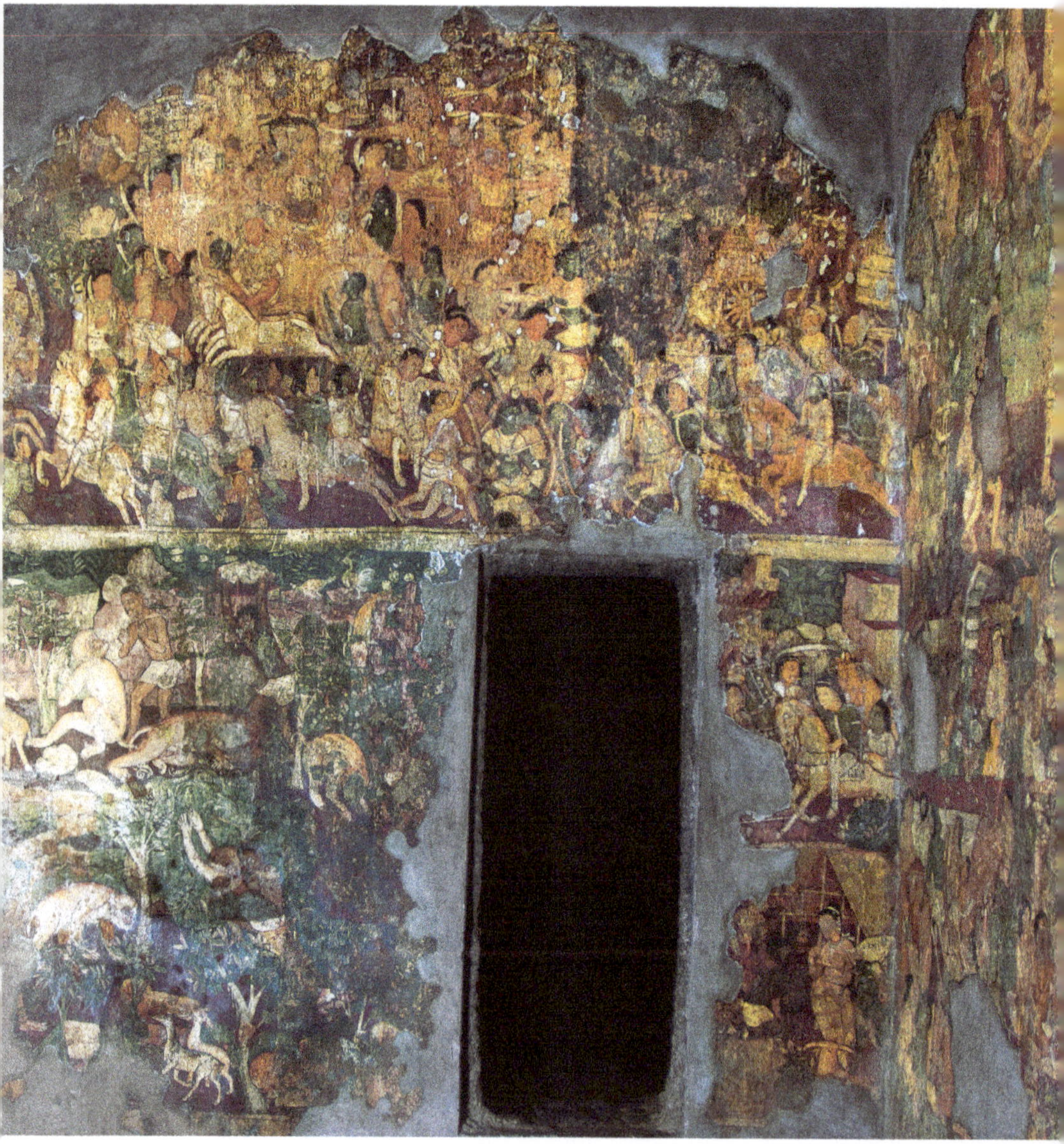

No. 63. Upper half: *battle of Indra*

No. 29. Lower half: *the legend of a* vānara *(monkey)*

Hall, rear aisle, left wall.

him his power and glory. So, Indra had to battle them with an army of chariots, elephants, cavalry, and infantry. The battle began on the shores of the ocean of heaven. After heavy fighting, the gods were defeated and were forced to flee while Indra alone shielded his side from the chariot, till finally his charioteer turned to follow his retreating troops. Suddenly, Indra realised that his flying chariot was fast approaching a silk cotton tree with a nest of young *garuḍas*. Indra immediately ordered his chariot to be turned, risking death in hands of the enemies rather than letting innocent creatures die. The sudden volte-face alarmed the *asuras* and the resultant confusion prompted their summary defeat. Indra's warriors also surged forward and celebrated the victory of their king.—Indra, the king of the Gods, was none other than the Buddha in a former existence.

No. 29. Vānara.

Identification: episodes 2 to 7 by Oldenburg (1895, narrative no. 7).—There lived a big monkey in a remote Himalayan area where a peasant lost his way searching for a stray cow. The peasant climbed a Tinduka tree to pick some fruit. The branch broke off and he crashed into a ravine from where he could not get out. After several days, he was found by the monkey, who gave him fruits to eat. Then, after doing some climbing exercises with a load of stones, he lugged the peasant out of the ravine. Exhausted, the monkey lay down to rest and asked the peasant to guard him. The peasant, however, thought that he would need a lot of energy as he had miles to travel to reach home. He reasoned that only a big meaty meal would give him that kind of energy. So he hit the sleeping monkey with a huge stone. The monkey survived the attack, though he was severely injured, and pointed out to the peasant the wantonness of his deed. The monkey then took him through the wild mountains to a settlement. The peasant was struck with leprosy as punishment for his immorality. Scorned everywhere for his loathsome appearance, he wandered around, until one day he met a king, who asked him about his situation. The peasant told the king that he was paying the price for his shameful deed.—The monkey was none other than the Buddha in a former existence.

No. 57. Sutasoma.

Identification: Foucher (1921, narrative no. 20).—King Sudāsa

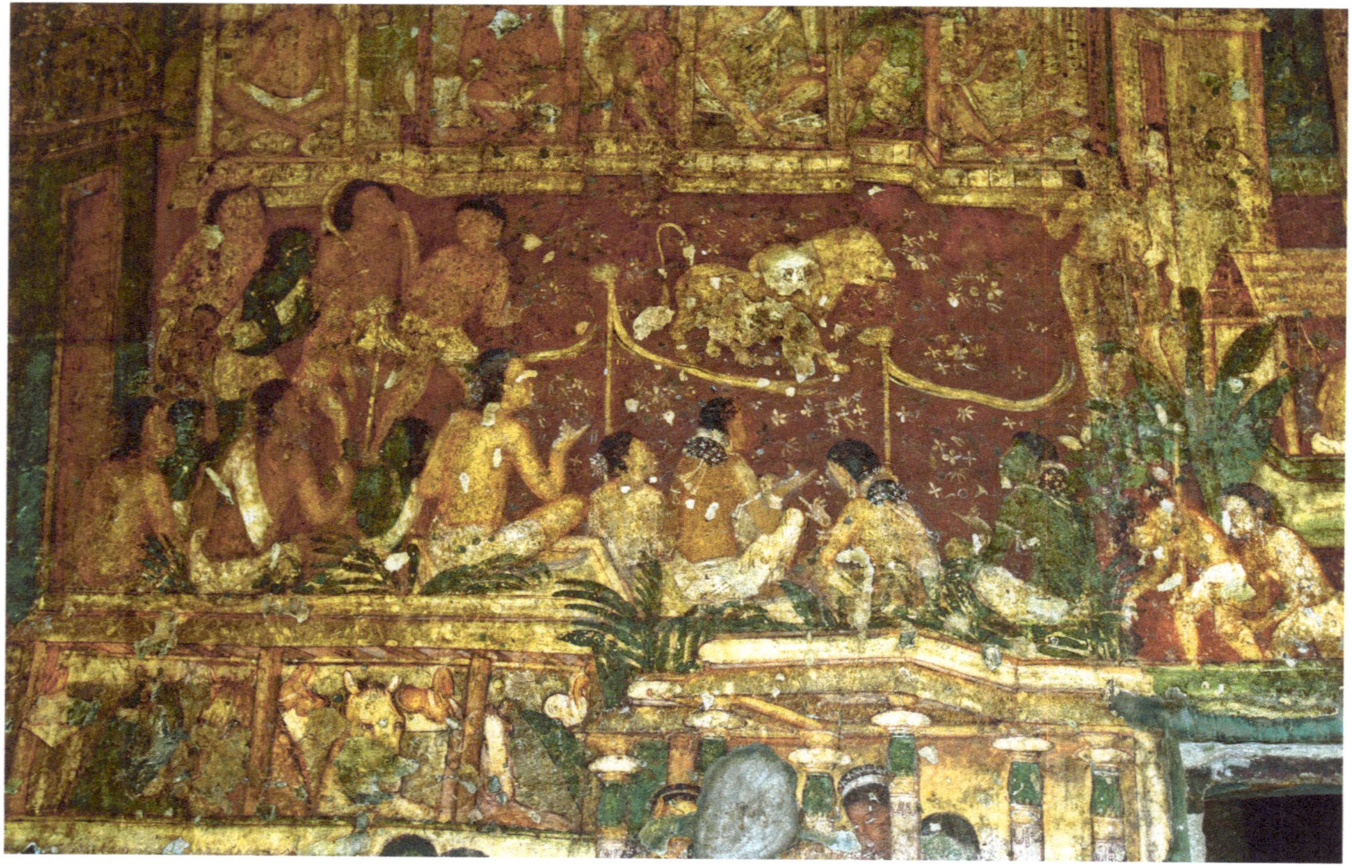

No. 57.1. *Sutasoma, scene 5: The inhabitants of the city gaze in astonishment, as the lioness carries the child, whom she has born to the king, through the main street of the town to the royal palace.* Hall, left of rear wall.

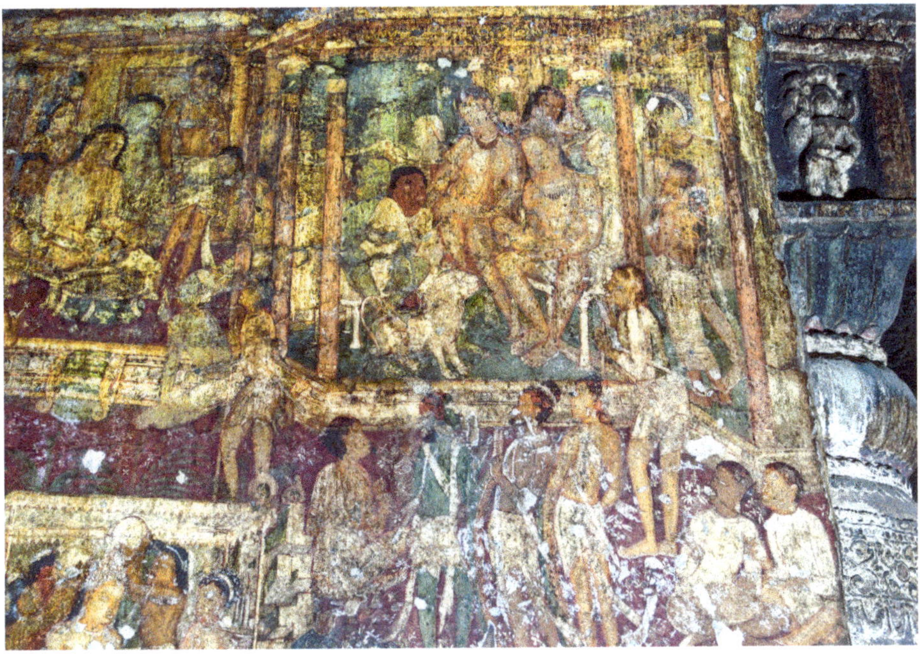

No. 57.2. *Sutasoma, scene 6: The king, who has taken the son born to him by the lioness into his arms, names him Saudāsa and designates him as heir to the throne.* Hall, left of rear wall.

of Banaras got separated from his entourage while on a hunting expedition. As he rested, a lioness in heat approached him. The king understood her predicament and kindly obliged. The lioness became pregnant, gave birth to a child, and brought the child through the main street of the city to the king's palace. The king accepted his son and named him Saudāsa, the successor of his throne, as he had no other offspring. Saudāsa was crowned after his father's death. He appointed the best chefs to prepare meat dishes as he had inherited his great appetite for meat from his mother, the lioness. Once, he got a piece of meat he had not tasted earlier. What had happened was the drunken cook had dozed off and a dog had stolen the meat kept for the king. To cover up his carelessness, the cook served human flesh to the king, who quickly realised that all was not right. He demanded the truth from the cook, who immediately confessed. But the king had developed a taste for human flesh. To keep up the supply, the cook had to secretly kill humans. The citizens' lives were at stake and they requested the king to tighten up their security.

One day the citizens caught the cook red-handed and presented him in the court, where Saudāsa confessed his approval behind the murders. The citizens, in turn, banished the king from the state. When he was staying in the forest, the king was once

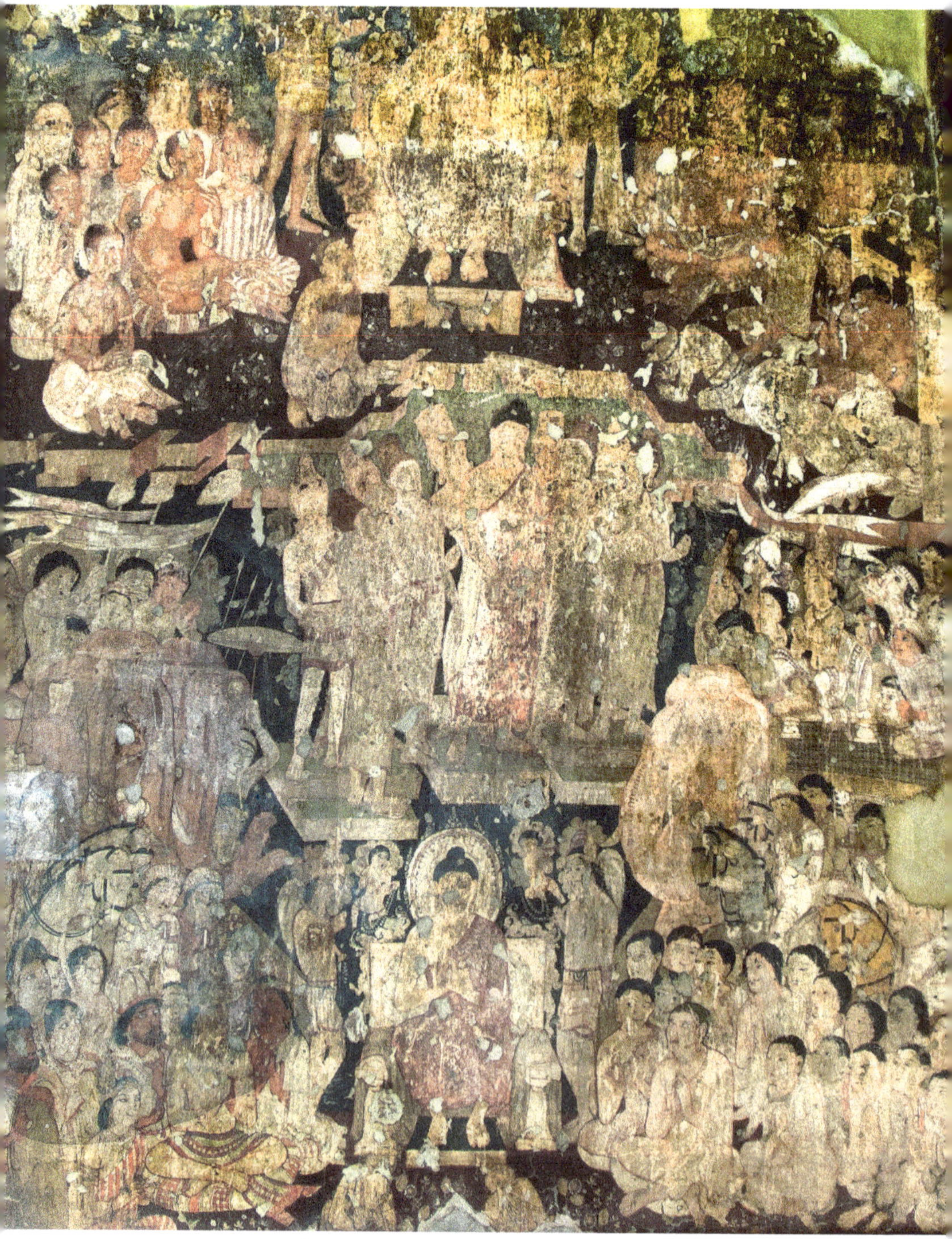

No. 86. *Devāvatāra*. *Hall, shrine antechamber, left wall.*

attacked by armed citizens; but he somehow managed to escape from them by assuming the form of a man-eating demon. He fled to the mountains and became the head of the man-eating demons. They decided to slaughter 500 kings for a luncheon, and they had already captured 499 kings. Saudāsa captured Sutasoma, the king of Indraprastha, when he was bathing in a forest pond. Saudāsa was taken by surprise when he saw Sutasoma weeping, for Sutasoma was famous for courage and bravery. When asked, Sutasoma explained that he was weeping because he had failed to keep his word given to a brahman prior to his bath; he had promised to present the brahman with alms. Saudāsa then released him to fulfil his promise. Thereafter, King Sutasoma paid alms to the brahman and returned to the man-eater. In admiration Saudāsa decided to give up his disastrous man-eating habit on Sutasoma's advice. Even the other kings were set free and Saudāsa returned to Banaras. He managed to win back his royal dignity with the help of Sutasoma.—King Sutasoma was none other than the Buddha in a former existence.

No. 86. Devāvatāra.

Identification: Schlingloff 2013. For the story, vide Cave 16, No. 84.

No. 70. Rāhula.

Identification: Yazdani (IV, 1955, p. 70 f.). The legend is from the life of the Buddha.—Rāhula was born after the Buddha's enlightenment. When the Buddha visited Kapilavastu, Rāhula was six years old and his mother wanted the Buddha to return to the worldly life. So, she made a dumpling with a sorceress's help, which could enthral the one who ate it and bind him to one who offered it. She instructed her son to offer it to the Buddha. As Rāhula approached, the Buddha aware of the spell magically multiplied into 500 identical Buddhas. Rāhula identified his father among the apparitions and offered him the dumpling. The Buddha, aware of the spell, offered Rāhula the dumpling rather than have it himself. Rāhula, thus, could not be restrained from following his father and became a monk.

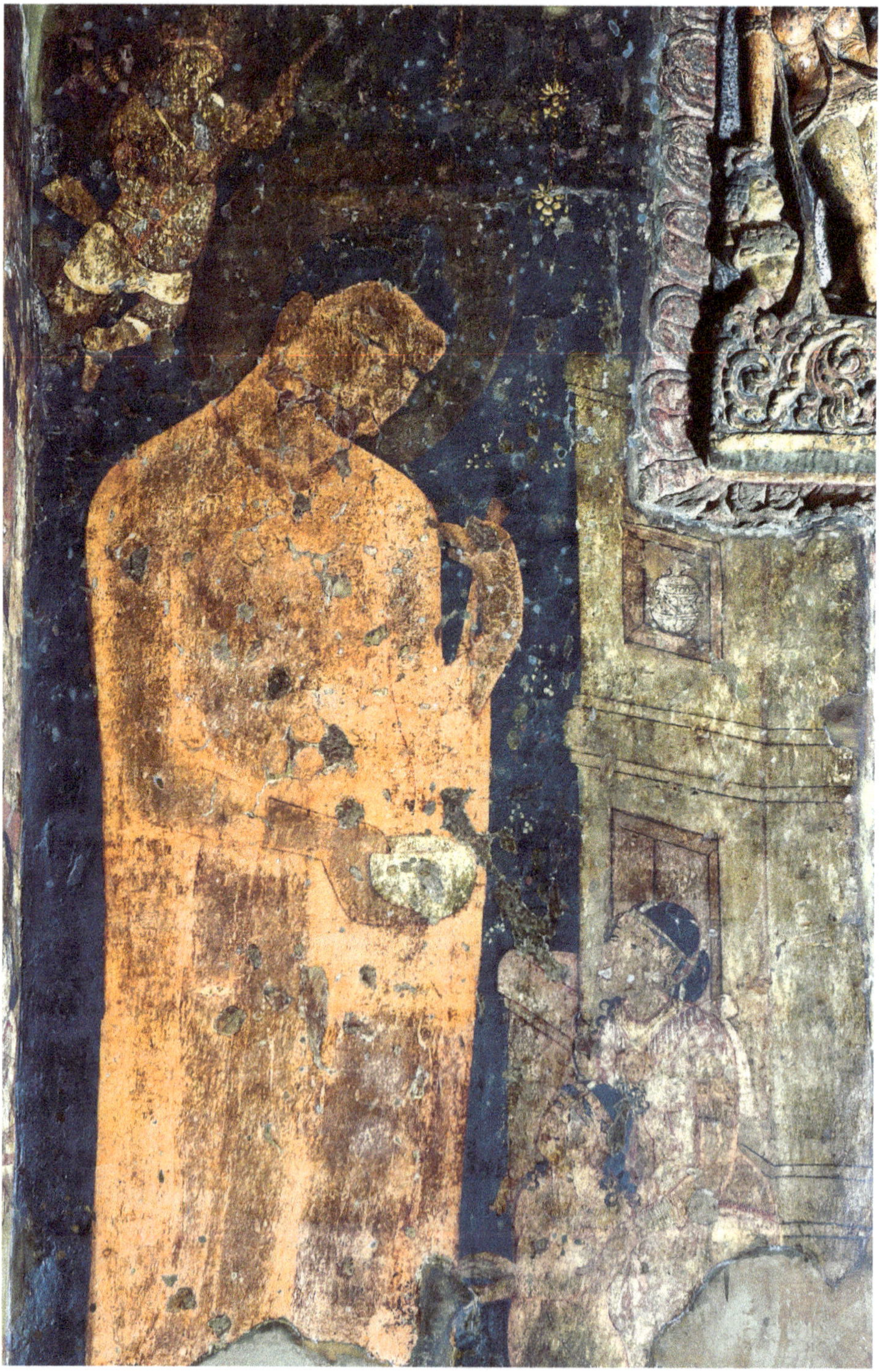

No. 70. ***Rahula's ordination.*** *Shrine antechamber, left of shrine doorway.*

No. 92.
Mahāprātihārya or the Great Miracle of Śrāvastī. Shrine antechamber, right wall.

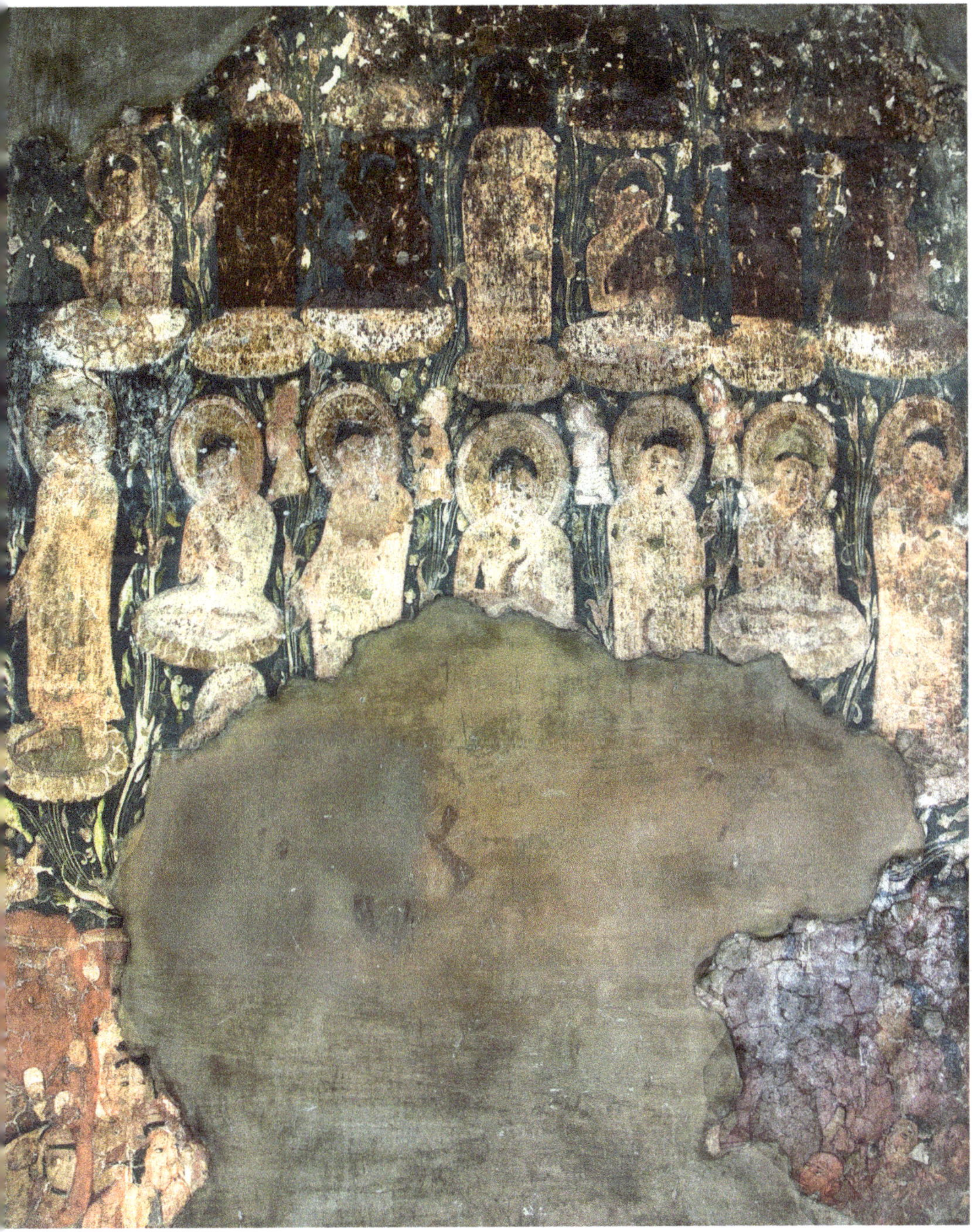

No. 92. Mahāprātihārya.

Identification: Foucher (1921, narrative no. 57). For the story, vide Cave 1, No. 88.

No. 20. Śarabha.

Identification: Foucher (1921, narrative no. 14).—A *śarabha* or *sāmbhara* (ibex or a type of antelope) lived in a remote forest. He was chased by a king, who had separated from his retinue. Fearing for his life, the ibex jumped across a wide crevice. The king's horse abruptly halted, throwing the king off his back into the crevice. The ibex, not hearing the sound of the horse's hoofs, turned around and saw the injured king. He promised to help him out. After a few exercises which involved carrying a burden of rocks on his back, he descended and came up with the king on his back, and guided him to the horse. The king, filled with remorse and struck by the ibex's generosity, promised to renounce hunting thenceforth. The king discussed the incident with the royal priest after returning to

No. 20.1. *Legend of a* śarabha *(deer).* Left: *scenes 1–3, while hunting, the king gets separated from the entourage.* Far right: *scenes 4–7, after some practice, the ibex carries the king out on his back from the crevice.* Right of centre: *scene 8, the ibex guides the king back on his horse. Hall, rear wall, right side.*

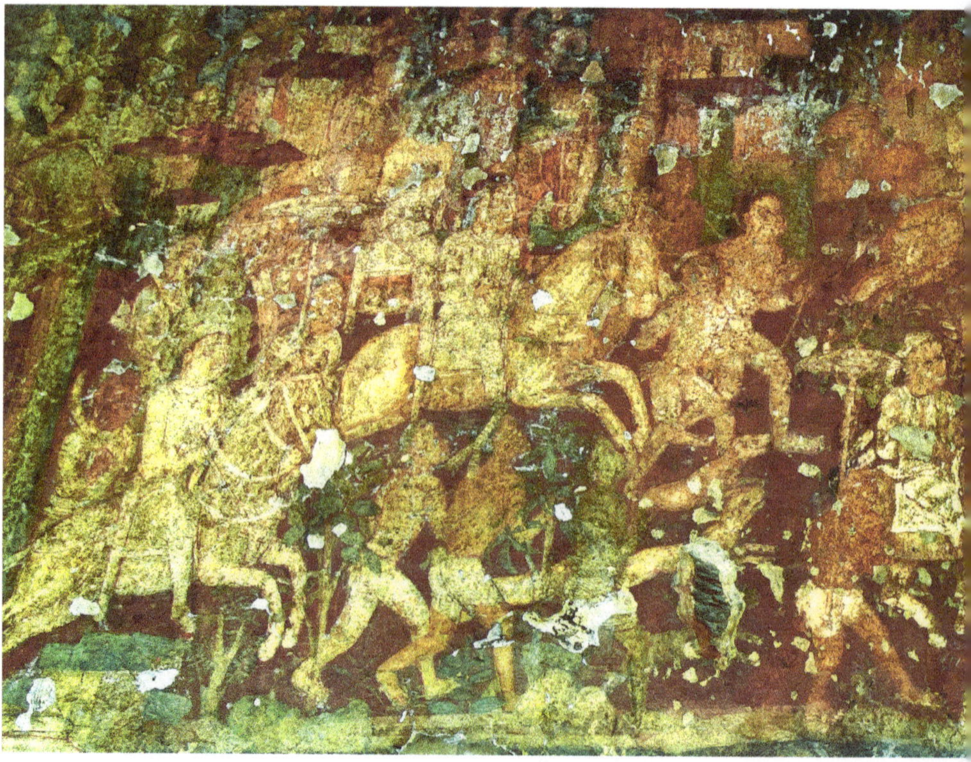

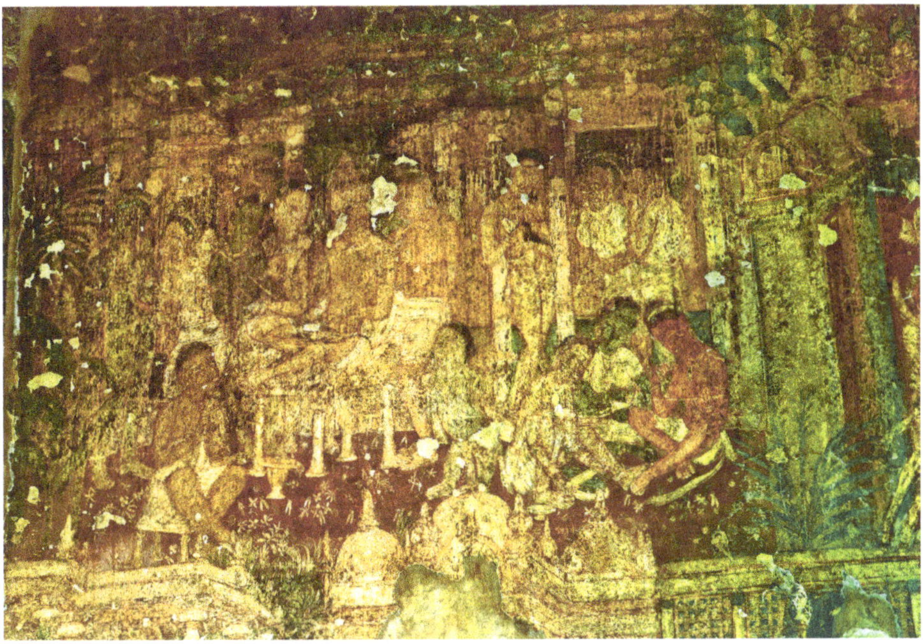

No. 20.2. *Śarabha, scene 9. The king is discussing the event in his palace.* Hall, rear wall, right side.

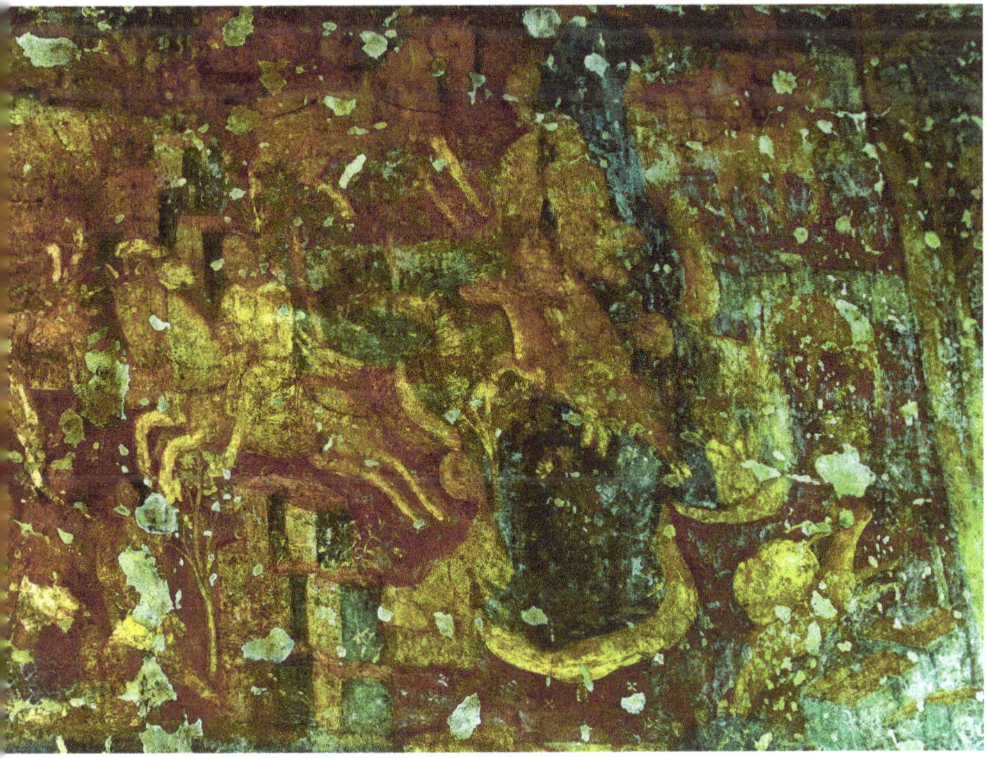

his palace.—The ibex was none other than the Buddha in a former existence.

No. 15. Śaśa. (No photo.)

Identification: Schlingloff (1971, p. 61–67).—In a forest contoured by a rivulet lived a *śaśa* (hare), who had an exemplary demeanour and devout character. He always led by example. An otter, a jackal, and a monkey had a soft spot for him. One evening, the hare pointed out to them that the religious custom of food offerings should be followed on a full moon night. The hare soon realised that his food habits would not allow him to offer any food; instead, in his mind he decided to offer his own body. Heaven and earth were shaken by this thought and the hare even grabbed the attention of Indra, the king of gods, who decided to check him out. So, on the following day, Indra appeared in the forest disguised as a hungry brahman. Mindful of the hare's teachings, the otter offered him seven fishes, the jackal offered a lizard and a pot of curdled milk left by someone; the monkey offered him ripe mangoes and cool water. The hare offered himself and asked the brahman to roast him over a fire, as he could not offer anything else. Indra then ignited a fire, into which the hare flung himself. Filled with admiration, Indra assumed his original form and personally carried the hare to heaven, praising his magnanimity. He immortalised the hare by adorning the gable of his palace, the hall of gods and the disk of the moon with the hare's image, thenceforth named 'The One Bearing the Hare's Mark.'—The hare was none other than the Buddha in a former existence.

No. 27. Mātṛpoṣaka.

Identification: Oldenburg (1895, narrative no. 8).—A hunter told the king about an extraordinarily beautiful elephant he had spotted in the forest. Royal orders were issued to catch the elephant and train him. Hunters caught him and soon presented him to the king, who himself tended to the splendid-looking elephant. Surprisingly however, the elephant starved himself, grieving over his separation from his parents, who were alone in the forest. The king was moved by his filial loyalty and set the elephant free. The elephant trudged back to the forest and found his mother near the lotus pond, blind. He sprayed a trunkful of water over her and

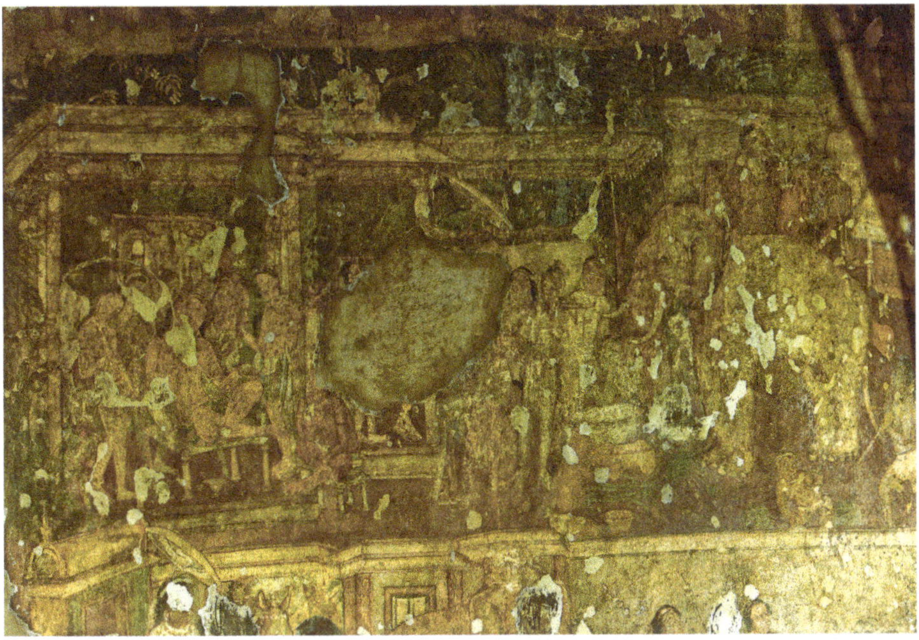

No. 27.1. *The legend of an elephant* mātṛpoṣaka *(the one who takes care of his mother).* Left: *scene 1.* Right: *scene 3. Hall, rear wall, right side.*

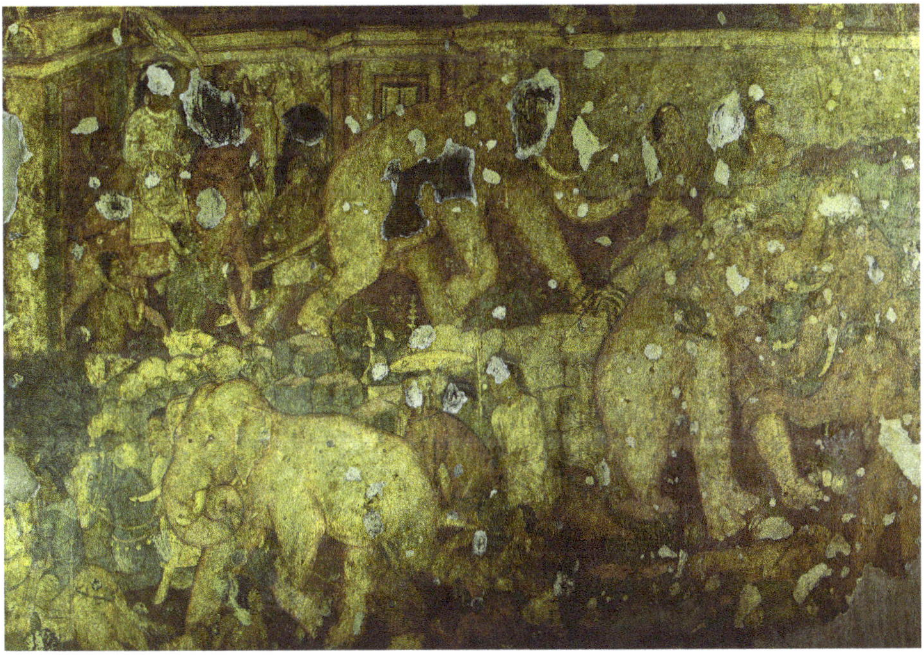

No. 27.2. *Mātṛpoṣaka.* Below left: *scene 2.* Above left: *scene 4.* Right: *scene 5. Hall, rear wall, right side.*

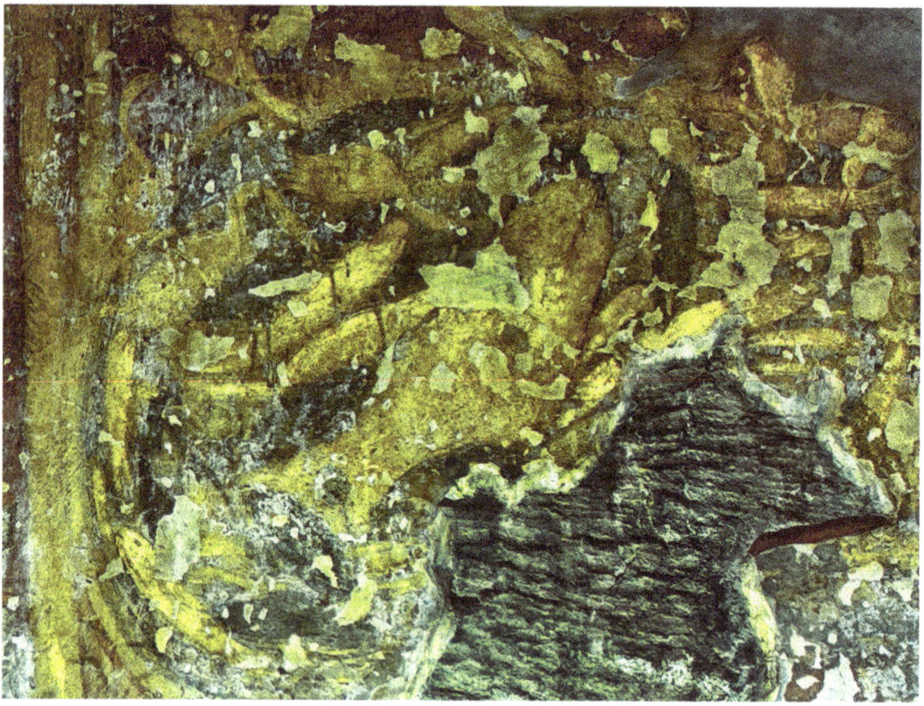

No. 11. *Legend of a* matsya *(fish). Severely damaged. Rear wall, far right.*

she regained her eyesight.—The elephant was none other than the Buddha in a former existence.

No. 11. Matsya.

Identification: Foucher (1921, narrative no. 4).—In a lotus pond, there lived a big *matsya* (fish), the leader of the shoals. During a particularly hot summer, the pond started drying up and shrinking in size. As a result, the fish became easy prey for crows and other birds. In utter distress, the big fish beseeched God Indra for help. Because of his truth spell, rain came pouring and filled the pond despite the dry season. The fish were saved. Then the big fish begged again to the rain god not to stop, fearing a fresh dry spell.—The fish was none other than the Buddha in a former existence.

No. 32. Śyāma.

Identification: Oldenburg (1895, narrative no. 9).—Śyāma was

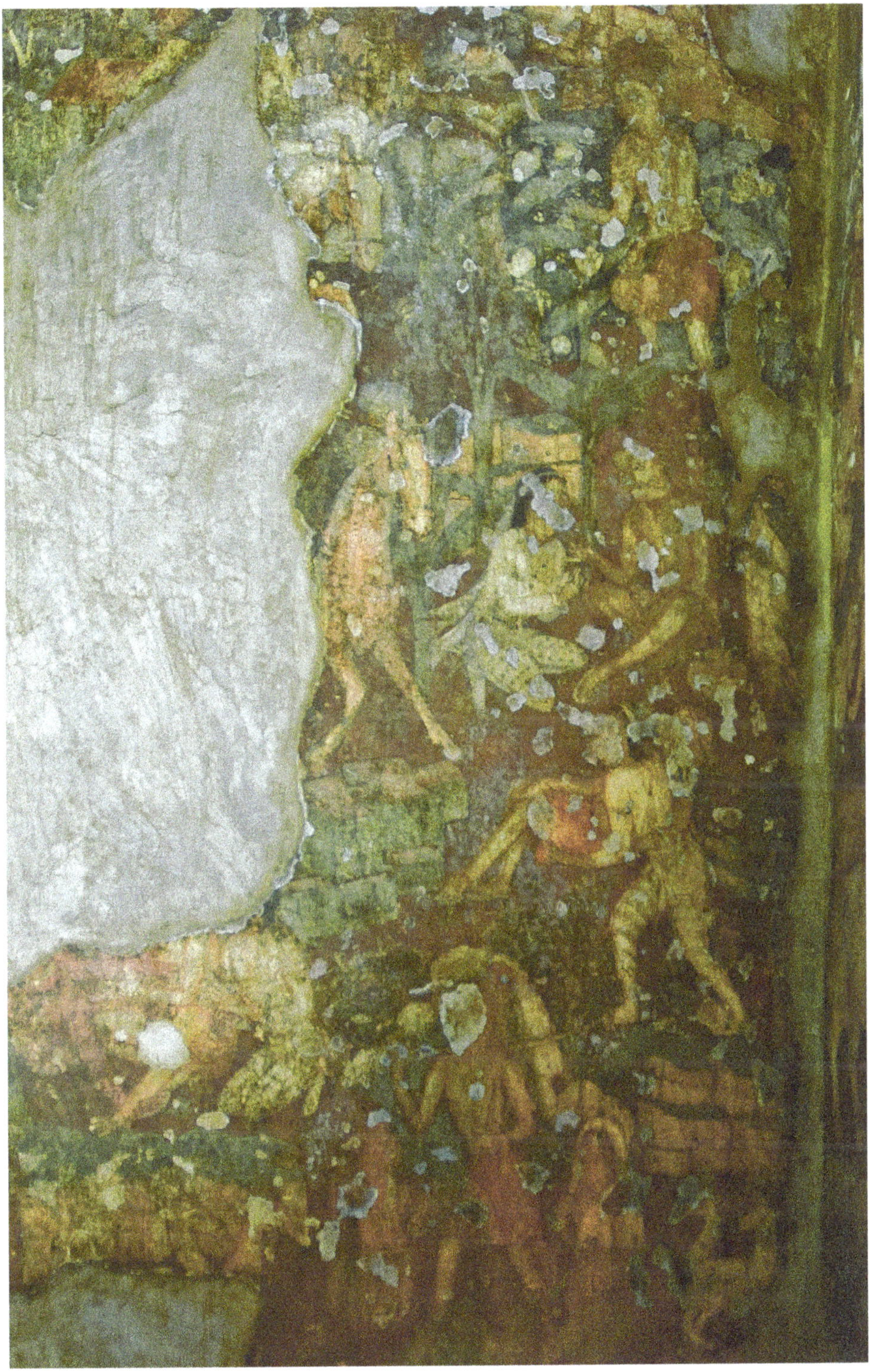

No. 32. *Five scenes from the legend of Śyāma. Hall, rear wall, far right.*

the court priest's devoted son. As the priest and his wife grew old and blind, he asked the king to institute Śyāma as the court priest so that he could retire with his wife in the forests. Śyāma refused to accept the post and went along with his parents to the forest so that he could take care of them. Once, as he was fetching water for his parents, the king, who had come with a hunting party, accidently hit him with his arrow. The king immediately recognising him as the son of court priest, asked him to pardon the curse. Śyāma asked him to calm down and take the water to his parents. Having come to know about the fatal injury to their son, the priest and his wife overcame their initial shock and requested the king to take them to their dying son. They swore on their son's virtue, and Lord Indra descended from heaven to grant Śyāma back his life.—Śyāma was none other than the Buddha in a former existence.

No. 22. Mahiṣa.

Identification: Oldenburg (1895, narrative no. 10).—A *yakṣa* (genius, a class of semi-divine beings) once observed a monkey tormenting a buffalo by climbing on the back and doing a balancing act on its horns, even covering up its eyes. The *yakṣa* was amazed at the buffalo's patience. On inquiry, the buffalo explained the value of humbleness. The *yakṣa* admired the buffalo's virtue, pushed the monkey off from its back, and gave the buffalo a protective charm.—The buffalo was none other than the Buddha in a former existence.

No. 55. Prabhāsa. (No photo.)

Identification: Foucher (1921, narrative no. 28). For the story, vide Cave 1, No. 53.

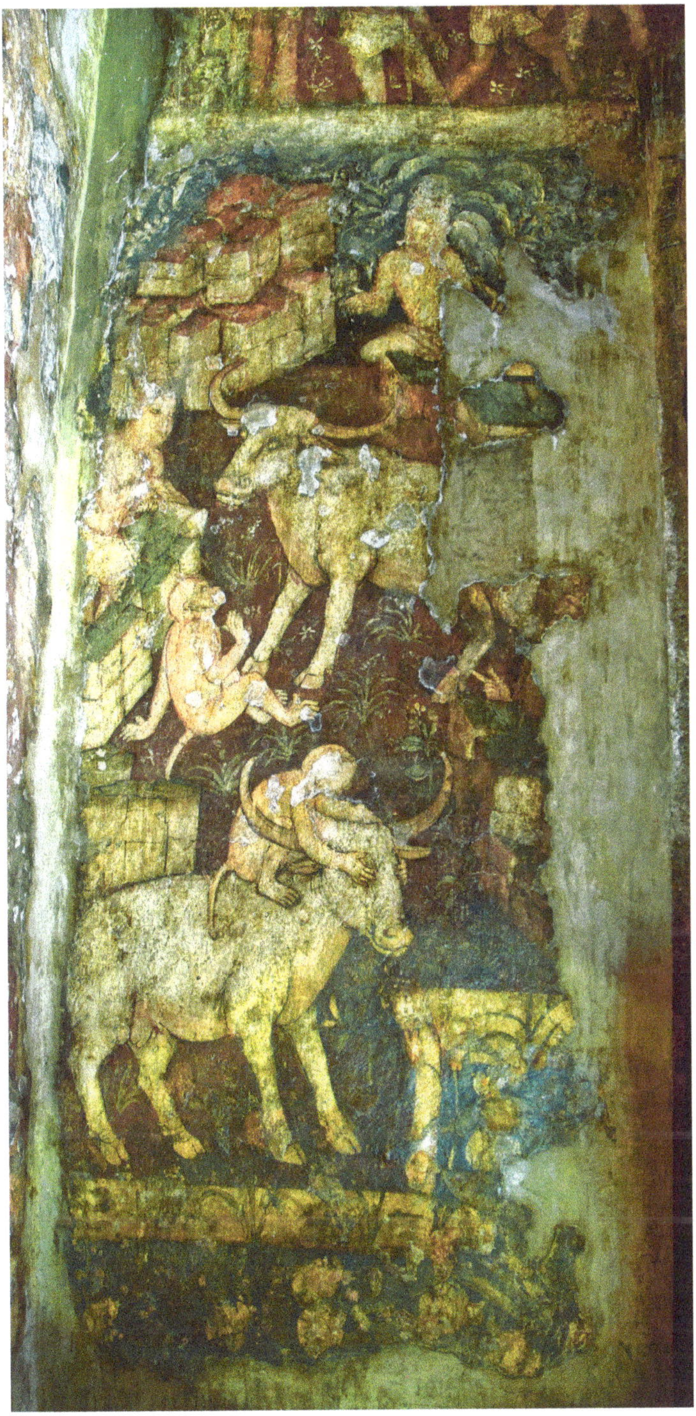

No. 22. *The legend of a* mahiṣa *(buffalo).* Below: *scene 1, a monkey is tormenting a buffalo by covering the buffalo's eyes who wants to bath in the pond.* Above: *scene 2, a* yakṣa *on the left has thrown the monkey down to help the buffalo, while the God Indra looks on from the skies.* *Hall, rear aisle, right wall.*

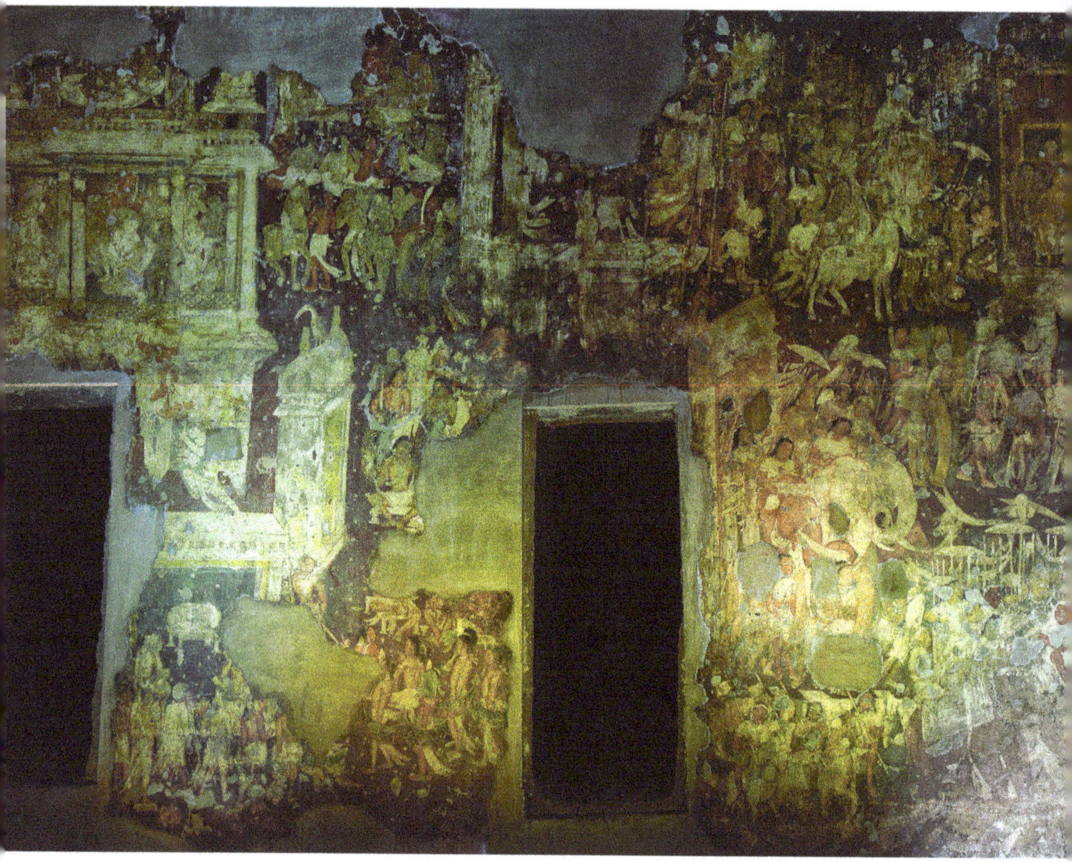

No. 58.1. *The legend of Siṃhala. Three photos merged digitally. Hall, right wall.*

No. 58. Siṃhala.

Identification: Foucher (1921, narrative no. 19).—The rich merchant, Siṃhala, went on a voyage along with a group of merchants. They were shipwrecked and found refuge in an island, keeping afloat by various means. Here they were charmed by beautiful women, who married them and kept them happy. The only hitch was that they were forbidden to go to the south of the island. They lived in pleasure for a while. However, hounded by curiosity, Siṃhala slipped away southwards one night.

It turned out there was an iron tower with captive wailing men, who were also shipwrecked merchants. They too were taken by the beauties (who were really man-eating *rākṣasis* or demonesses) till the new batch of shipwrecked people was ushered in. Then, some of them were devoured and others were kept in the tower, meant to be eaten later. The men saw no hope for themselves but

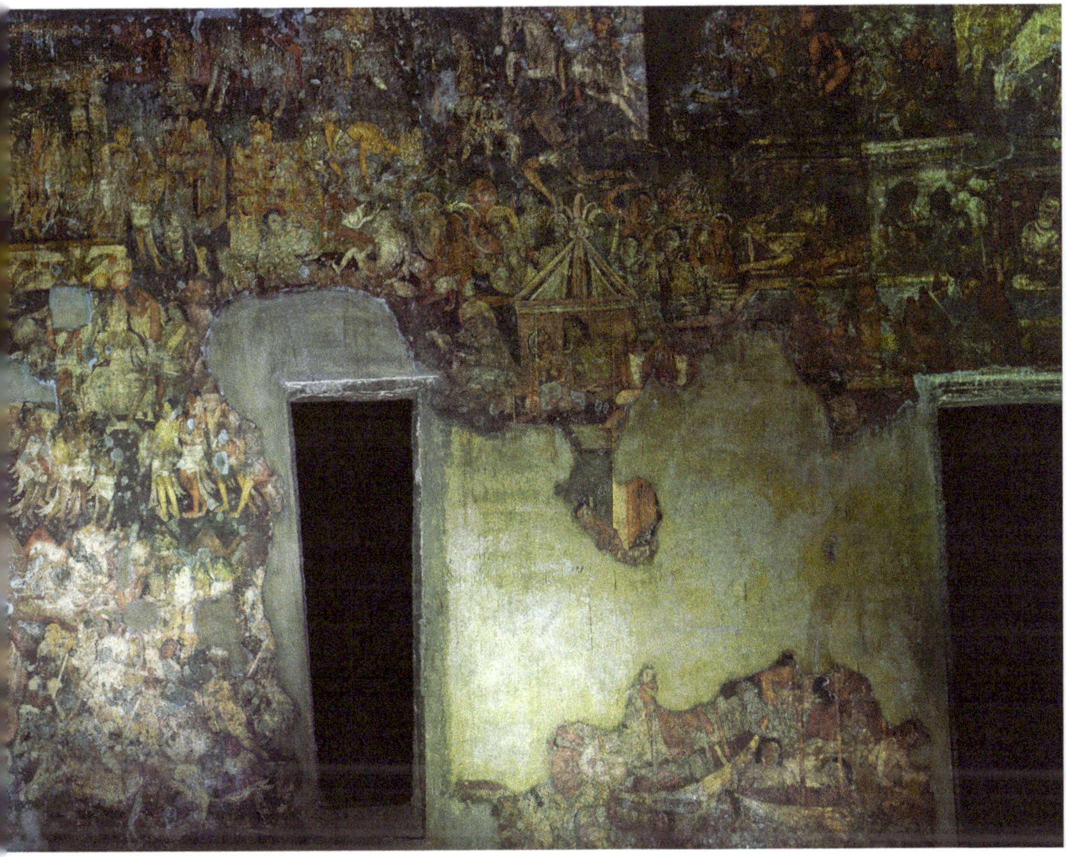

told Siṃhala that he and his accomplice could escape by going to north on a certain day, where a winged horse would come, and would fly them to India safely.

The next morning, Siṃhala gathered the others, told them about his experience, and following the prisoners' advice, found the winged horse on the north shore. They bowed and requested the horse to rescue them. The horse asked them to mount or cling to him and rose in the air. The women, however, caught them in the act. They used emotional blackmailing tactics and showed them their children. All of the men were beguiled and jumped down and were immediately devoured by *rākṣasis*, but Siṃhala alone, unperturbed, fled to safety.

His *rākṣasi* wife, however, was encouraged by other *rākṣasis* to devour him. In her alluring best, and with a child exactly like Siṃhala, she went to his door and told everyone that she was a

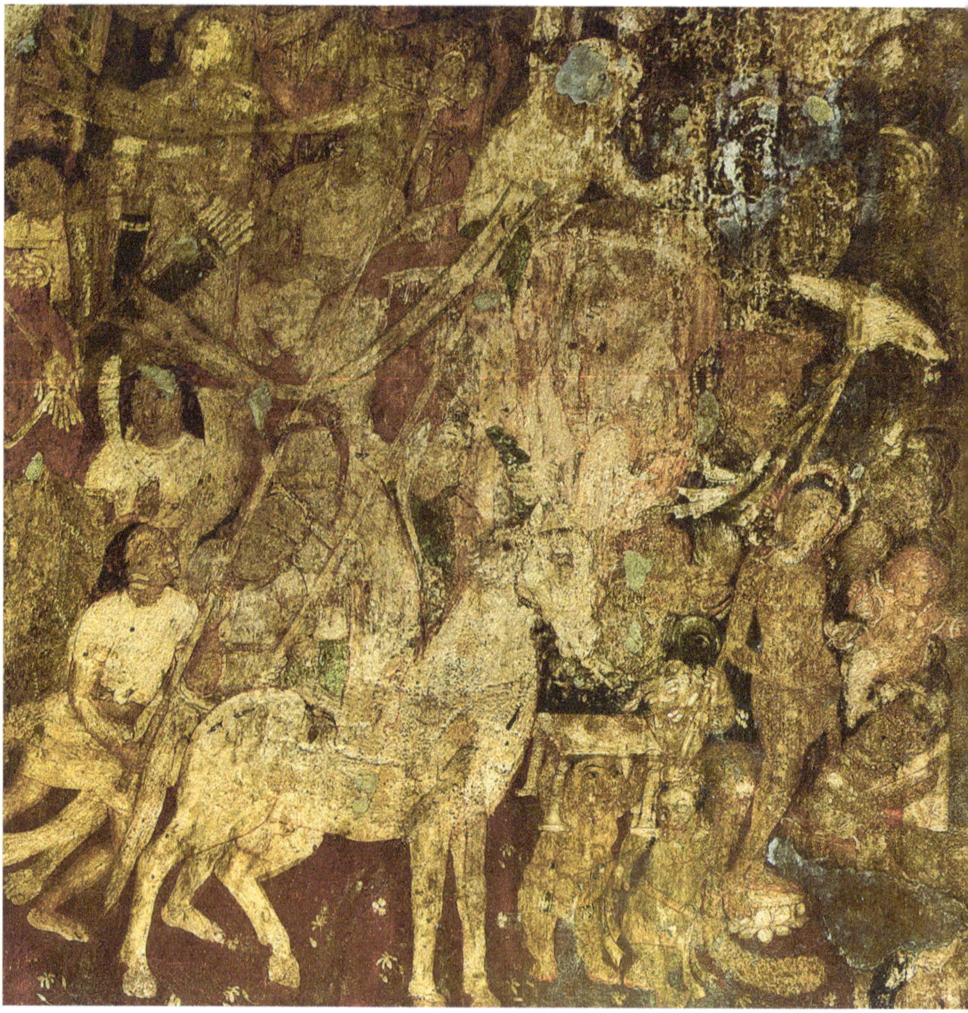

No. 58.2. *Siṃhala: scene of the demoness queen in the garb of a beautiful princess who has come to the royal palace with a child claiming that Siṃhala is the father of the child.*

princess, abandoned by him. People, on hearing the story, asked Siṃhala's parents to accept her, but since they were well-informed by Siṃhala about her real form, were unmoved. Having failed, the *rākṣasi* went to the king, who was completely taken up by her charm. In spite of warnings from Siṃhala, the king made sure that she was accepted in the royal quarters. One night, the *rākṣasi* called all her companions and devoured the entire royal household. The next day, when the royal gates remained closed and the palace was encircled by vultures, the citizens summoned Siṃhala, who knew what had happened. He climbed over the palace wall, slaying the *rākṣasis* with a sword. As the palace gates opened, people saw that their king and his family had been killed.

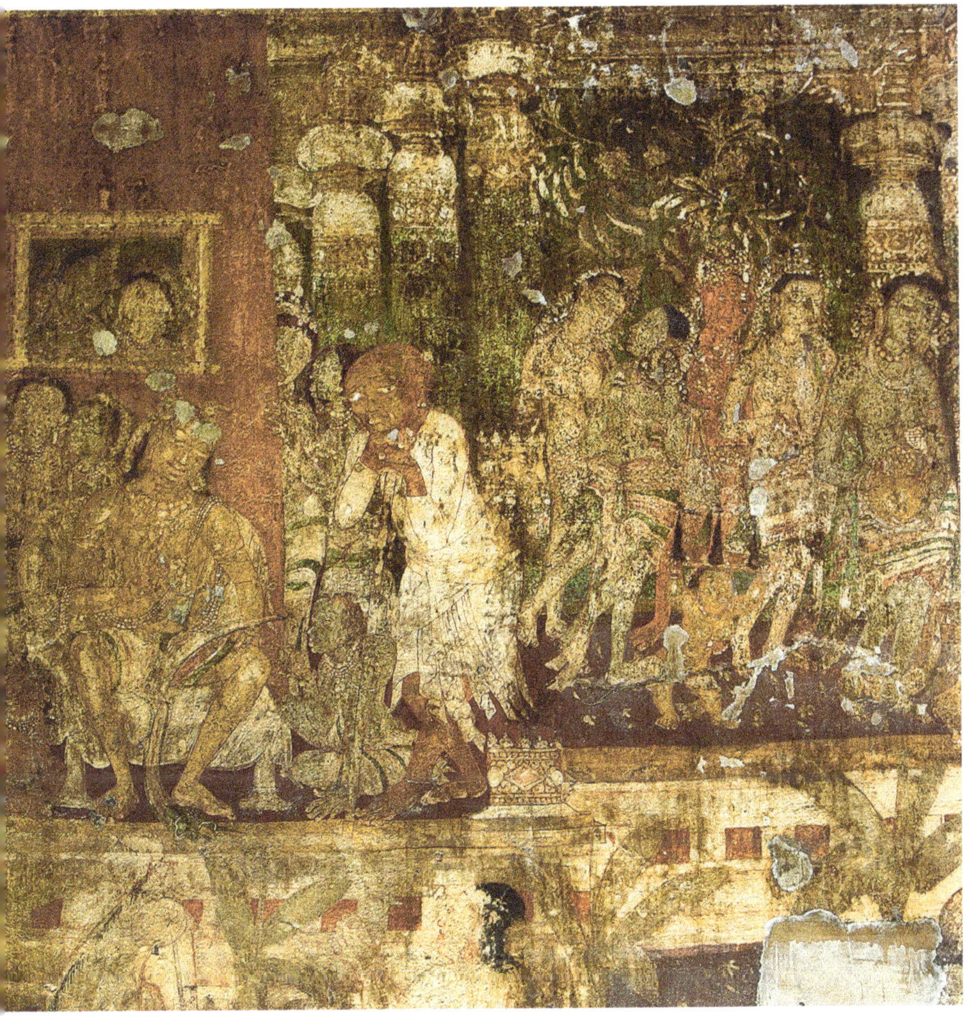

On public demand, Siṃhala agreed to become the new king on the condition that he would be given far-reaching powers. Soon, with a highly-equipped army he attacked the island of the *rākṣasis*, who battled with full force, but ultimately lost to the superior archers of Siṃhala's army. The demonesses were granted mercy only on the condition that they would leave the island and settle elsewhere.—Siṃhala, the merchant turned king, was none other than the Buddha in a former existence.

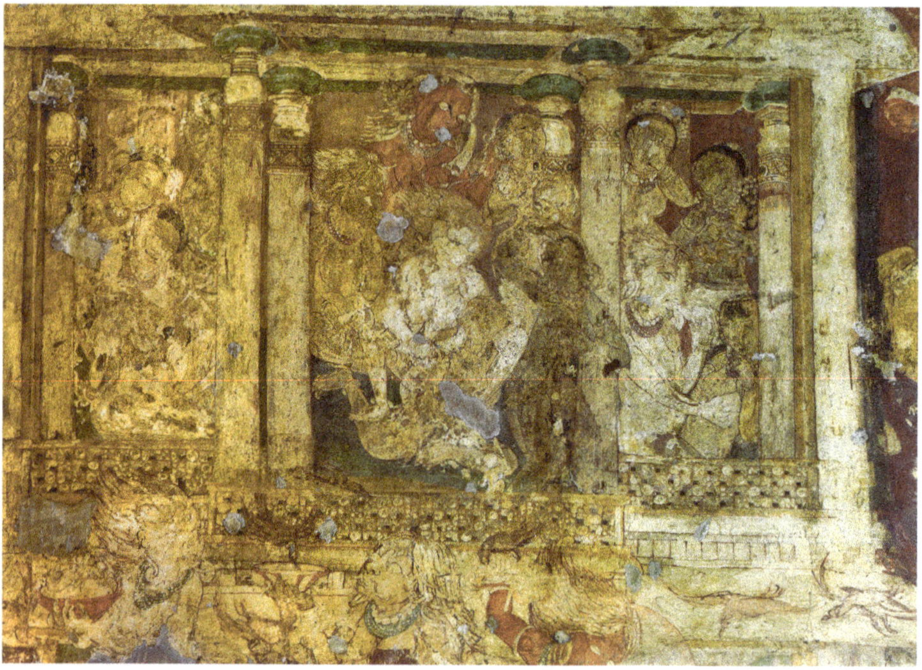

No. 58.3. *Siṃhala: at night, the beautiful women come in their real form of demonesses and create a bloodbath in the palace.*

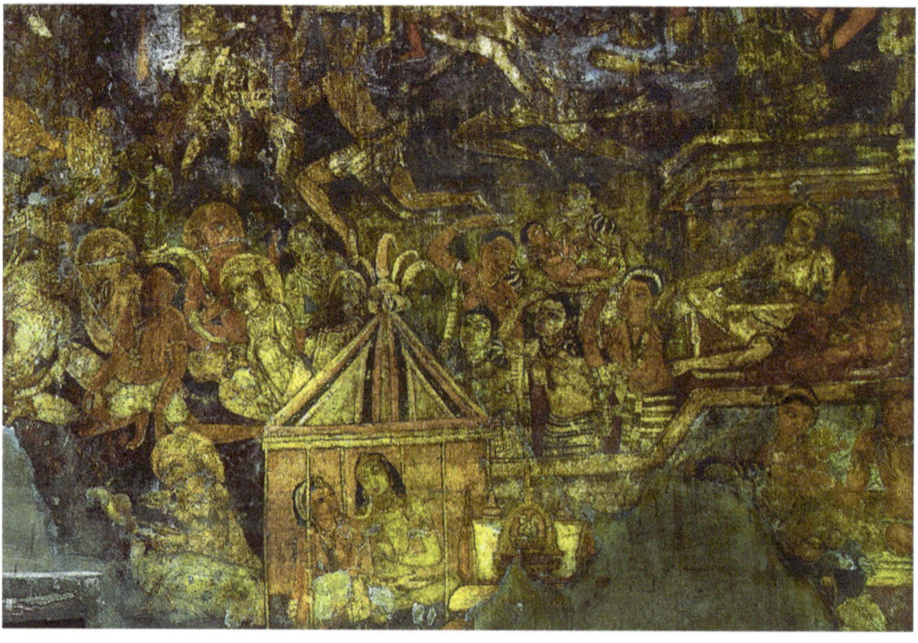

No. 58.4. *Scenes from the Siṃhala narrative*

SOME NON-NARRATIVE THEMES.

No. 44.4.[1] Bodhisattva Avalokiteśvara.

The Bodhisattva Avalokiteśvara is the guardian saint of travelling merchants, in the shape of a brahmin.

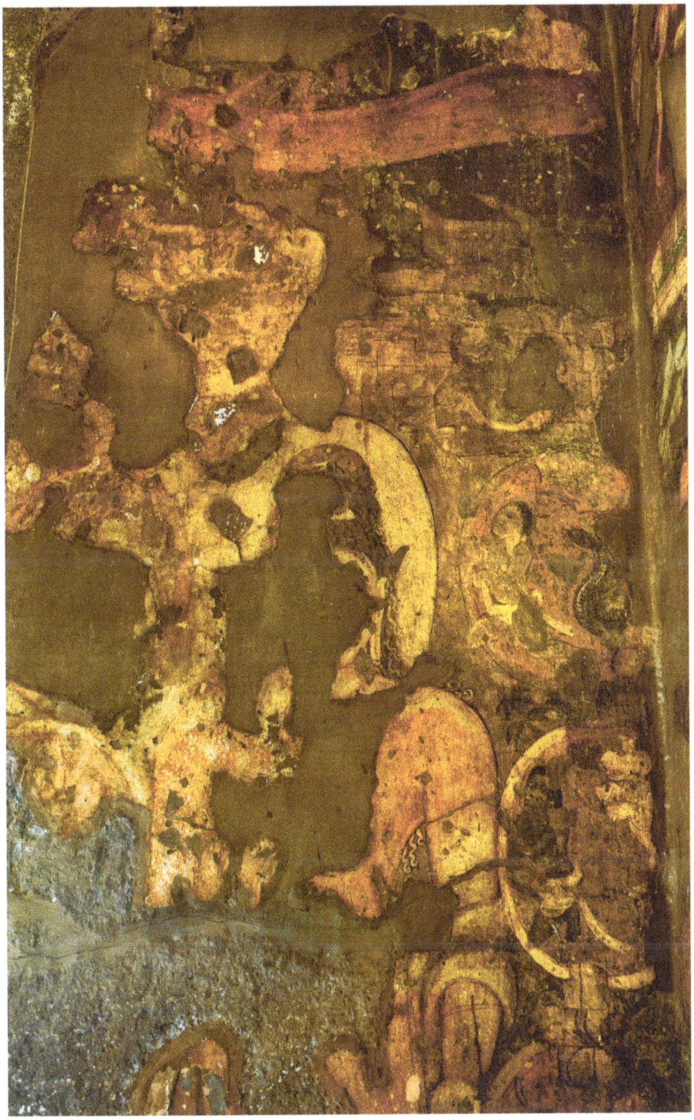

No. 44.4.
Avalokiteśvara dispelling aṣṭabhaya *(eight fears). The surrounding medallions depict the eight kinds of perils faced especially by travelling merchants.*
Porch, left pilaster.

1 The numbers under the *non-narrative* themes including the captions refer to those assigned by Monika Zin to the *non-narrative* themes of the Ajanta paintings, vide Zin 2003a.

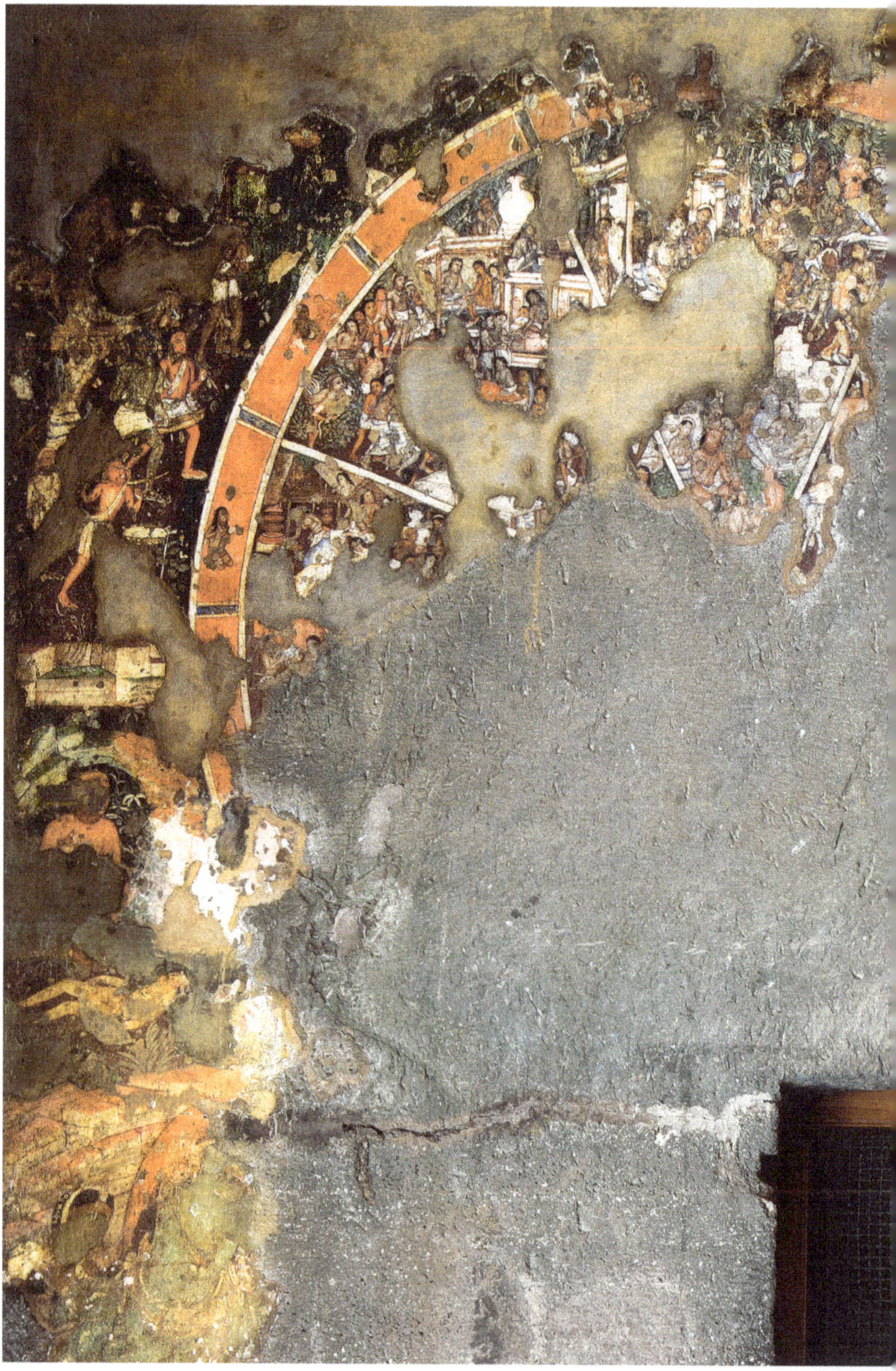

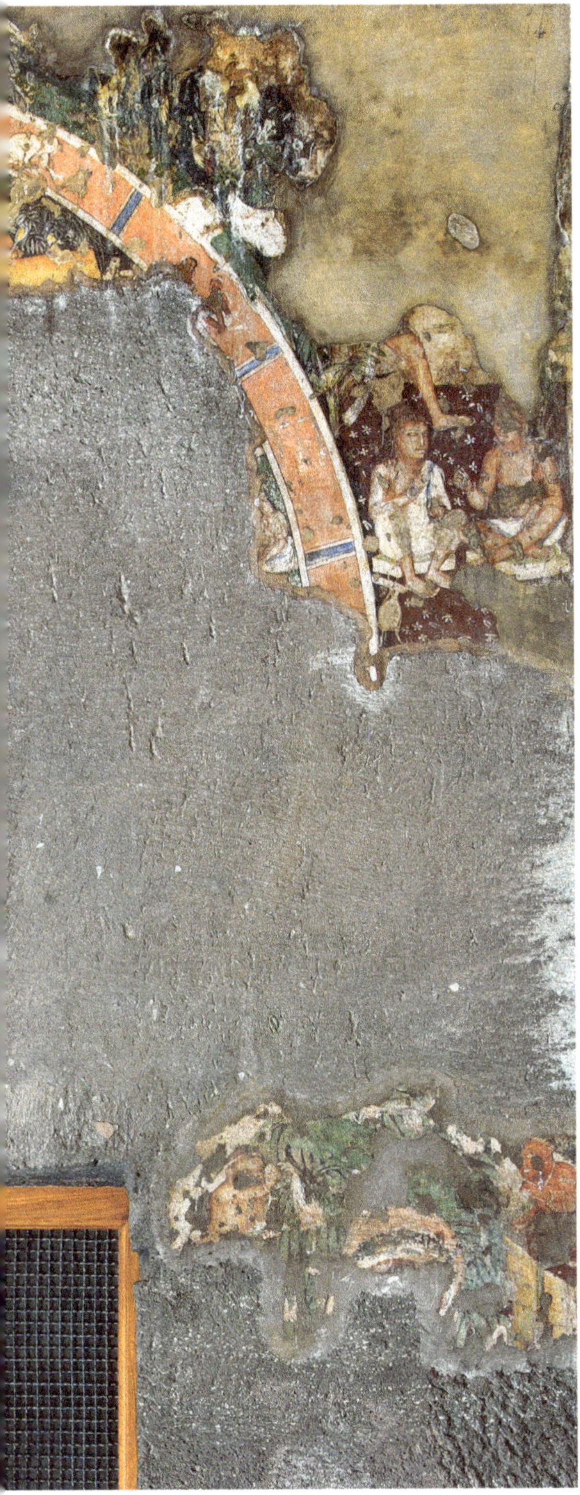

No. 46. Samsāracakra.

Samsāracakra (The Wheel of Transmigration) is seen in the clutches of the demon transitiveness. Four sections of the wheel are partially extant towards the middle and upper areas of the wheel. Clockwise, the section to the left depicts the world of the animals; the section on the upper left corner depicts the world of the *asuras* (titans); the uppermost section depicts the world of the gods; the upper right section depicts the world of the humans; while the section on the right, of which only some traces are preserved, depicted the world of the ghosts (*preta*). Most likely, there were three further sections on the lower areas of the wheel, which are no longer extant. They probably depicted the creatures in the different hells (*naraka*). Cf. Zin and Schlingloff 2007.

No. 46. *Samsāracakra (Cycle of Life). Porch, left wall.*

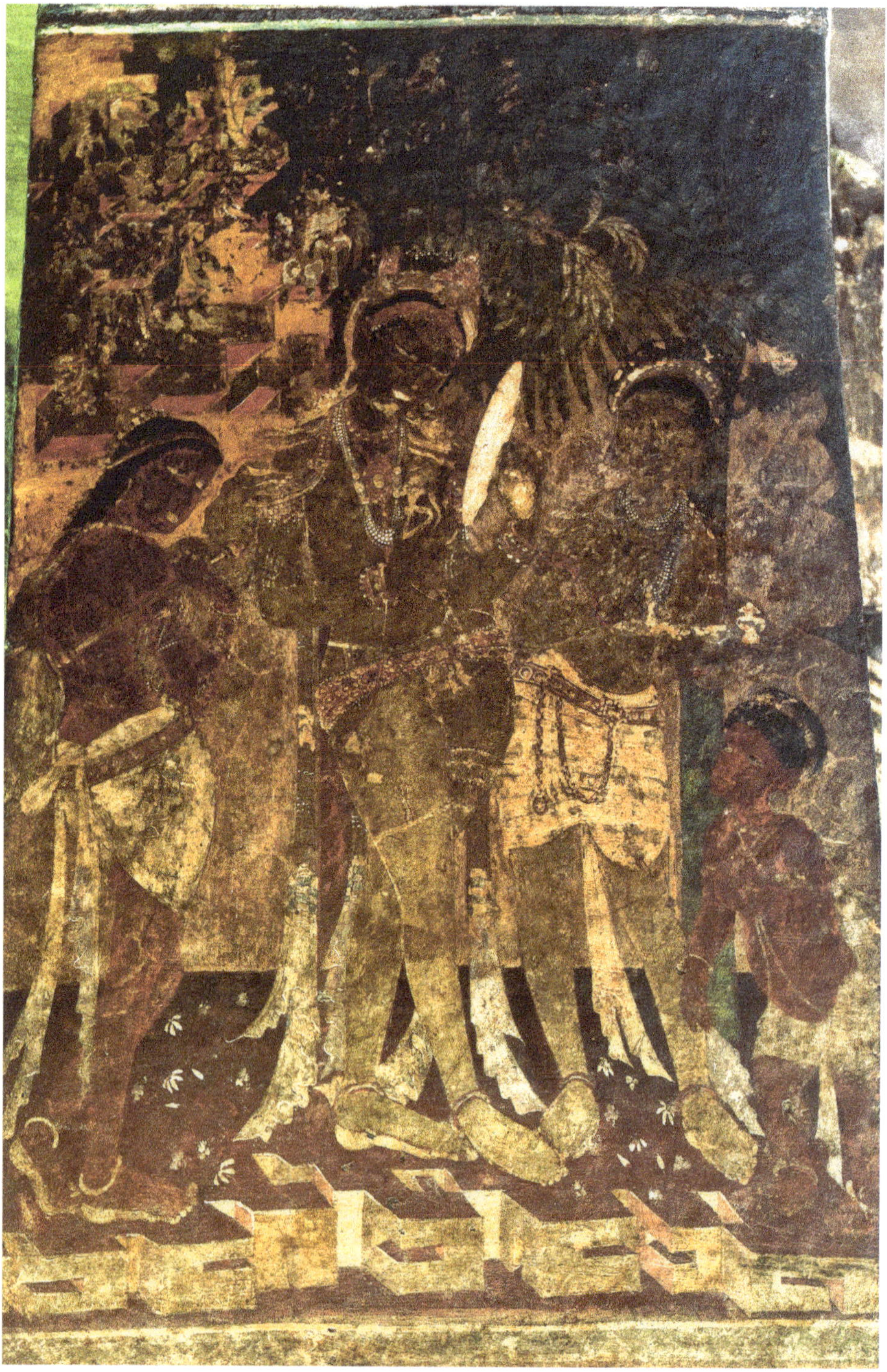

No. 23.7. *A* yakṣiṇī *with a mirror. Her attendants carry cosmetics. Hall, front right pilaster.*

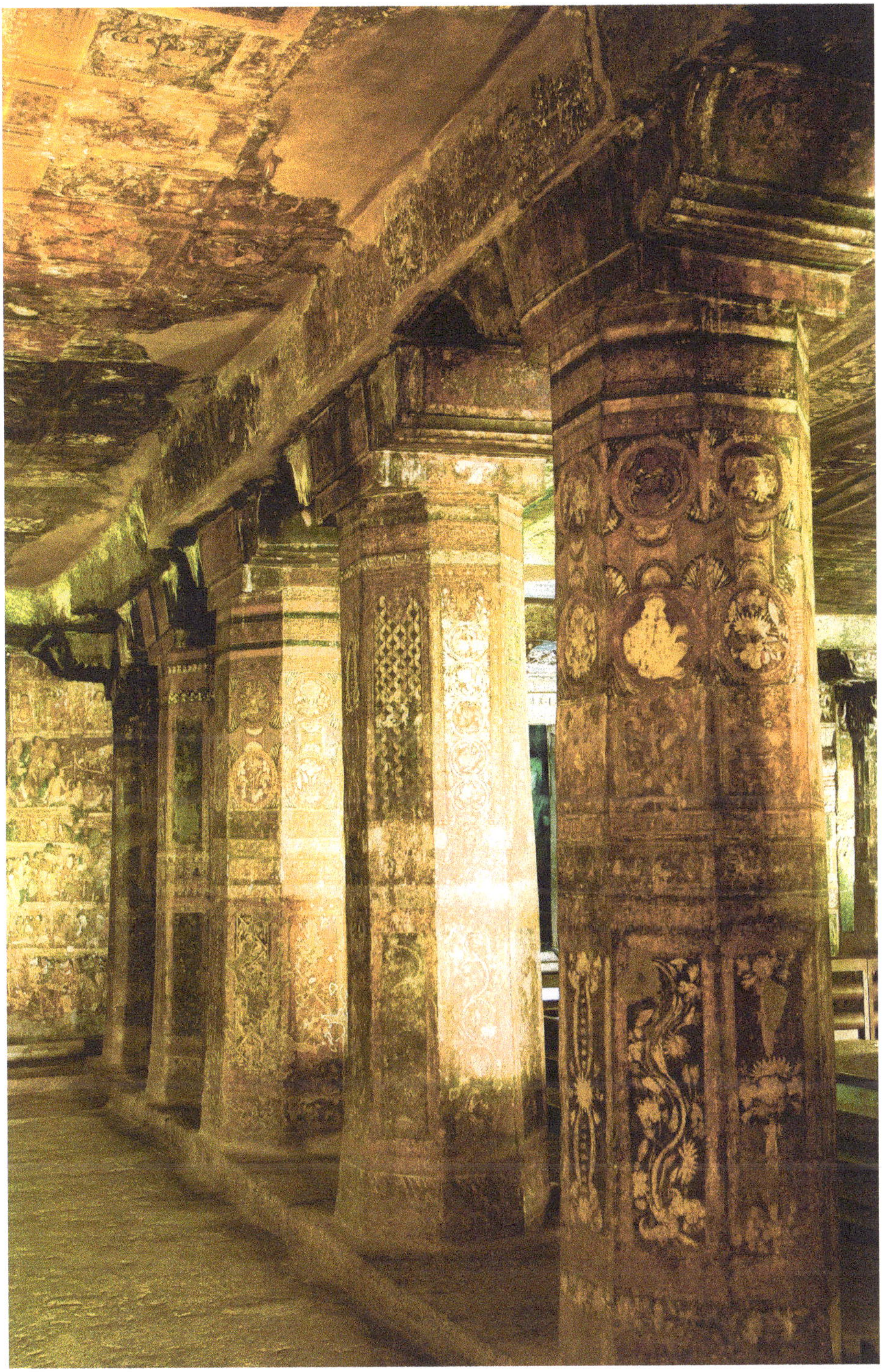

Painted decorative and ornamental motifs and symbols on pillars. Left aisle.

REFERENCES

Begley, W. E. 1966. The Chronology of Mahāyāna Buddhist Architecture and Painting at Ajaṇṭā, = Ph.D. thesis, University of Pennsylvania, Ann Arbor.

Burgess, James. 1879. *Notes on the Bauddha Rock-Temples of Ajanta, their Paintings and Sculptures, and on the Paintings in the Bagh Caves, Modern Bauddha Mythology etc.*, = Archaeological Survey of Western India 9, Bombay.

Fergusson, James, and James Burgess. 1880. *The Cave Temples of India* (London: W. H. Allen). Repr. Delhi: Munshiram Manoharlal, 2000.

Foucher, A. 1921. 'Lettre d'Ajanta,' in: *Journal Asiatique*, p. 201–245; = Rapport préliminaire sur l'interprétation des peintures et sculptures d'Ajanta, Bombay 1920; (trans.): 'Preliminary Report on the Interpretation of the Paintings and Sculptures of Ajanta,' in: *Journal of the Hyderabad Archaeological Society* 5, 1919–1920, p. 50–111.

—. 1919. *Les représentations de Jātaka dans l'art boudhique*, = Memoires concernant l'Asie Orientale, 3, Paris.

—. 1911. 'Essai de classement chronologique des diverses versions du Ṣaḍdanta jātaka,' in: *Mélanges Sylvain Lévi*, Paris; (trans.): 'The Six-Tusked Elephant, An Attempt at a Chronological Classification of the Various Versions of the Shaḍdanta-Jātaka, in: *Beginnings of Buddhist Art and Other Essays*, London 1918, p. 185–204.

Goloubew, V. 1927. *Documents pour servir à l'étude d'Ajanta, Les peintures de la premiére grotte = Ars Asiatica* 10, Paris.

Griffiths, J. 1896–1897. *The Paintings in the Buddhist Cave-Temples of Ajanta, Khandesh, India, 1, Pictorial Subjects, 2, Decorative Details*, London; repr. New Delhi 1983.

Lalou, M. 1925. Trois récits du Dulva reconnus dans les peintures d'Ajanta, in: *Journal Asiatique*, Paris, p. 333–337.

Lüders, H. 1902. 'Ārya-Śūra's Jātakamālā und die Fresken von Ajantā,' in: *Nachrichten von der Königlichen Gesellschaft der Wissenschaften*, Göttingen, p. 758–762; repr. in: *Philologica Indica*, Göttingen, 1940, p. 73–77; tran. J. Burgess, in: *Indian Antiquary* 32, Bombay, 1903, p. 326–328.

Oldenburg, S. F. 1895. 'Zamétki o buddijskom iskusstve,' in:

Vostocnyaja Zamétki, St. Petersburg, p. 337–365; (trans.): 'Notes on Buddhist Art,' in: *Journal of the American Oriental Society* 18, New Haven, 1897, p. 183–201.

Schlingloff, Dieter. 2013. *Ajanta—Handbook of the Paintings 1, Narrative Wall Paintings*, I-III (New Delhi: IGNCA).

—. 1999. *A Guide to the Ajanta Paintings 1: Narrative Wall Paintings* (Delhi: Munshiram Manoharlal).

—. 1995. 'A Fortified Palace in an Ancient Painting,' in: *Śri Nāgābhinandanam, Dr. M. S. Nagaraja Rao Festschrift*, Bangalore, p. 435–44.

—. 1993. 'Wandmalereien aus dem alten Indien,' in: *Einsichten, Ludwig-Maximilians-Universität, Munchen* 1, p. 9–14.

—. 1987. *Studies in the Ajanta Paintings, Identifications and Interpretations* (Delhi: Ajanta Publications).

—. 1986. 'Śibi-Sarvaṃdada,' in: *Ṛtam* 16–18, Lucknow, 1984–1986, p. 299–308.

—. 1983. 'Ein Zyklus des Buddhalebens in Ajanta,' in: *Wiener Zeitschrift für die Kunde Südasiens* 27, Wien, p. 113–148; trans. in: Schlingloff 1987, chapter 2.

—. 1977a. 'Die Jātaka-Darstellungen in Höhle 16 von Ajanta, in: *Beiträge zur Indienforschung, E. Waldschmidt zum* 80. Geburststag gewidmet, Berlin, p. 451-478.

—. 1977b. 'Zwei Malereien in Höhle 1 von Ajanta,' in: *Zeitschrift der Deutschen Morgenländischen Gesellschaft, Supplement*, 3, 2 (Wiesbaden: Otto Harrassowitz GmbH & Co. KG), p. 912–917.

—. 1977c. 'König Prabhāsa und der Elefant,' in: *Indologica Taurinensia* 5, Torino, p. 139–152.

—. 1976. 'Kalyāṇakārin's Adventures,' in: *Artibus Asiae* 38, Ascona, p. 5–28.

—. 1973a. 'Prince Sudhana and the Kinnarī,' in: *Indologica Taurinensia* 1, Torino, p. 155–167.

—. 1973b. 'A Battle Painting in Ajanta,' in: *Indologen-Tagung* 1971, Wiesbaden, p. 196–203.

—. 1972. 'Jātakamālā-Darstellungen in Ajanta,' in: *Wiener Zeitschrift für die Kunde Süd- und Ostasiens* 16, p. 55–65.

Singh, Rajesh Kumar. 2017. *Ajanta Cave No. 1: Documented According to the Corpus by Dieter Schlingloff* = Photographic

Compendium of Ajanta Narrative Paintings, vol. 1 (Baroda: Hari Sena Press).

—. 2013. *Ajanta Paintings: 86 Panels of Jatakas and Other Themes* (Baroda: Hari Sena Press).

—. 2012. *An Introduction to the Ajanta Caves: With Examples of Six Caves* (Baroda: Hari Sena Press).

Vogel, J. Ph. (Review). 1948. G. Yazdani, Ajanta, 3, in: *Artibus Asiae* 11, Ascona, p. 153–157.

Yazdani, G. 1955. *Ajanta: Monochrome Reproductions of the Ajanta Frescoes Based on Photography*, vol. IV (London: Oxford University Press).

—. 1946. *Ajanta: Monochrome Reproductions of the Ajanta Frescoes Based on Photography*, vol. III (London: Oxford University Press).

Zin, Monika, and Dieter Schlingloff. 2007. *Saṃsāracakra: Das Rad der Wiedergeburten in der Indischen Überlieferung*, = Buddhismus-Studien, 6 (Dusseldorf: Eine Veroffentlichung des EKO-Hauses der Japanischen Kulture e. V.).

—. 2003a. *Ajanta — Handbuch der Malereine / Handbook of the Paintings 2, Devotionale und Ornamentale Malereien / Ornamental and Devotional Paintings* (Wiesbaden: Otto Harrassowitz), German. English trans. in press (New Delhi: IGNCA).

—. 2003b. *A Guide to the Ajanta Paintings 2—Devotional and Ornamental Paintings*, I-II (Delhi: Munshiram Manoharlal).

—. 2000. 'Two Nāga-stories in the Oldest Paintings in Ajanta IX,' in: *South Asian Archaeology 1997*, Roma, p. 1171–1199.

NUMERICAL INDEX OF THE PAINTINGS

Non-narrative nos./cave nos./keywords/ page no.

Note

Due to certain inadequacies the following narrative paintings could *not* be included in this book:

No. 6.	Cave 10. Śyāma.
No. 7.	Cave 10. Ṣaḍdanta.
No. 8.	Cave 10. Bhagavān.
No. 9.	Cave 10. Udayana.
No. 66.	Cave 7. Bhagavān.
No. 81.	Cave 6. Māravijaya.
No. 87.	Cave 21. Devāvatāra.
No. 90.	Cave 6. Mahāprātihārya.

Due to the vastness of the material, more than 90% of the non-narrative themes have *not* be included in this book.

ALPHABETICAL INDEX OF THE PAINTINGS

Narrative nos./cave nos./keywords **page no.**

Non-narrative nos./cave nos./keywords/page no.

OTHER PUBLICATIONS BY THE AUTHOR

Monographs

2017. *Ajanta Cave No. 1: Documented According to the Ajanta Corpus of Dieter Schlingloff*, =Photographic Compendium of Ajanta Narrative Paintings, vol. 1 (Baroda: Harisena Press). 218 pp.

2013. *Ajanta Paintings: 86 Panels of Jatakas and Other Narrative Themes* (Baroda: Hari Sena Press). 160 pp.

2012. *An Introduction to the Ajanta Caves: With Examples of Six Caves* (Baroda: Hari Sena Press). 260 pp.

Articles

In press. 'The Ajiṇṭhā Caves, Part III: astronomy of the age.' In: Prof. Ratan Parimoo Felicitation Volume, ed. by Gauri Parimoo Krishnan and Raghavendra Kulkarni.

2019. 'Devil in the Details: Spink's Imaginations 1. Did the Aśmakas Really Destroy the Front Cells of Ajanta Cave 19?,' *Berliner Indologische Studien* 24, 257–264.

2018. 'Rock-cut architecture of western India 1. Momentum I: origins of leṇa-cetiyaghara, ca. 120–300 CE,' *History Today, Journal of the Indian History & Culture Society* 19, 216–231.

2016. 'Ajanta: An Overview.' In: *Sahapedia.org, an Encyclopaedia of the Indian Arts, Culture, and Heritage.* http://sahapedia.org/ajanta-caves . Accessed on 2 May 2017.

2016. 'The Ajiṇṭhā Caves, Part I: Aspects of Historical and Political Background.' In: *Sahapedia.org, an Encyclopaedia of Indian Arts, Culture, and Heritage* (New Delhi: Sahapedia.org). Accessed on 1 May 2017. http://www.sahapedia.org/aji%E1%B9%87%E1%B9%ADh%C4%81-cavespart-i .

2016. 'The Ajiṇṭhā Caves, Part II: Aspects of Anthropological and Sociological Background.' In: *Sahapedia.org, an Encyclopaedia of Indian Arts, Culture, and Heritage* (New Delhi: Sahapedia.org). Accessed on 1 May 2017. http://www.sahapedia.org/aji%E1%B9%87%E1%B9%ADh%C4%81-cavespart-ii .

With Singh, M. 2014. 'Ajanta.' In: *Encyclopaedia of the History of*

Science, Technology, and Medicine in Non-Western Cultures, 3rd ed. Ed. Helaine Selin. (Verlag Berlin Heidelberg: Springer).

2012a. 'The Early Development of the Cave 26-Complex at Ajanta,' *South Asian Studies* 28.1 (London: BASAS and Routledge), 37–68.

2012b. 'Buddhabhadra's Dedicatory Inscription at Ajanta: A Review.' In: *Pratnakirti: Recent Studies in Indian Epigraphy, History, Archaeology, and Art, Professor Shriniwas S. Ritti Felicitation volume.* 2 vols. Ed. Shriniwas V. Padigar and Shivanand V. (Delhi: Agam Kala Prakashan), vol. 1, pp. 34–46.

2009. 'Enumerating the Sailagrhas at Ajanta,' *Journal of the Asiatic Society of Mumbai* 82, 122–126.

2009. 'Ajanta Cave 8: Historiography and Fresh Look at the First Mahayana Sailagrha,' *Jnana-Pravah Research Journal* (Varanasi) 12, 68-80.

2008-2009. 'Some Problems in Fixing the Date of Ajanta Caves.' In: *Kalā, the Journal of Indian Art History Congress* 14, Ed. R. D. Choudhury (Guwahati and Delhi: Indian Art History Congress and Sharada Publishing House), pp. 69–85.

2005. 'The Writings of Stella Kramrisch: A Review of Reviews,' *Lalit Kalā* [journal] 30 (New Delhi: Lalit Kala Akademi), 41–54.

2003. 'Role of Stella Kramrisch in Indian Art History,' *East & West* 53.14 (Rome: Istituto italiano per il Medio ed Estremo Oriente), 127–48.

CD-Rom

2004. [Anonymous (Ed.)] *Ajanta: A Digital Encyclopaedia and Virtual Walkthrough* [CD-Rom]. (New Delhi: Indira Gandhi National Centre for Arts).

Doctoral thesis

2014. 'Ajanta's Antiquity: Sources and Problems.' PhD thesis. Faculty of Fine Arts, M. S. University of Baroda.

Videos

2016. 'Built spaces: Ajanta Caves: In conversation with Rajesh Singh.' [Video interview] *Sahapedia.org*. https://www.sahapedia.org/ajanta-caves-history-and-practices . Accessed on 6 May 2017.

2016. 'Built spaces: Monika Zin in conversation with Rajesh Singh on Ajanta cave paintings.' [Video interview] *Sahapedia.org.* https://www.sahapedia.org/ajanta-cave-paintings. Accessed on 6 May 2017.

2016. 'Built Spaces: Dr. Rajesh Kumar Singh in Conversation with Padmashree M. K. Dhavalikar.' [Video interview] *Sahapedia.org.* https://www.sahapedia.org/interview-mkdhavalikar. Accessed on 6 May 2017.

2016. 'Built Spaces: Dr. Rajesh Kumar Singh in Conversation with Naomichi Yaguchi.' [Video interview] *Sahapedia.org.* https://www.sahapedia.org/conversation-naomichi-yaguchi . Accessed on 6 May 2017.

2016. 'Built Spaces: Ajanta and the Vakatakas: Rajesh Kumar Singh in Conversation with Hans Bakker.' [Video interview] *Sahapedia.org.* https://www.sahapedia.org/interview-mkdhavalikar. Accessed on 6 May 2017.

Reviews of Singh's works

Visvas, Anamika. 2015. 'Review of An Introduction to the Ajanta Caves by Rajesh K. Singh,' *Purātattva* 43 (New Delhi: Indian Archaeological Society).

Bhalerao, Manjiri. 2017. 'Review of An Introduction to the Ajanta Caves by Rajesh K. Singh,' *Journal of Asiatic Society of Mumbai* 87.

Raghu, G. 2013 (2 June). 'Spinkam-Singham,' *Mathrubhumi, Weekend Supplement.* [Newspaper in Malayalam] Kochi.

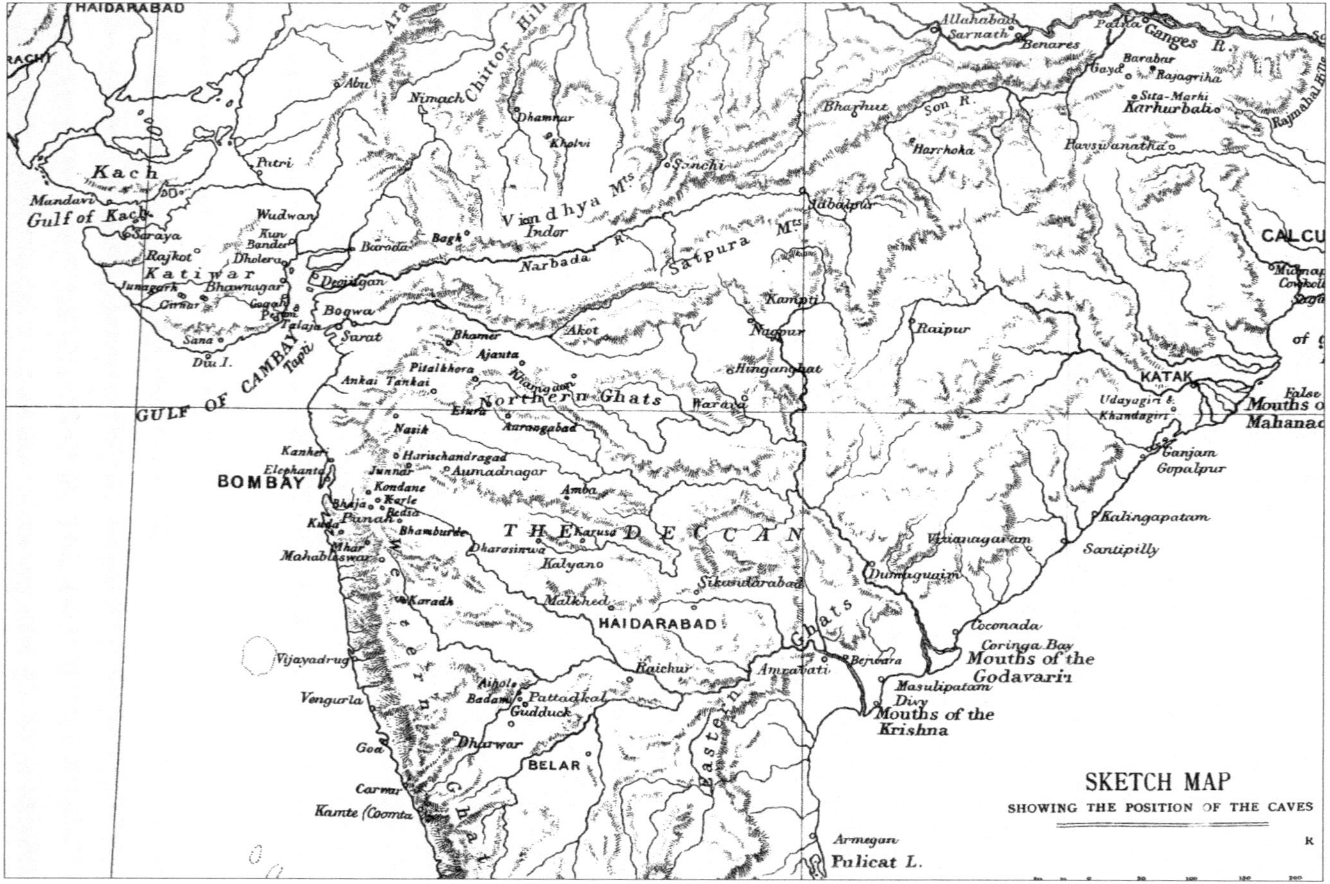

Map of rock cut cave sites in India. Fergusson and Burgess 1880.

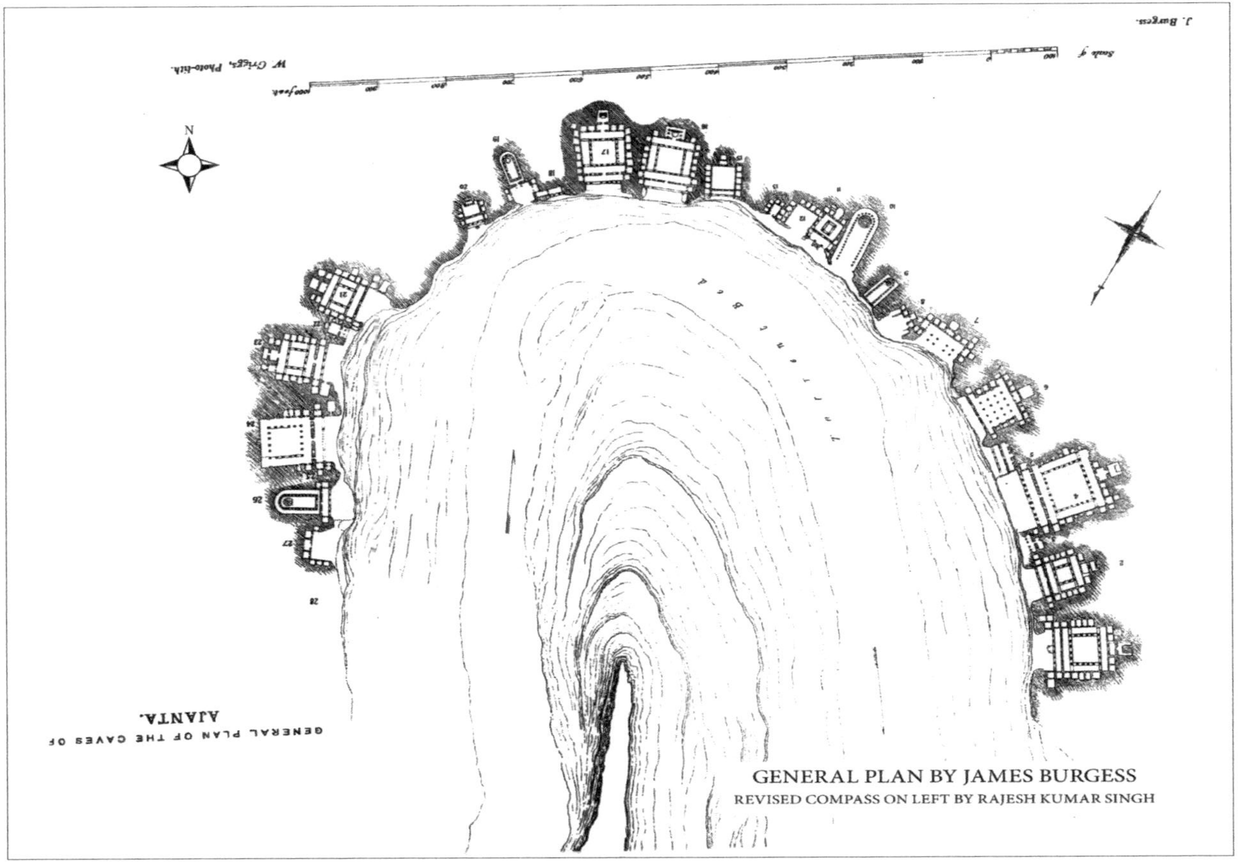

General Plan of the Ajantā Caves. The compass on top left showing the true north is placed by Singh after clockwise rotation of the plan by 92 degree. Adapted from Burgess 1883.